# STUDENT

# SAILOR

# SKIPPER

# SURVIVOR

---

*How WWII Transformed
the Lives of
Ordinary Americans*

# JULIA GIMBEL

*with journal excerpts from Robert T. McCurdy*

For information on bulk orders or author visits, please contact:

Orange Hat Publishing
www.orangehatpublishing.com
Waukesha, WI

Editor: Denise Guibord
Proofreader: Lauren Blue
Cover design by Kaeley Dunteman
Cover photo: National Archive Photo Media# 06671429: V-J Day Celebration in San Francisco, used with permission. Original photo taken by George De Carval and first published by the *San Francisco Chronicle* newspaper, 1945.
All interior photos courtesy of Julia Gimbel, unless otherwise noted

To Dad – and all the others like him

# TABLE OF CONTENTS

**THE DISCOVERY**................................................................*9*

**SECTION ONE: THE TRANSITION**..............................*19*

So It Begins – The V-12 Program................................*21*
Midshipmen's School – 90-Day Wonders....................*36*
A Lot of Goodbyes – Off They Go..............................*47*
Al Exner – From Studies to Syringes..........................*58*
LCT-977 – A Navy Workhorse...................................*72*
Cast of Characters on LCT-977.................................*88*
John Eskau – Young Man, Big Adventure...................*99*
The Navy Way.........................................................*107*
Forces Combined Yet Also Conflicted.......................*120*

**SECTION TWO: SETTLING IN**..................................*133*

Feeding the Force....................................................*134*
Smoke 'Em If You Got 'Em.......................................*149*
Boys and the Booze..................................................*158*
The Ties That Bind – How V-Mail Kept Love Alive....*172*
Boredom + Ingenuity = Fun......................................*186*
Wash.Dry.Fold.Repeat – Sailor Style..........................*203*

**SECTION THREE: HARSH REALITY**............................211

Danger Lies in Wait.............................................216

Ed Knight – Brave Army Medic...............................227

"Medic, Medic!" – From Injury to Recovery..............244

African Americans Fight Two Wars..........................257

**SECTION FOUR: WAR'S END**............................275

A V-J Day Like No Other – Chaos in San Francisco............279

The GI Bill – Our Men Come Home......................283

**I LEAVE YOU WITH THIS**............................299

**ACKNOWLEDGEMENTS**............................304

**ABOUT  THE  AUTHORS**............................308

**REFERENCES**............................310

YOUNG ENSIGN McCURDY - 1944 JAN
age 22

# THE DISCOVERY

It all started with a high school homework assignment.

In winter 2014, the freshmen students in Mr. Mewes' history class at Whitefish Bay High School were charged with an open-ended final project with just two requirements: it had to cover one of the subjects discussed that semester, and it had to be creative. My daughter, Lena, knew that she wanted to focus on World War II, but the creative part stymied her. Knowing that my late father served in the Navy during the war and that his scrapbook was still in the family, I suggested she take a look at it for inspiration.

The album itself is worn black leather, with a portrait of Dad in his newly earned ensign's stripe and star anchoring the cover—the leather beautifully tooled with intricate swirls, softened and cracked over many years. Inside, the worn pages are filled with hundreds of photographs, scraps of paper, letters, and other memorabilia that Dad sent home to Mom for safekeeping during the war.

Together, Lena and I pored over the artifacts taped inside, with me trying my best (and often failing) to answer the many questions she had about them. What was V-Mail and how did it work? Why is there a booklet of drink coupons for an officers' club? What was a Service flag? What is a K-Ration?

As we turned the last page in the scrapbook, we were startled to find a sixty-page handwritten journal tucked into the back flap. I'd known about the scrapbook for years, but this was new. This was Dad's voice coming straight off the page, telling me stories he never mentioned when he was alive.

Here is how his chronicle begins:

*Lots of luck to anyone who wades through all these comments.*

*I started this memoir of World War II one January just after I retired—maybe 1985 or so. I was bored and sick of hearing a lot of what I considered false history. Each year in January—during the winter doldrums, I added six or seven pages and presently, January 2000, I see that I have quite a wad of paper. I have resisted the urge to discard the notes and have hung onto them as a pleasant winter diversion. Someone else can fling them out after I retire permanently. If I live long enough, I could easily accumulate 80 or 90 pages—enough for one proper bonfire.*

Lena did her best to wade through the whole journal, the task made more difficult by Dad's scratchy penmanship. To her it was history come alive. Here was an actual person she had loved, telling her what it was like to leave home at twenty-two to spend three years serving in the South Pacific. Lena was especially delighted to find the love letters between her as-yet-to-be-married grandparents taped inside the journal.

I spent the next several months transcribing Dad's journal in order to send a legible copy to each of my siblings. I wanted to introduce them to the part of our dad that they had never known. Honestly, I didn't expect to get so caught up in the story. Sipping coffee as I typed away, I found myself stopping often to Google things he mentioned. That search would lead to another, and another, and so on. There was a lot I didn't know about the war: how people enlisted or were drafted, how they were trained, how they got to their assignments, and what life was like aboard those ships.

What they ate.

Some people might laugh at that last statement, but in my budding research, I began trying to find out what everyday life was like for the millions who served. Just like Lena and me, most Americans have been taught and quizzed about the famous battles, powerful people, and critical dates of World War II that are such important parts of the historical record. The folks swept up in the Allied efforts were under the near-constant threat of danger, injury, and death. It became clear to me that there was a whole other layer of war stories lying beneath those familiar ones, ones that focused on the *people* aspect of winning a war—the friendships, the food, the downtime, the chores.

As I transcribed Dad's journal, I felt a connection to him and a budding desire to learn more about that pivotal time in American history. Over the next year, a series of events propelled me to dig deeper into my father's past and the experiences he shared with other WWII veterans.

In August 2014, several months after Lena's assignment had earned an "A," I dropped my son, Elijah, off for his freshman year at Washington University in St. Louis, the city that is also home of the National Archives for Navy service records. I planned a return visit that winter to spend some time with my boy, treat him to a few special meals out, and view Dad's file. Predicting that it would be difficult to schedule an appointment with a government facility, I filled out and submitted all the necessary paperwork some four months before my visit.

Then, I twiddled my thumbs.

Back and forth I communicated with the staff at the National Archives. Some of Dad's records were archival and some were not, so to see his entire file I had to request permission from two separate offices. Then I had to provide his birth or death certificate—neither of which I possessed—for proof of our next-of-kin relationship.

After jumping over all these hurdles, I still failed to pin down an appointment. Repeated phone calls to each office denied me the guarantee of a timeslot, or that the records could even be located before I arrived in St. Louis. I put aside my disappointment and instead spent the six-hour car ride looking forward to being with Elijah.

On the Thursday afternoon before my planned departure for home on Friday, I had a few hours to kill while Elijah was at class. I wandered into a fabulous, old-school record store called Vintage Vinyl and was greeted by the store's speakers blaring The Sex Pistols—the music of my youth. As I flipped through the stacks of new and vintage albums, I smiled as I thought about how some of the coolest things, like record stores, never stop being cool.

The last song reached its crashing climax followed by a moment of relative silence as the employee put a new platter on the turntable. Soon, the scratchy crackle and snap sounds of what was surely a very old album began. Plaintive trumpet notes filled the room and I knew instantly it was side two of Miles Davis' *Porgy and Bess*—one of my father's favorite LPs. It's a total writer cliché to say this, but as I listened to "Prayer (Oh Doctor Jesus)," the hairs on the back of my neck stood at attention and the air around me began to feel close and odd.

At that very moment, my cell phone rang, and on the other end of the line, I heard Archive Specialist Susan Nash say to me, "Mrs. Gimbel, we've located your father's records. If you're still in town, we'd be happy to show them to you at 9 a.m. tomorrow morning."

~ ~ ~ ~ ~

Pulling off the highway, I saw that the National Archives was an enormous building with a somewhat severe edifice, the entry marked by governmental lettering and a crest.

The Navy's National Personnel Records Center holds the health and service records of millions of military personnel who served during the 20th century. The government is very particular when allowing access to the records. After signing in, an employee trained me regarding how to handle the documents and described which things I could copy. I would be required to stow my personal belongings during my visit, and these items would be inspected (and weighed) as I exited the building to make sure no unauthorized documents left with me.

After an archivist directed me to a small desk where I sat down, she handed me the archival (oldest) portion of Dad's records to me. I was surprised to see that everything was enclosed in one small envelope that measured about four by ten inches. I reached out and slid it across the tabletop toward me, wondering what I might find inside. I somehow hoped that it would connect me to my dad when he was just twenty-two years old. Holding that little sliver of information, it felt amazing to be sitting in this giant building where every packet like this, holding a single individual's military history, added up into such a tremendous volume of files. The envelope seemed so meager and insignificant, and yet it represented my father's efforts during three full years of his young life. I opened the envelope's clasp and began to follow in his footsteps.

My personal journey into the war years continued about a year after my visit to the Archives, when Lena and I headed to New Orleans for a college tour. We agreed that squeezing in a visit to The National WWII Museum was a top priority while we were in town. After purchasing our tickets, we decided to include

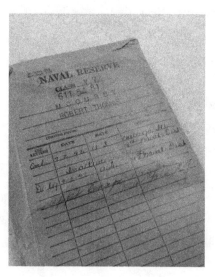

the screening of "Beyond All Boundaries," the 4-D immersive film with special effects shown on a huge panoramic screen. In thirty minutes, the experience encapsulated the timeline of the war as it played out around the world and on the home front. To me, it was awe-inspiring and moving, and as the lights came up, my eyes glistened, and I found it hard to speak around the lump in my throat.

To Lena, however, the patriotic fervor of the film made her feel a little unsettled. Obviously, she was glad that the Allies prevailed, but she pointed out that they did so at such a great and unnecessary cost of life. From her perspective two generations removed from that of the WWII era, she has never known a time when the United States was NOT at war. She wonders why our leaders haven't learned any lessons since then. She wishes so fervently that stronger efforts at diplomacy could replace what she has witnessed her entire life: a continuous stream of U.S. combat forces sent around the globe to support often futile efforts overseas. Many of these troops come back injured or suffering from PTSD—or worse, in coffins. She wonders if the American ideals of peace and prosperity that her grandpa fought for will ever become a reality.

As I straddle these two generations, I am pulled in both directions: back in time to try to understand my father more completely and forward in an effort to try to help my daughter better comprehend the sacrifices made by her grandpa's generation.

In the 1940s, young people who enlisted or were drafted during WWII certainly didn't plan to die. It cannot be denied that many willingly served their country, and they agreed to defend the American way of life. While luckily Dad's assignments kept him from experiencing the worst dangers of the war, he served proudly, and along with millions of his peers, came home and went on with his life.

But it wasn't as if the war didn't have a profound effect on him. Why else would he spend so many winter afternoons in the late 1980s and '90s recording as much about his WWII experience as he could recall for posterity? From the opening paragraphs of his journal, his voice jumps off the page as he gives us some insight:

*On my trip home from my second tour of duty in 1946 on the USLSM 148, I had prepared a nice neat compilation of the things I did during my Navy career. It was entitled "Robin on the Wing" after a popular hit record of the era. It covered 20 pages of single space typing on legal size paper. Rather than waste a lot of time discussing World War II with friends, family etc, I proposed to simply shove "Robin on the Wing" at them. We lost the original sheets during our household moves in the fifties which is why I started these papers. I hate war stories and to this day have kept pretty mum about the services. In fact, my son Bob was quite startled many years ago when he learned that I had spent "time"—in the Navy that is. Actually, I have found that most veterans who served overseas talk very little, if at all, about their time in the services.*

*Mom started and abandoned the accompanying scrapbook and I, of course, finished it. I used to send her bits of life in the Navy. A lot of items probably look pretty sappy now—sand from New Guinea, barnacles, etc. I said earlier that we were frequently hard-pressed to amuse ourselves. The sequence of the snapshots stinks, but some day one of our ancestors may peer at it and be mildly amused. I enjoy reviewing the scrapbook, usually in January. I get a kick out of seeing Mom and me when we were young. I think I have accepted growing old more easily than Mom and also the fact that nothing lasts forever.*

Well, I guess that *I* was that ancestor who would not only take a look at the scrapbook and journal but would spend the next few years following the "pathways" that sprung from the memories he jotted down. As I became immersed in the research, the idea for a book covering the war from a different perspective began to take shape in my mind. With Dad's journal creating the backbone for the narrative, the two of us together could help other children and grandchildren of WWII veterans understand the universal experiences of millions of sailors, soldiers, Marines, and pilots. Dad had a lively wit and engaging manner and it will shine through as he does a lot of the "talking."

He unknowingly sent me on this "mission" after I discovered his journal, and while writing, I often felt frustrated and sad that I was unable to turn to him for answers to the questions that cropped up. Thankfully, I met three generous and wonderful men who stepped into his shoes to fill in a lot of the blanks for me. These veterans became like surrogate WWII fathers to me, so their contributions and stories are also included.

Finally, this book was ultimately the perfect opportunity to honor my father and, by extension, all the other brave young men who left their comfortable lives back home to cross the globe and stand up to fight for America—a chance that I would not let slip away.

## SECTION ONE: THE TRANSITION

Americans stood stunned on December 7, 1941, watching in horror as the Japanese launched their fierce attack on Pearl Harbor. Within days, President Franklin D. Roosevelt asked Congress to declare war on Japan, and soon after, the other members of the Axis, Germany and Italy, declared war on the United States. There would be no more sitting on the sidelines for America.

What began in shock soon mobilized into resolute action to take on three formidable enemies on two distinctly different fronts. Not only would the United States have to recruit and train a vast military force, we would have to accomplish it while doing our best to aid our allies in material ways such as supplying weapons, ships, and military vehicles. In this effort, everyday citizens would join American businesses and the government to create what Roosevelt called "the Arsenal of Democracy." Some folks contributed by collecting scrap metal or wrapping bandages; others uprooted their lives and went to work in manufacturing plants converted to produce much-needed equipment such as airplanes and ships. Millions would serve in the military.

In the years just prior to the events at Pearl Harbor, the

threat of war was building, leading to the creation of the nation's first peacetime draft in the fall of 1940. The draft was one of several national security measures enacted after France fell to Nazi Germany. While isolationist sentiment remained strong, many Americans were unsure whether Great Britain could defeat the Axis on its own and thus believed that the United States would eventually be drawn into the conflict. While the draft helped the military grow to almost 2.2 million members by that fateful Sunday in 1941, it was still woefully unprepared for war, and many, many more men would be required for the fight.

Patriotism (or the feeling of inevitability) drove scores of men from all walks of life and every corner of the country to volunteer at local military recruitment offices. However, in the end, the draft claimed responsibility for the majority of recruits—roughly ten million men in all, most assigned to the Army.

Some of these young men were rushed into the war zone with little preparation. Others were selected for specialized duties that required up to a year of training. Somewhere in between is where Dad found himself as he embarked on his journey toward becoming a Naval Officer.

## SO IT BEGINS – The V-12 Program

When the Japanese bombed Pearl Harbor in December 1941, plunging the United States into World War II, my twenty-year-old father was halfway through his sophomore year at the University of Wisconsin-Madison.

Robert Thomas McCurdy continued his studies while the American war machine ramped up around him. Factories geared up production to meet the coming needs of war. The military would soon require hundreds of thousands of items: airplanes, ships, weapons, and clothing just to name a few. Millions of American young men would be compelled to participate in this war—as sailors, soldiers, pilots, and officers.

The Navy would need 70,000 officers to fully staff the burgeoning wartime fleet. While career Navy officers were graduating as usual from the Naval Academy in Annapolis, it became evident that many more officers would be required to helm the scores of ships that were to come. Navy brass pondered how to identify and select tens of thousands of bright young men, quickly train them as commissioned officers, and get them out to sea.

By the summer of 1942, just as Dad made his way to the naval recruiting center in Chicago to enlist, the Navy zeroed in on college students as the prime source for their future officers. While they hashed out the details of the program, the recruits were put on inactive reserve. This meant that they were officially members of the Navy but were waiting for their eventual assignments. This status allowed them to return to their schools and continue their studies without the risk of being drafted before the program could be rolled out.

*Card proving that Dad was a member of the Naval Reserve for the next four years.*

*My assignment was to enter a special Navy program called V-12. The Navy wanted to procure young Ensigns. Their stated goal was to maintain a certain standard of college education in their officers and at the same time alleviate some of the pressures on the other midshipmen schools around the country. Another goal—unstated— was to keep us out of the Army draft. Most of my colleagues in V-12 there thought that staying out of the Army was a good idea.*

Two separate programs would work in tandem to turn these young students into officers. First, the Navy College program, or V-12 as it was randomly named, would mold the recruits into well-trained sailors. After successfully completing V-12, the men

THE UNIVERSITY OF WISCONSIN
MADISON

S. H. GOODNIGHT
DEAN OF MEN
DEAN OF THE SUMMER SESSION
CHAIRMAN, COMMITTEE ON STUDENT LIFE AND INTERESTS

May 27, 1942

TO WHOM IT MAY CONCERN:

This is to certify that Robert Thomas McCurdy of Freeport, Illinois, is now completing his sophomore year in the University of Wisconsin. He has compiled a splendid scholastic record, attaining freshman honors, and is undoubtedly eligible for sophomore honors now. He had a legislative scholarship because of his good work and because he is almost wholly self-supporting. He is a boy of excellent character, diligent habits and fine reputation. I recommend him unhesitatingly for any branch of our national service, and I am sure that he will prove himself loyal, dependable and worthy of every trust.

Respectfully submitted,

Dean of Men

SHG:ea

would continue on to V-7, the number assigned to the Naval Reserve Midshipmen's Program. Neither program was ready to go at the time Dad enlisted, so he headed back to campus in Madison to start his junior year.

From the records I saw in St. Louis, Dad's military file contains some of the documents he provided for consideration for the V-12 program: his birth certificate, a college transcript, three letters of recommendation, some pictures, proof of good health and eyesight, and a short letter describing why he wanted to participate.

The United States' entry into the war had a profound effect on enrollment at the nation's colleges and universities. After witnessing Pearl Harbor and hearing President Roosevelt's call to arms, many young men felt they should forgo their dreams of a college education in order to join the armed services. This would be especially true after November 13, 1942, when the draft age was lowered to eighteen, forcing those already in college to put their educations on hold. As students left to serve in the military, college enrollments nationwide fell into a steep and rapid decline. Subsequently, without tuition forthcoming from these new soldiers and sailors, many schools faced the threat of closure.

After Pearl Harbor, universities and colleges across the U.S. rushed to volunteer their facilities for anything that the armed forces might need. Schools recognized that hosting fees paid by the Army and Navy for use of their campuses could keep their institutions afloat.

But first, the details of the V-12 program had to be ironed out and the locations selected. There were just six months between the announcement of the V-12 program and the target beginning date of July 1, 1943, so the Navy set about hustling to make the deadline.

President Franklin D. Roosevelt received both the Navy and Army plans for their training programs on college campuses in December 1942. He urged the armed forces to create a fair program that created opportunity for schools of all sizes throughout the country to participate.

Over 1,600 schools quickly applied for consideration, and that number was soon whittled down to the 500 that seemed best able to house, feed, and educate the participants in the program.

First, the Navy reviewed the physical assets of each school. Each potential host had to have either a pool or body of water nearby to make sure that every officer knew how to swim. Campuses also needed adequate gyms and athletic fields to carry out the critical physical training aspects of the program. Planners considered other logistics, such as adding extra bathrooms in dorms where two men would share every room formerly used by just one civilian student.

Debates ensued regarding the financial ramifications of the program: if any part of the facility was deemed lacking, who would be responsible for investing in the improvements, the school or the Navy? If a building needed remodeling, could the Navy or school afford the construction materials now in such short supply due to the war? Some of these debates were resolved in universal decisions as the program details were ironed out; some were handled on a case-by-case basis as the program rolled out.

As Roosevelt hoped, the 131 schools that made the final cut

spanned the whole country, and they ranged in size from large to small and were both private and public—some had religious affiliations as my dad would discover. Each school signed its own contract covering the Navy's use of campus buildings, as well as how it would reimburse the school for meals, physical training fees, and teacher salaries.

Men who already attended a school selected to host the V-12 program had a good chance of remaining there to begin their training. In Dad's case, although the University of Wisconsin-Madison was a V-12 school, the Navy ordered him to report to the University of Notre Dame in South Bend, Indiana, on the very first day the program rolled out nationwide, July 1, 1943.

*On July 1, 1943, with a somewhat heavy heart, I left Freeport, Illinois* [his hometown] *and headed toward South Bend, Indiana.*

*I was not much of a world traveler at the time—had been to Chicago a few times, Fort Dodge, Iowa, and of course, my original hometown of Madison, Wisconsin. It was a real treat then, as a stranger in a strange world, to find all kinds of classmates from the*

Future War Hero
1943 = NOTRE DAME U.
V-12

*University of Wisconsin and my accounting class. There were 2500* [This number was closer to 1,800 according to Notre Dame] *sailors and young marines in our group at Notre Dame and also many regular civilian students mixed in our classes. The Marines were pretty well segregated from the sailors—in different dorms. The paying students as far as I could see ate separately and lived separately . . . I think they got second-rate attention from the University officials.*

On their first day, the men assembled and went through a complete physical examination. Those who didn't pass this test were put back on inactive duty for reassignment. If something about a man's health made him entirely unfit to serve, he was discharged.

During the following days, the recruits received their Navy-issued clothing. After using a stencil to paint their name and service number on their sailor whites, they laid the clothes to dry on the campus lawns. Because their regular studies would continue while they trained, the young men registered for classes and collected their books. They also signed up for life insurance policies and purchased war bonds, both paid for with deductions from their future monthly pay.

*I paid $6.60 a month for life insurance—in case I got killed. The policy was for $10,000. It still seems odd to me that a member of the armed forces would have to pay for his own life insurance.*

The V-12 program ran year-round with three 4-month terms each year beginning July 1st, November 1st, and March 1st. At Notre Dame, for convenience sake, the civilian student terms eventually lined up to coincide with the V-12 "trimesters."

Men in the program were sorted into two designations.

"Regulars" were those who had not yet attended college. The Navy selected their curriculum, and it was heavy on science and math—subjects determined to be most relevant to their future duties at sea. With all the extra sessions of science and math required, some liberal arts professors shifted gears to teach those subjects to meet the increased demand.

"Irregulars," the second designation of recruits in the program, were men who had already completed up to seven semesters of college. They were assigned classes in their chosen majors because the Navy decided it wouldn't be fair to make them start over from scratch. My father, an accounting major at the time, was one of these men.

The academic rigors of the V-12 program overwhelmed some of the new sailors, and if they couldn't keep their grades up, the Navy discharged them. Dad, however, thought it was a breeze. *Needless to say, we made mincemeat out of the meager academics at Notre Dame. To save time, they gave us our schedules. There was no free choice in South Bend; the schedule came in a simple white envelope and was the same for all seniors majoring in accounting. Mine was as follows:*

1. *Advanced Accounting Problems*
2. *Business Law*
3. *Corporate Finance*
4. *Money & Banking*
5. *Logic (a freshman course)*
6. *Five hours a week for Physical Education*

*After three weeks, our accounting professor realized that we all had already taken the advanced accounting course, so he transferred us to auditing. Our professor at Notre Dame paid us all a nice compliment—he wrote the accounting department in Madison extolling our virtues and wondered what and how they were teaching us. I had previously taken Money & Banking at Madison—made this a no brainer. The course in Logic was equally a no brainer. It was interesting to me, at least, that one of the students in Logic had actually flunked the course the prior year. How he did that, I'll never know.*

Dad had a natural affinity for numbers and a keen and quick mind. It is impossible to know now if the two universities' accounting programs were really that different or if Dad just personally felt the Notre Dame classes were a breeze.

Occasionally, there were flare-ups when the schools and the Navy disagreed about who should pay for expenses that cropped up. For example, mealtime metal trays were a "commissioned" expense paid for by the Navy at all schools. Most often, repairs or supplies were considered part of the school's deferred maintenance and were therefore deemed the school's responsibility. The Navy's position was that if classroom or dormitory lighting was not sufficient, it was up to the school to make these improvements. Dad weighed in on this:

*The University once raised a big stink when one of the sailors allegedly stole a light bulb—we hadn't been furnished any for our study lamps. The Navy reacted in the only way it could to find the thief—mustered us out on the Drill Field at 6 a.m. and forced us to run double time around the outer perimeter of the football stadium. After one round, most of us, even though innocent, were ready to confess. The Navy chiefs called off the torture after the lap and we eventually got the light bulbs from Father "Light Bulb." It turned out that the academics were so incredibly simple that we probably could have gotten passing grades studying in the dark (there was a ceiling light in the room)—or just going to class and writing the exams.*

Dad jokingly named the character he writes about "Father Light Bulb," but since Notre Dame was a Catholic university, priests did indeed teach the courses. Dad spent several years during his childhood in a Catholic elementary school, the nuns teaching classes and also doling out the occasional rap on the knuckle with a wooden ruler to those who misbehaved. Here at Notre Dame it was the priests that made a lasting impression on him. *There were some interesting priests and teachers, of course. The very eccentric Father McGinn who taught logic gave us some sage advice one day out of the clear blue sky. Simply put it was "don't 'kadiddle' with any young girls in South Bend, but if you must 'kadiddle' be sure you wear a good condom." In 1943 that was far-out advice, especially from a priest and at a Catholic University—a University which actually attempted to bar the showing of a standard Navy film dealing with various sexually transmitted diseases, and what to do about them. It was a standard movie shown to all Army and Navy personnel. I must admit the film was a bit gruesome.*

Academics aside, many of the recruits to V-12 had a long way to go before they reached the peak physical shape required of them. Ideally, an instructor from the college's athletic department took on the task of whipping the young men into shape. When such a staff member wasn't available, the Navy provided an athletic officer to run the sailors through calisthenics drills—running, jumping jacks, squats, and the like.

Hands down, one of the worst parts of training was the obstacle course, something that every sailor, soldier, Marine, and airman encountered during their training. Meant to build the men's physical fitness, agility, and confidence, the courses consisted of things like climbing walls, swinging and climbing on ropes, running, crawling through trenches and tunnels, and throwing. The specialists who devised these rigorous courses were devilishly renowned for trying to make theirs the hardest in the district, using whatever materials they had access to. *I suspect that I would never have survived the regular phy-ed course taught by Navy chiefs and Marine sergeants. I used to marvel as Paul Ziemer—a fairly burly chap* [Paul was a Marine also training at Notre Dame]*—would come back to the dorm literally whipped by the obstacle course, the toughest in the country they said. The rough Marine sergeant, a little guy, also delighted in torturing Paul on the karate mat with body slams. He was bloody but unbroken. Paul was not nearly as good in accounting as most of us, but he had leadership qualities that really paid off in his business career—he became president of Wisconsin Public Service Co in later years.*

Knowing how to swim was a necessity in the Navy because a sailor's life might depend on it. Soon after arriving at Notre Dame, the recruits were tested for their ability in the water and then separated into groups of swimmers and non-swimmers, with skill levels rated under each designation. *I was very lucky. During the first week we were marched to the Rockne Memorial Hall swimming pool, ordered to strip and swim the length of the pool, or stand aside and enter the beginner's swimming class. I stood aside* [to be a beginner] *and became a survivor and master of the breast and backstrokes—the elementary ones where there is a minimum of splashing. It was a bit of a challenge at first since we were served dinner at noon and then raced three or four blocks for our swim—on full stomachs. Mr. Gill, our main instructor, assured us there was no such thing as stomach cramps—even on full stomachs. He was on the University staff and I rank him as one of the best in his line—a fine man too, and great teacher. Mr. Gill did not bully or try to humiliate us.*

There were only four months to get the recruits ready for their assignments, so the non-swimmers like Dad went through a rigorous training routine. Almost every day of the week, the guys reported to the pool for intensive swimming drills until they finally passed the swimmer's test. The participants who were already good swimmers when they entered the V-12 program only hit the water once per week.

Life for the young sailors was not all laps, books, and drills—there were also opportunities for fun during their time in V-12. When "off the clock," the recruits did all the things regular students do at college: go to dances, write for campus newspapers and yearbooks, put on musical shows, join bands and choirs, and attend church. At some schools, men even joined fraternities.

The Navy allowed the trainees to leave campus for designated amounts of time with passes for short breaks off or "liberty." Curfew was strictly enforced, though, and all men had to "muster" (gather for inspection, drills, or battle) and be accounted for at liberty's end.

Their studies and military training came first, but soldiers, sailors, and Marines in V-12 could join intercollegiate sports on campus as long as traveling to compete took less than two days at a time. Many schools suspended their sports programs for the duration of the war because their best athletes left school to serve. Other schools persevered and, in an ironic twist, went from having weak athletic programs to suddenly excelling in sports due to the influx of vigorously healthy V-12 athletes. Dad talked about this in his journal: *Notre Dame had a wonderful football team in 1943—the most polished bunch I ever saw perform. They not only had their regular players from the prior year (a couple of "all Big Ten" players the year before) but picked up a few who were in the V-12 program: Julius Rykovich and Vic Kulbitski from Illinois and Minnesota. They fit right in—names and all. It was also the first time that I got a decent seat at a football game—as seniors we rated 40-yard line viewing for only 50 cents a ticket. A dear friend of mine, Bill Schmelzle, had a lifetime dream to attend Notre Dame. I always told him I'd die before I would go.* [Dad was a loyal Badger] *He went to the University of Illinois and visited with me before the Illinois-Notre Dame football game in 1943. He was green with envy. I believe Notre Dame won—49 to 0 or something like that.*

Actually, the score was 47-0. Dad was close. With a nearly perfect record that season, Notre Dame earned the National Football Title for 1943. In addition to its civilian players, the team consisted of fourteen Navy apprentice seamen, twelve transfers who were part of the Marine branch of the V-12, as well as seventeen Marine privates.

One big downside for the V-12 athletes was that their Navy training might end in the middle of their sport's regular season, abruptly cutting off their athletic career as they were sent on to midshipmen's school. Unfortunately, the stark reality of wartime meant that V-12 athletes were on these campuses to serve their country first, not just to further their college education or play ball.

Dad would have to wait to complete his accounting degree until after the war. On September 21, 1943, he joined his new friends in Company C as they "graduated" from the V-12 program. For the next two years, thousands more young men would follow at Notre Dame and other training campuses until the Navy chiefs agreed that they had all the officers they would need already participating in the training process. During the summer of 1945, men in the program with five or fewer semesters were moved into the Naval Reserve Officer Training Corps program, while those with six or more continued in the V-12 program until graduation.

*Happy group of new sailors*

At the close of V-12, the program commissioned 60,000 officers from the total of 125,000 men who enrolled. Prior to this point in American history, most young men never dreamed of attending college. For these special young sailors, the V-12 program opened the door to getting a college education that would likely have been closed to them otherwise. Many graduates of the program returned to school after the war and completed their educations to go on to successful careers. Further, V-12 helped colleges and universities across the United States remain open and even thrive while doing their part for the war effort.

In four months' time, my father had left the life he knew to become part of something much larger. He was now a sailor in the United States Navy, and well on his way to obtaining that officer's star and stripe.

*Here's a little invite to my mom for a date when Dad was home between the training programs*

# MIDSHIPMEN'S SCHOOL – 90-Day Wonders

With the goal of producing 36,000 Naval Reserve officers, President Franklin D. Roosevelt announced the Navy Midshipmen's Program, known as "V-7," in June 1940. Over the next five years, candidates for this program streamed out of V-12 and into one of four schools hosting midshipmen training—Northwestern, Notre Dame, Cornell, and Columbia University. There, they remained apprentice seamen in the Naval Reserve until successful completion of the V-7 program when they became ensigns—the lowest rank of commissioned officer in the Navy.

*Pop and Mom – waxing emotional –*

*October 1943*

Upon completing his four months of Navy V-12 coursework at Notre Dame, Dad spent a few days' leave catching up with his family and my future mom before boarding a train to New York City to continue his training at Columbia University.

*Around November 1, [1943] I further broadened my travel experience and was enrolled in the 16th class of mid-shipmen at Columbia University in New York City. Sleeping in the Pullman berth* [these were single beds that pulled down from the ceiling of the train car—usually four to a compartment] *was another big thrill. We didn't get much time off between gigs.*

*I worried a lot about being sent to midshipmen school. A fate worse than death waited the majority of apprentice seamen—four months in Little Creek, Virginia or Norfolk, and then out to sea. What I was trying to say is that I really wanted to go to Midshipman School, but we were all deathly afraid of failing.*

I assume that his fear of failing refers to making it through training to become an officer. He and everyone in the program knew that life as an officer would be preferable to that of an enlisted seaman. Being a bookish sort of person, Dad was likely daunted by the physical rigors of the training. Most importantly, I'm sure that he did not want to disappoint his family by not achieving the officer rank.

Even before Roosevelt's summer announcement of the V-7 program, the Navy was already tinkering with establishing a Reserve Midshipmen's Program at both Northwestern and Columbia universities. In fact, in the spring of 1940, Columbia University hosted a class of the V-7 program in an off-campus location.

Soon after, the midshipmen school at Columbia moved onto the Morningside Heights campus, using about twelve buildings there for housing and training. It was here where Dad arrived and, along with the other trainees, made his home in John Jay Hall. When this dorm first opened in 1927, it was called The Skyscraper because at fifteen stories, it was twice the height of any other dorm on campus. The design included areas for student social life, a large dining hall, meeting and club spaces, and lounge areas on each floor. Single rooms meant for graduate students would now bunk pairs of sailors.

*My roommate was also from the University of Wisconsin. We were on the 14th floor of John Jay Hall—and required to run double time up the stairs and down. We could not use the elevators.*

The Navy ran the building as if it was a ship, referring to it as the USS *John Jay*. The officers-in-training, now following strict Navy discipline as they transitioned from civilians to officers, entered the building by snapping to attention and requesting "permission to come aboard, sir?" from their superiors.

The pairs of trainees in each room were expected to maintain strict cleanliness and military order. Dad learned to dread the daily white glove inspections that included checking to see if he'd made his bed with precise corners.

Harold R. Stark, Admiral of the U.S. Navy, welcomed the members of the 16th class to their training with these words, later included in their keepsake yearbook the *Sideboy*:

> "To you who are just joining the Naval Service I send my best wishes. Never in the history of our country has the Navy been so much in need of the

best of our youth, with ruggedness of character, loyalty, high courage, and – THE WILL TO WIN. I hope you all may have opportunity to cross swords with the enemy. The country has every reliance and confidence in your ability to come out victoriously. To do so, hard work, singleness of purpose and devotion to the tasks in hand are essential; for as you have trained, and as you continue to train today, and tomorrow, so will you fight. Keep fit, physically and mentally, and keep the FIGHTING EDGE sharp. Congratulations on the great privilege for service that is yours. Good luck."

The challenging first month of the program, known as indoctrination, was meant to cull the recruits who didn't have what it took to become an officer. The Navy expected the men to both quickly adapt to the strict rules and protocols of Navy life and prove their physical fitness, intelligence, and ability to lead others. Those who didn't make the grade were demoted and sent on to enlisted seaman training. The men who prevailed during indoctrination would continue with three months

of additional training to become Ensigns. They earned the nickname "90-Day Wonders" since they accomplished in three months what it took an Annapolis Naval Academy graduate to achieve in four years.

*There were about 1200 of us to be molded into proper Navy line officers—in four months. We all fretted for the first three weeks awaiting the first "cut." This had been 20 to 25% in previous classes. Less than 75 of us washed out—Navy for fired. The four months at Notre Dame obviously had helped us get used to the ways of the Navy.*

*The Navy had an interesting method of advising which of us had washed out after the third week testing period. They mustered us out in the halls at 10pm and on the PA systems made this announcement: "The following men, I repeat, the following named men will not send out laundry on Monday, 22 November 1943." (It's odd but service people always seemed to repeat phrases when giving orders.)*

*They then read the names in agonizing slowness and in alphabetical order. Once your letter in the alphabet was passed, you could hear midshipmen and their sighs of relief. At the very end of the alphabet, however, the announcer doubled back to list 10 or 12 fellows who had been overlooked in the original reading. This was Navy-type torture. It's odd but we all stood at rigid attention outside our rooms. We were afraid to move though there was no one supervising us in the hall—they really had us cowed.*

*Those who washed out weren't discharged. They simply were sent to Great Lakes and other bases to become apprentice seamen. This was a great humiliation for men with seven semesters of college under their belts—and life was a lot tougher as enlisted trainees.*

According to the *Sideboy*, the 16th class had fewer washouts than any previous class, and the men who made the cut officially became midshipmen, now poised to continue further training to become officers. In dramatic fashion the book reads, "As Indoctrination drew to a close, the three weeks past seemed

distant and dream-like, but it was no dream that we stood in the cathedral and took the midshipman's oath together. 'I, having been duly appointed . . . a midshipman . . . will uphold the traditions of the Navy . . . so help me God.' We were midshipmen, and that single stripe and star seemed infinitely closer."

*We officially became midshipmen late in November with better uniforms and a raise in pay from $21 a month to $54. Columbia University was thoroughly high class and still is, I guess. No more* [sailor] *bellbottoms.*

Dad could breathe a sigh of relief that he survived Indoctrination. The next three months would be a whirlwind of orders, drills, and further training for the job ahead.

*Once we got accustomed to Columbia, it was a much better spot than Notre Dame. I will admit that the Navy had us scared. For example, we had marched past Grant's Tomb for two months before we realized it was even there—we were afraid to avert our eyes to the left. We marched in our usual straight lines and we really barked out our responses in unison. We learned the crisp responses in the first three weeks from the 15th class of Midshipmen. We really sounded great—no mumbling. We said it like we meant it.*

The men traveled in strict formation with their company for review, the companies pitted against each other for the highest rankings. The Navy handed out demerits for such things as uniform infractions, being out of step, not moving in sharp columns, or failing a part of the room inspection. Physical training continued with drills, obstacle courses, and practice performing watches. The *Sideboy* states that officers strictly scrutinized the men, watching for any traits that could someday endanger the lives of their shipmates.

Excerpts from the Executive Department of Training in Dad's midshipmen yearbook read almost like propaganda:

> "RIGHT FACE!" Look ahead. Don't wait for the torpedo to hit and then run for your book to look up damage control instructions. Forehandedness will often save your skin.
>
> "KEEP IN STEP! DRESS IT OFF!" Move together. Cooperation and teamwork are the lubricants for a perfectly operating Naval machine. If, from the corner of your eye, you can size up a situation at a glance, Tojo will find it hard to catch you off guard."

Even with the threat of demerits, Dad and the other midshipmen eased in for the duration of their training. *Once we were midshipmen the balance of the training was a cupcake—partly because those of us from the North were obviously better schooled in both high school and in college than 98% of the lads from the South. It's hard, for example, to learn celestial navigation if somewhere along the line you haven't had a course in Trigonometry.*

Celestial navigation is the art of figuring out your location by taking measurements of the angles between the horizon and navigational stars, the sun, or the moon. To do this, the men used a sextant, a device with a viewing sight and a sliding semicircle that measured the angle between the two visible objects. Daily tests made sure the sailors understood how to take the measurements and could translate them to longitude and latitude.

The men also learned to use a magnetic compass, a tool used by mariners for centuries.

Using the magnetic pull of the north and south poles to determine a course or location, this type of compass was tricky to master because the accuracy of true north varies depending on where the person using it is located on earth. Dad learned that being able to correct his measurements was almost as important as figuring them out to begin with. The ships themselves were magnetic which could skew the reading of the compass, so the midshipmen had to factor in this effect to be sure they had accurate readings.

The midshipmen acquired basic seamanship skills such as keeping a ship's records, understanding Navy terms and slang, recognizing aircraft, mastering the art of signaling, and handling a ship in crowded waters. They absorbed how to use and store weapons, otherwise known as ordnance.

Dad learned Damage Control, or how to keep the ship afloat in an emergency. If his ship collided with another or was bombed, torpedoed, or grounded, his goal was to try to minimize the damage to the ship until help could arrive. Later, he would assess the damage and report it up the chain of command. Fires could become a major hazard for the men on their ships, so they familiarized themselves with basic firefighting equipment and how to use it.

Dovetailing with the damage control classes were engineering courses that taught the men about the ship's basic mechanical operation. They learned all about the engines, boilers, and electrical workings of the ship. The *Sideboy* nicknamed one of these courses "How to Sink a Ship in Ten Easy Lessons," because the men came out of it wide-eyed and with a complete knowledge of both how the ship was built and everything that could destroy it.

To apply the things they learned in the classroom, the men set sail on three different training cruises. This was how they got hands-on experience casting off, steering, performing lookout duty, manning the bridge, and navigating. As they stopped for lunch, they went over signal drills before returning the ship to the mooring. This is a photo of Dad taken on one of his training cruises in the cold New York Harbor.

While the ninety days of training were full of classes and practice, the men also participated in pursuits other than their studies just as they had in the V-12 program. Many joined band, choir, and sports teams during their free time. The Navy required attendance at religious services, but the men had their choice of a Protestant service at Riverside Church, a Jewish service led by a lieutenant commander named Joshua Goldberg, and a Catholic service at Corpus Christi Roman Catholic Church.

*I have never been a religious man, but I enjoyed the Sunday night services at Corpus Christi Church. This was required, of course, although Sunday mass wasn't. I skipped Corpus Christi one Sunday to attend the service at Riverside Drive Church. This was a big time Protestant church at the time, but the service was dull, dull, dull.*

*I still remember the last service at Corpus Christi conducted by a young, fiery, fluent and articulate Irish priest who pleaded with us to fight the honorable fight in battle and added, "if you die, then die like men." To tell the truth, most of us hadn't thought much about battles—and certainly not about being killed. It was a stirring sermon that obviously I have never forgotten—*

A whole generation of young men were now forced to confront their mortality, something they likely never dwelled on before. Would they make it home alive? Would they be able to pursue their dreams of work and family? Time would tell. With the words of the Irish priest ringing in many of their ears, 141 members of the 16th Class of Midshipmen at Columbia graduated as Ensigns on February 24, 1944. *We became Ensigns late in February. The pay was much better—$150 a month plus a lot of travel perks.*

In just seven months, Dad left home, acclimated to Navy life in the V-12 program, and completed midshipmen school to become an officer. Now, as he waited for word about his future assignment, he was left to wonder about where he was headed and how soon he would leave the life he knew behind.

The Commanding Officer
of the
United States Naval Reserve
Midshipmen's School
New York, N. Y.
announces the graduation of the
Sixteenth Class of Reserve Midshipmen
and their commissioning as
Ensigns in the United States Naval Reserve
Thursday, the twenty-fourth of February
Nineteen hundred and forty-four

# A LOT OF GOODBYES – Off They Go

*After a week's leave in Freeport, Illinois, I headed west for San Francisco to report to a landing craft unit. The train left Chicago at 7 p.m. on Sunday and arrived in San Francisco around noon the following Wednesday (it might have been Tuesday.) It's hard to believe that this is maybe a four-hour flight nowadays. I remember when I kissed Muriel* [my mother] *goodbye. It was always very, very hard to do, saying goodbye that is. There were a lot of goodbyes in those days—many of them were, of course, forever. I also remember how I envied Ensign Herbie Webb from my class at Columbia. He had his young bride with him on the trip west while dear old Muriel was languishing in Freeport (and unmarried). Herbie had many things going for him—mainly a very rich father and a nice family business to inherit.*

There was a great deal of commotion at the dock in San Francisco on February 11, 1944. My father joined a sea of over a thousand other men, all dressed in white or navy blue, pouring onto the gangways to climb aboard the USS *Ommaney Bay*—the ship that would deliver them to their assignments in the South Pacific.

Each sailor balanced a heavy canvas sea bag awkwardly over his shoulder, freshly stenciled with his name, containing all his worldly possessions. His uniforms, sleeping gear, and towels were tightly rolled inside in a specific order, drilled into his memory through repeated practice of packing and unpacking the bag. Additionally, for the enlisted men, a hammock and mattress were wrapped around the exterior of the bag and bound fast with a line.

Dad didn't need the hammock because, as an officer, he wouldn't be sleeping with the masses—"Rank has its privileges," as they say. But like the other officers catching a ride that day, he still had a full bag to hoist onto his shoulder as he boarded the ship in search of his quarters.

*I sailed out of San Francisco on a brand new light aircraft carrier named the U.S.S. Ommaney Bay (hull classification CVE). The food and service were excellent. There were some ground swells right outside of San Francisco that caused the first bout of seasickness and then we ran into a vicious storm that lasted four days. As a passenger officer, I shared quarters with another young Ensign. He was seasick for at least a week. Being seasick is a good way to lose weight.*

As Dad mentioned, the USS *Ommaney Bay* CVE-79 was a new escort carrier and like Dad, the ship was making its maiden voyage. Packed with passengers, troops, supplies, and aircraft, it was bound for Brisbane, Australia, where the passengers would go on to find their permanent assignments.

The USS *Ommaney Bay* had a hull designation of "CVE Escort Carrier," but these types of ships were often casually referred to as "baby flattops." They were about half the length of the regular fleet aircraft carriers and held far fewer aircraft— only about twenty-eight. Slow and barely armored but cheap and quick to build, they filled a gap in the fleet. According to Lincoln Cushing in his article about Kaiser CVE's, these ships were also sarcastically known as "**C**ombustible, **V**ulnerable, and **E**xpendable" due to their many inferior qualities.

*The Ommaney Bay was probably ill fated from the start. It was on its maiden voyage and the crew, as well as the officers, were having difficulty adapting to life at sea. The Navy didn't have the "practice" option in 1943. They went right to work—on the job training—just as we did on our LCTs* [Landing Craft, Tank is the type of ship Dad served on].

It would take the real-life scenarios of long voyages and battle duties to show these new members of the Navy that they could rise above their minimal boot camp and officer training.

*There were 50 passenger officers* [being delivered to their assignments] *and for the first week only five or six of us showed up for meals. I had never been able to endure carnival rides, so I was quite proud that in my whole career at sea—mostly on small craft, I never once was sick.*

*There were about 1000 enlisted men passengers on board. They were cooped up in the well deck—like the hold of the ship. I strolled down there one day and discovered that 1000 men can create one monstrous amount of vomit. Shower facilities were also very limited for the young sailors. Needless to say, they were not traveling first class. There was no air conditioning on the ship.*

Al Exner, a veteran Navy Corpsman Surgical Technician from Waukesha, Wisconsin, served in both the European and Pacific theaters of war and he shared his experiences with me. He was never on a boat or ship at all during his training at Great Lakes after joining the Navy at age seventeen. Soon after boot camp, he found himself on a converted ocean liner with 7,000 other men on his way to England. He recalled the conditions in the hold of his ship for me: "On the ship, the quarters were very tight. There were fabric pieces stretched onto pipes to act as beds, and these were stacked four high. There was only about eighteen inches between each canvas. The fellow above me was very heavy, and if I didn't get into my bunk before him, I would have to squeeze into the small space left below from his weight sagging the canvas."

I later saw one of these bunks at the National World War II Museum. The fabric was pulled tight as a board, and it looked as if it was as uncomfortable as sleeping on the ground.

I read how other veterans recalled climbing over the sea bags littered all over the narrow aisle between the bunks every time they made their way to and from their bunk. The quarters were below the waterline, with no portholes, so the conditions were stifling for the men crowded into these confined spaces. According to Al, the food was very poor—kidney stew served from wooden pails, for example—and many men were seasick.

As my father said, the personal hygiene options for the troops were minimal. The only showers were with saltwater, and the little brick of soap provided produced barely any lather at all. I wondered if the young men actually felt dirtier after their shower once the saltwater dried to a crust on their skin than they had before taking it.

Dad continued in the journal, further describing the USS *Ommaney Bay*: *We couldn't get over how well the ship was equipped. It had a beautiful sick bay, at least one M.D. and the usual assistants. One of the ensigns who was right out of dental school looked longingly at the equipment. He was also a passenger. I heard the two ships' company dentists complaining about having to spend the next 18 months doing amalgams—silver fillings. They were "gold crown" type chaps.*

Meanwhile, Al often slept up on the deck or in the sick bay of his ship to escape the suffocating conditions in the bunks down below. While sick bays were primarily set up to treat those wounded in battle, they often served a secondary purpose as the ship's barbershop. Here there were twenty-five or thirty bunks, a couple of barber chairs, and medical supplies stored in lockers. Al had access to the sick bay because he served as a Navy surgical technician.

Dad had plenty of time to explore the USS *Ommaney Bay* since his trip to Brisbane, Australia, would last sixteen or seventeen days. He was happy to discover the ship's library, where he found plenty of books to read en route.

Deck space was at a premium as troops and sailors clad in lifejackets sprawled about just to get some sunshine and fresh air. Sailors could stretch their legs exploring the ship or join one of the card games that quickly sprang up. Training exercises and daily inspections continued for all. On larger transport ships, the crew even produced daily newsletters with news of the world gathered from the radio. Some lucky men were on transport ships where Special Services put on entertainment such as plays or movies.

Many ships the size of Dad's escort carrier or larger had a snack bar, called a gedunk (usually pronounced "gee-DUNK with a hard "g") in addition to the regular mess hall. No one is 100 percent sure where the term gedunk came from, but one theory is that it was derived from a popular newspaper comic strip called "Harold Teen" that had called ice cream "gedunk" since the 1920s. The use of the term spread from ice cream to snacks and candy, and finally extended to the actual place on board where sailors could come to purchase these items, as well as cigarettes, when the mess was closed.

Feeding all the troops was a major daily undertaking. On a typical transport ship, the men sometimes had to line up for hours to get their chow. In an article titled "Life Aboard a Troop Transport," Arthur Cott recalled finally getting into the mess hall after waiting in line, having food plopped onto his tray, and moving along a chest-high table, eating as he went. When he reached the end of the table, he washed his tray and left the mess hall, only to repeat this process later for the second meal of the day.

Al remembers that the mess hall on his ship was large enough to feed several hundred men at one time. Officers were served their meals in their own quarters, or in officer dining rooms, so Dad never commented on the mess hall on his transport ship.

While some of these transport ships sailed in safe waters, the Navy still took precautions to ensure their safe arrival, Dad recalled: *At night we traveled under blackout conditions and of course, were on a zigzag path to make it more difficult for submarines to aim their torpedoes. One night all hell broke loose, we came to a dead stop, sirens blaring, lifeboats were lowered and every searchlight on board turned on. At this point we would have been a prime target for any Japanese submarine nearby. A harried muster (roll count) had indicated that one of the passenger sailors was missing (man overboard). The search continued for several hours and then was abandoned. The missing sailor happily was found—in one of the lifeboats. He had thought it would be fun to join the search.*

*The Captain was obviously a humanitarian and did what his heart dictated. I would think his naval superiors would have thought differently—endangering perhaps 2000 men to rescue one chap.*

*It was on the* Ommaney Bay *that I realized I was never going to be the gung-ho type guy with dangerous weapons. The ship's gunnery officer offered to conduct some target practice off the stern of the ship—we being the shooters. I took my trusty .45, aimed carefully at some floating cans and then shot just once. The noise was deafening, so in a daze I turned toward the instructor pointing the weapon directly at his stomach asking him casually, "what do I do now?" He quickly turned my hand away uttering some unkind profanities and that was the end of target practice. I could very easily have killed him and to this day have never fired another weapon—in vain or otherwise.*

Could it be possible that Dad never learned how to fire his own war-issue pistol?

This is a telling example of how some men's harried training could have sent them off to war without even knowing how to use their own weapons. When Dad left the service, he was allowed to keep his gun. Years later, he told me he unleashed a firestorm from my mother when he placed the weapon on their kitchen table to show to a neighbor. Mom wanted it gone, so just like that, the neighbor became the proud owner of a Navy-issued pistol.

Dad stepped off the USS *Ommaney Bay* in Australia, where he spent a week before moving closer to his final destination— LCT (Landing Craft Tank) 977. He said: *We landed in Brisbane (that's in Australia, land of emeralds) and for a week while waiting to 'ship out' we visited a lovely seaside cottage type place. It was run by an English woman who referred to herself as Lady Coot. We romped in the sand and surf and in general had lots of fun. I was able to use my new swimming skills having learned the art at South Bend. We played a lot of blackjack to kill time and Jack Forgeson really cleaned us out. Eventually he confessed that he had been a part-time blackjack dealer in Reno, Nevada, during the summers while in college. I never saw him again either. He was a real nice chap.*

*We sailed on a smaller vessel up north and west to Milne Bay in Southern New Guinea. All I can remember is that we slept on deck—fortunately it did not rain. Our voyage was along the Great Barrier Reef that I understand is quite an attraction—for tourists—at 22, who cares?*

I was curious about what happened to the USS *Ommaney Bay* after it dropped Dad off in Brisbane, and I discovered it had a storied and ultimately tragic journey. First it served as a training vessel back at Pearl Harbor. From there, it sailed to the Philippines to provide air cover for what is widely considered the fiercest Navy battle of the war—The Battle of Leyte Gulf.

A kamikaze attack later sealed the fate of the USS *Ommaney Bay*, the beautiful new ship that Dad hitched a ride on. On January 4, 1945, in the Sulu Seas in the Surigao Strait during the Luzon campaign, she was struck on the starboard side, the Japanese plane hurtling right through the flight deck and into the fully fueled planes stored below. There was no power or water to control the fires that erupted, and when the flames began to spread toward the ship's torpedo storage, the captain ordered all hands to abandon ship. A nearby destroyer, the USS *Burns*, launched a torpedo to deliberately sink the ship, presumably to keep it from the enemy. Ninety-three of the *Ommaney Bay* crew were killed and scores more were injured.

There's a clip of the kamikaze attack on the USS *Ommaney Bay* for anyone who is interested to take a look:

https://www.criticalpast.com/video/65675024972_USS-Mississippi_USS-Ommaney-Bay_Japanese-plane_General-Kruger.

The seven-decades-old film clip shows the Japanese plane elude frantic anti-aircraft fire from the CVE's deck before it crashes into the ship, billows of thick, black smoke erupting in the aftermath.

It was chilling for me to see this piece of history, knowing that my father traveled aboard this vessel. I was struck by the pure luck involved—that Dad returned from the war unscathed while others, including members of the crew he traveled with on that ship, met their fates.

*Use of this photo permitted by Bruce Leininger*

*Photo courtesy National Archives 80-G-273153*

## AL EXNER – From Studies To Syringes

In September 1940, Congress passed the Burke-Wadsworth Act (The Selective Service and Training Act) and sent it along to Roosevelt for his signature. When the ink dried, the first peacetime draft in the United States began. After Pearl Harbor and the U.S. entry into the war, the government required all men between the ages of eighteen and thirty-eight to register. At the same time, it became possible for seventeen-year-old young men to willingly join the armed services with the signed permission of their parents.

One of these selfless teenagers was Al Exner. Born in Racine, Wisconsin, he graduated at just seventeen from Washington Park High School. He was particularly interested in the sciences and hoped to become a doctor one day. However, the war would soon delay his plans. Al knew that the draft would randomly select a military branch for him, so he decided to exercise some control over his future by enlisting.

Still a minor, Al first needed to convince his mother to allow him to join up. She was reluctant to do so since Al and his younger brother were all she had left. Her husband had been a police officer, shot and killed in the line of duty when Al was just a boy. Pushing past her reservations, she agreed to send Al on a train to the recruitment center at the Plankinton Arcade in Milwaukee.

A Naval representative soon swooped down on Al and did his best to convince him to choose the Navy. He assured Al that with so many math and science courses under his belt, he wouldn't have to start at the lowest rate of seaman but would instead be assigned the rate of Hospital Apprentice Second Class. So, after an interview that lasted less than five minutes, Al began his military career.

Before long he reported to Naval Station Great Lakes in Lake County, Illinois, for boot camp. Basic training in peacetime normally took thirteen weeks—for Al it was only nine.

The Navy typically sent the young men desiring medical assignments to a Corps school with a six-month training schedule. Al didn't realize until much later that his abbreviated training was unheard of at the time. He can only surmise as he reflects about this now that they were rushing the staff through training to meet the needs of the upcoming planned invasions.

"The push was on to get people to those invasion spots," recalled Al.

At the close of boot camp, the men lined up in front of a table where two petty officers sat waiting to give them their assignments. Al confidently approached them and said that he wanted to learn something, not just do regular duty like the other guys. He has always felt that his cheeky approach to that table that morning landed him on the meningitis ward right there at Great Lakes.

Al had never seen anything like it in his life. Whole groups of men had come down with the disease and lay quarantined in the ward. Every one of the twenty beds contained a man in a coma and in danger of dying. Al had never done anything as simple as taking someone's temperature and was rightfully daunted facing this grim scene.

A kindly woman, Nurse Kennedy, showed him the ropes. Al was eternally grateful to her, because everything she taught him on that ward came in handy later during his service abroad.

Dressed in a gown and gloves, Al learned to administer what little quantities of medicine they had into IVs and watched as doctors injected it directly into the patients' spines. Meningitis was a mystery in those days, and the doses of medicine used to treat it were exceptionally small compared to today's protocols. Al spent thirty days working tirelessly on the ward until he finally received his orders to ship out.

*Photo of Al taken in the Philippines*

The very first ship he ever found himself aboard was a transport ship, the RMS *Aquitania*, bound for Europe. What he remembered most from the journey was that the ship was huge, carrying thousands of Army soldiers along with his own group from the Navy. As they approached Scotland, he was startled to see German planes leisurely circling in the air over the ship, casually keeping an eye on their enemy.

Al continued on to Netley Hospital in Southampton, England, where he drove jeeps and ambulances to and from the almost century-old facility. Although Al didn't witness this personally, records indicate that the Americans often drove jeeps inside the building from ward to ward along the main corridor that stretched a quarter of a mile long. He recalled that the hospital had a thousand beds, half of which were designated to his unit.

In 1944, the English handed the hospital over to the U.S. Army and Navy, and between that time and the end of the war, over 68,000 patients were treated there, including many injured in the battles on D-Day, as well as thousands of German prisoners of war—as many as 10,000 according to Al.

Since there were only six surgical technicians when Al arrived, he saw an opportunity and volunteered for this job. After a brief interview, he received the promotion and underwent a whirlwind two-week training period. Dr. George Novak from Harvard was a worldly fellow who spoke several languages, could converse on any subject, and took Al under his wing, making a huge impression on the young sailor. He never hesitated to stop a procedure to explain what he was doing.

"I ate it up, I was just gung ho. If another technician got a call and complained, I'd say, 'Just stay in the sack, I'll take the call.' I made notes, I made drawings, I studied on the side because I wanted to learn," Al recalled. His dedication soon earned him a promotion to a 3$^{rd}$ class rate.

Al was fascinated by how Dr. Novak used the Gigli saw to open skulls. This apparatus was like two rings with a length of braided wire between them that the surgeon would stretch tight, pulling the saw back and forth to make the cuts. Sometimes the wire got so hot with the friction of the rapid movement that it snapped in two.

The wounded arrived at Netley by land and sea to be triaged, or to receive emergency surgery before being transferred by train to other hospitals in England, or by ship back to the United States for further treatment. Because of the risk of gangrene, doctors only sutured closed belly wounds—they left other injuries open to drain during the transfer out of the hospital.

In the two weeks after the invasion of Normandy, the hospital was a scene of frantic activity. The staff worked on the wounded from six in the morning to midnight, after which they cleaned up and tried to relax a little (sometimes by drinking a little medicinal alcohol mixed with water). They grabbed some sleep between 3 and 6 a.m. when the cycle would start up again. Al remembered often staying awake for several days at a time.

"Our hands got so tender from scrubbing in that we put two pairs of gloves on at 6 a.m.," recalled Al.

During those harrowing two weeks while he assisted on almost 200 cases, he lost twenty-two pounds. Al sent a picture of himself home to his mother, and she could barely recognize her own son in the image, something that must have given her pause as she recalled granting her permission for his enlistment.

According to Al, the Germans bombed the area around the hospital over 800 times, but miraculously, they never hit the building directly. Many of the bombs were V-1 bombs, called "buzz bombs" because of their distinctive sound. You can hear the sound for yourself at this link: https://www.youtube.com/watch?v=Q1qsBGTkVSk. Al said, "As long as you could hear them, you knew you were okay—once the motor cut out you were in trouble."

Buzz bombs were like the original cruise missile—the tiny craft were either launched from a catapult-type device or, later in the war, dropped from German bombers in the general direction of their target. They had gas-powered engines that fired fifty times a second, creating the distinctive sound that terrified the citizens below. The engine was set to cut at a certain time, and the little aircraft would fall from the sky, its one-ton warhead exploding on impact. Luckily for Al and the British, buzz bombs were highly inaccurate. To illustrate, only about one-fifth of the thousands of V-1s launched at London reached the city.

English anti-aircraft gunners protected Netley Hospital, but it is likely that barrage balloons were another defense used to protect it. These huge balloons, nearly sixty feet long, were filled with a gas lighter than air. Steel cables kept them in place and served to raise or lower the balloons, which could also potentially snag a low-flying plane. Floating above the building, these balloons forced enemy bombers to fly at higher altitudes, reducing their aim and the element of surprise.

Inside the hospital, the medical staff treated thousands of German prisoners of war. There was no preference given to wounded Americans for who was seen first by doctors or for how they were treated. Of the POWs, Al remembered, "they were tough as nails."

Eight hundred German POWs traveled back to the United States on the same ship as Al after he completed his nine months of service in Europe. Many of them worked in the mess hall of the ship, and Al remembered seeing them sneak food left on the plates by the American troops. Al remembered feeling annoyed that the POWs got priority to be deloused and leave the ship before he and the other Americans who had served in Europe.

Al received a much needed twenty-five-day leave at this point and returned home to Racine, Wisconsin. He managed to get two tickets to see the drummer Gene Krupa at Memorial Hall and called a nurse in training he knew to ask her to go with him. Her roommate, Norma Mae, told him his potential date was working the night shift, so Al asked Norma if she would like to go. She said yes on one condition—she absolutely had to be home by curfew.

"We danced the night away and I was in love right then and there. That was the end of me, I was just smitten," Al said of the woman who would later become his bride.

After his leave, the Navy assigned Al to the amphibious ship USS *Lubbock (APA 197)*.

The *Lubbock* was an attack transport ship, designed to carry a full battalion of assault troops and the landing craft and any other equipment they needed for amphibious operations. The *Lubbock* had a regular crew of 56 officers and 480 enlisted men and could transport more than 1,500 additional men, each one needing a place to sleep and eat. The ship was approximately the length of one-and-a-half football fields—more than three times the size of the ship Dad served upon.

Al recalled transporting hundreds of Marines at a time for battle. During an invasion, the *Lubbock* waited in nearby waters, poised to evacuate troops, casualties, and POWs.

The ship's roster included one doctor and one dentist with additional doctors brought onto the ship during invasions— usually ten to fifteen at a time. Some of these doctors were armed and went ashore with the Marines to provide emergency medical care on land.

*Photo of Al in Hilo, HI where the* Lubbock *picked up the Marines for the Iwo Jima invasion*

After stopping in Hawaii to pick up 600 Marines who had trained there, the ship headed to Iwo Jima, arriving on the night of February 18, 1945. Iwo Jima is the tiny volcanic island about 600 miles from Tokyo that the Japanese used as an airbase. The Allies needed to capture Iwo Jima to secure protection of their own planes for the future advance toward mainland Japan.

"All hell was breaking loose there," Al recalled of the naval and air bombardment going on before the actual invasion began. "It looked like the 4th of July with loads of these red projectiles going through the sky toward Iwo Jima."

As the convoy headed to Japan, the Lutheran chaplain aboard Al's ship contacted another ship that had a Catholic chaplain. He spoke to the Catholics on the *Lubbock* over the ship's PA system, absolving them of their sins. In hearing his words, a somber Al realized the danger he would soon face.

On the drizzly morning of February 19, the troops on the USS *Lubbock* headed for battle. They woke at 1:30 a.m., dressed, and arrived at the mess hall fully loaded down with their weapons, grenades, and other equipment. Hundreds of men soon filled the huge room, tucking into a large breakfast of steak and eggs.

After eating, the men scrambled down the nets into the waiting LCVPs (the small boats that transported troops to the beaches) bobbing in the ocean beside the ship. Al and other *Lubbock* crewmembers offered two little bottles of liquor to each man—some waved them away, but most took them. Al and the other guys encouraged the men to do so knowing the liquor might provide some medicinal relief later in the event of injury.

Once the LCVPs were packed tight with Marines standing shoulder to shoulder, the men had to wait until they got their orders to the beach, in many cases for hours in the rolling waves. Seasick Marines had nowhere to be sick but on each other. Al's heart went out to these poor souls as they awaited battle under such grim conditions.

The invasion was supposed to last just three days but ended up taking over a month. The Americans knew the Japanese were waiting, but what they didn't know was that there were so many—estimates differ, but there were close to 22,000 Japanese soldiers in all. These tenacious and, in many cases, fanatical men entrenched themselves in a series of well-built, zigzagged tunnels and caves that led off the beach and headed inland. It was an ingenious strategy for battle, and the Americans had an extremely difficult time finding and destroying these bunkers.

Many of the LCVPs waiting on the beach to release or take troops back became sitting ducks for enemy fire. The men struggled to move as their feet sank into the quicksand-like volcanic beach, hampering their efforts to both advance and evacuate the wounded. LCVPs filled with wounded men returned to the USS *Lubbock* for treatment, where the crew worked frantically to empty them. Orders aboard the *Lubbock* stood to sever ties with any LCVP that hadn't been emptied by nightfall, as the larger ship might receive orders to leave the area and could not be encumbered and become an enemy target. Once untied from the *Lubbock,* these little boats would be left to fend for themselves. Al remembered that some of these unfortunate LCVPs ran out of fuel and were left to float away on their own and, with luck, be picked up again later by other American ships passing by.

The volcanic sand continued to present problems back on the *Lubbock*. One young sailor lost both hands to a mortar shell, yet he was desperately trying to scratch the sand out of his curly mop of black hair as the medical team worked on him. Crewmembers stepped in and ran their fingers through his hair, offering a small gesture of mercy. Another young Marine was brought on board eviscerated and dying. Ashy sand filled every crevice of his belly wound, the terrified man cursing and screaming in pain as Al and the doctors frantically tried to help him, to no avail.

After seeing so many gruesome cases at Netley Hospital, Al was well-versed in tragic injuries. The ship's doctor, however, was green—he had no battle experience at all and was unprepared for what was to come. Al recalled that the doctor did, in fact, "go to pieces" in the first few days of fighting, but eventually he came around, bucked up, and carried on with his work.

Taking Iwo Jima required a grueling, inch-by-inch advance for the Americans, 6,800 of whom would die in the undertaking. According to the National WWII Museum, 70,000 American Marines fought in this battle, with 20,000 suffering injuries. After nine days, the Navy called Al and his ship away from Iwo Jima, but not before he saw the first American flag raised atop Mt. Suribachi. Al later told me about this in a letter:

"It was four days into the invasion D + 4 ~ a Tuesday. Things were not going well for our marines and sailors. The invasion beaches were a mess of wrecked boats and equipment. I was on deck watching what was going on. We had very few wounded at the time since they could not get them into boats and get them to us . . . The battle was intense! About 10:30 a.m. a small flag was raised from Mt. Suribuchi. Everyone was excited and thrilled to see it. Ship whistles, gun shots, etc. We were so proud—finally we were gaining on the enemy. About one and a half hours later, around noon, a bigger flag went up and the celebration continued. We were proud and thankful!"

The *Lubbock* had space for 500 wounded, but only 149 were on board when the ship received its orders to depart and head for a hospital in Guam. Before leaving the area, all nonessential materials, including the remaining LCVPs, were removed from the ship and taken to shore to be used by the invasion forces there. The *Lubbock* would be resupplied at the South Pacific American base in Espiritu Santo, Vanuatu, where it took on troops, supplies, and cargo for the coming assault on Okinawa.

Al served in the South Pacific for a total of seventeen months. He remained even after V-J Day, since corpsmen and radiomen were considered essential and were not allowed to muster out of the Navy. For a time, the Navy assigned him to the USS *Wildcat* in Manila Bay in the Philippines before they finally released him from duty on Easter Sunday, April 21, 1946.

Returning home to Racine, Al took a stab at attending the University of Wisconsin–Parkside. It didn't go well because it was hard for him to relate to people who hadn't lived through any of the things that he had.

"After the war, nobody asked us about anything, so we didn't really talk about it. I felt like we had missed so much, I really did. I didn't have a chance to participate in so many things."

He settled down with Norma Mae, marrying her in 1947. After suffering the loss of their first child, the couple went on to have four children. Their second baby was so eager to be born that Al himself made the delivery at home. He enjoyed a long career with Wyeth Laboratories, his interest in medicine driving much of his career.

His retirement involved lots of volunteering and helping others. Each year he spent a month working with a group of eye surgeons to help those less fortunate regain their sight. He traveled to Peru to distribute food and clothes to the poor. He spent countless hours sharing his WWII experiences with high school history classes throughout the Milwaukee area, and he encouraged other vets to share their stories with family and friends.

But part of him remained on that faraway beach in Japan. "I didn't know why," Al said, "but I wanted to go back to Iwo Jima."

It is nearly impossible to visit Iwo Jima nowadays—the Japanese army mans the island and no civilians live there at all. Once a year, the Japanese allow organized tours to bring small groups of veterans and family members to the beach for a memorial service.

In 2006, Al returned to that beach, and with some fellow American and Japanese attendees, witnessed a ceremony commemorating the battle. It should be noted that only 200 of the over 20,000 Japanese soldiers who fought there were taken alive—their code of honor meant fighting until death. Al shook hands with the grandson of the Japanese General Kuribiachi who met his death there. Profoundly moved by the experience, Al scooped up a big handful of volcanic ash to take home with him—some of which he later passed on to me.

He is still haunted by all the men he encountered during his months in the surgery ward and on the ship. Of the wounded Al said, "You know, we don't forget these things. I think of some of these guys every day of my life. What they went through and what they suffered."

The ghosts of the men Al lost may surround him, but the offspring of those he saved thrive in the world today. He was just a kid of seventeen, eighteen, and nineteen, sent to faraway places to do a job that most grown men could not fathom doing today. Of course, the experiences he had ultimately shaped his own life, but more importantly, the duty he honored to help save lives impacted the lives of others forever.

*An LCT (far right, #1326) joins larger LSMs dropping ramps to unload cargo.*
*Photo courtesy National Archives 080-G-321772*

## LCT-977 – A Navy Workhorse

The opening sequence of *Saving Private Ryan* at Normandy is one of the most harrowing battle scenes ever depicted on film, instantly plunging the viewer into the horrifying chaos of war. Terrified men stand packed into small landing craft, waiting for the ship's front ramps to drop. We are right alongside the soldiers as they pour off of these little amphibious transport ships, German gunfire everywhere around us, the water turning bright red from the injuries sustained in the effort to get to the beach.

Throughout the war in safer waters, the ramps of thousands of other amphibious ships dropped down in order to carry out the mundane but critical job of supplying the troops. This is where Dad came in. For every single man who saw combat, dozens more had to keep ammunition, food, and gasoline flowing to our soldiers who moved the grueling conflict further inland. Dad's Landing Craft, Tank delivered the goods as part of Flotilla 15, serving the invasion forces in the New Guinea and Philippine Liberation campaigns.

Before World War II, our Navy didn't have vessels capable of working on both water and land. When the tank was invented at the close of World War I, Winston Churchill began pondering a solution to the difficult problem of supplying invasion armies. At Churchill's urging, the British soon designed amphibious vessels capable of sailing to the coastline, beaching directly on land and unloading whatever the forces needed—all without the use of a dock.

In the United States, the Navy relied on the early British versions of amphibious vessels when it designed the first Landing Craft, Tank—commonly referred to with a hull designation of LCT. Dad describes them like this in his journal:

*LCTs were designed, at least in theory, to haul Sherman tanks to the beach. We hauled in just one Sherman tank in 14 months. Our ship was set up to carry in three tanks—the one we carried almost sunk us. It was commanded by a bright-eyed army lieutenant, complete with a pearl-handled derringer. He was nervous, pumped, and ready to go. When we hit the beach, we could see that we hadn't quite gotten in far enough. We cautioned the lieutenant—said we could give him a better spot. He said no, drove off our ship into about 4 feet of water and then just sat—engines drowned out. He said he'd call for help and that was that.*

The first American-made Mark 5 LCT models (the Mark being a number designation for the model's design progress, often abbreviated as Mk) sailed off the production line in June 1942, rapidly followed by about 500 more. As the LCT design evolved, improvements appeared in the newer Mark 6 models and almost 1,000 were produced by war's end. Dad's Mk 6 *LCT-977* had more comfortable living arrangements for the crew than the previous model. It could also be loaded and unloaded from either end. It was possible, though difficult, to use an LCT as a link between larger ships and the shore, with tanks or other vehicles driving right through the entire length of the vessel.

The LCT was about 120 feet long, with a flat "nose" that pushed awkwardly through the water. The "nose," or ramp, lowered upon beaching to allow trucks and tanks to drive on and off the small ship.

*Here's a photo of* LCT-33 *with its crew on the lowered front ramp. This gives an idea of the size and scale. (There are no clear photos such as this one of Dad's ship,* LCT-977.*) Photo property of Mark Dalzell, used with his permission.*

While the ramp worked perfectly to achieve the LCTs' goals, the lack of a pointed bow made the little vessels very difficult to control. In an article from the *Saturday Evening Post* in 1944, author Ira Wolfert says:

> To the layman, the LCT . . . looks like a tin shed with a false front, traveling upside down and backwards through the water . . . Instead of trying to ride the waves, it tries to club them to death. Another difficulty is the skippers of these crafts. They are all male ninety-day wonders, graduated as Ensigns, truculent, fretful, quarrelsome, eager and more friendly than anything else on two legs that I have found.

Tucked into Dad's scrapbook is a "greeting card" that he received from his crewmates after spending an aggravating twenty minutes attempting to moor his flat-bottomed ship alongside another LCT. They made quick work of hazing Dad— he opened the card to discover that it was blank inside.

All versions of the LCT were built in three large separate pieces. Sometimes these components were preassembled in the shipyards, and then the completed LCT was hoisted onto and transported to duty on larger ships, such as a Landing Ship, Tank (LST). When it was time to deliver the LCT, the larger ship would shift water in the ballast tanks below, making it tip to one side. The crew would loosen the tie-down chains holding the LCT on deck and the smaller ship would slide right off, landing flat in the water with a tremendous splash.

*Photo Courtesy: National Archives SC 188370*

Other times, the watertight LCT components were delivered to combat areas in pieces, thrown over the side into the sea and bolted together—frequently by their own crew as they stood in the shallow water.

Back in the United States, subcontractor businesses throughout the country prefabricated the LCT pieces, some in unlikely shipbuilding locations such as Nebraska, Ohio, and Wisconsin. A company in Denver, Colorado, put together the components for Dad's LCT, and the pieces were sent by rail to

Mare Island in California for final assembly. Huge shipyards on both the east and west coasts were perfectly situated to send ships of all sizes to the theaters of war in Europe and the Pacific.

Once built and delivered for duty, LCTs served as a workhorse for the Navy, slow-going and designed to operate along the shoreline with a range of only 500 miles. In general, there were no dock or harbor facilities at which cargo and Liberty ships could be unloaded, so those larger vessels remained anchored farther out at sea. On duty for twenty-four hours a day, LCTs transported cargo from these ships to the beaches, and vice versa. Flotillas of LCTs, broken into groups consisting of about a dozen ships each, worked together to empty the supply ships and fulfill the deliveries to shore.

Dad's LCT would have looked like a rowboat alongside the much larger cargo or Liberty ships (mass-produced cargo vessels manned by Merchant Marines) whose great decks rose twenty-five feet or more above the waterline. The two ships banged together wildly in the current until the crew properly secured them to each other. The two ships used hawsers (thick ropes) to pull the vessels in close, the larger ship dropping "monkey fists" (round balls with lead cores) between the ships to act as bumpers. Once the hawsers were secured—no easy feat—the two ships remained side by side for loading.

Huge arms from the bigger ship's crane lowered large boxes onto the LCTs. Each box had to be unhooked and distributed on the deck by the smaller vessel's crew. It often took many hours to fully load the LCT with supplies and ammunition.

*A nice example of cranes lowering crates onto the LCT parked beside the freighter.*
*Photo courtesy of NavSource #09350210*
*Original U.S. Navy photo from National Naval Aviation Museum*

Dad traded shifts with his skipper, Jim Harnack, the two officers working eight hours on, then eight off. *As skippers we would conn* [steer] *the ship by issuing orders to a helmsman who was at the "wheel" just below us. We also issued orders to the crewmembers in securing our vessel alongside the freighter. It was cargo to us from a large ship then to the beach.*

The bridge, or conning deck, on an LCT consisted of a ten-foot square elevated platform outlined by a canvas up to waist height to break the wind. The skipper stood on this platform and yelled directions down through a tube or trap door to the "pilothouse" below, where the helmsman and engine crew were manning the wheel and engine throttles. The ship was directed (conned) from above since it was nearly impossible to see out of the pilothouse. The big downside was that from this perch, the skippers and other executive officers on the conn deck had nowhere to hide in the event of enemy fire.

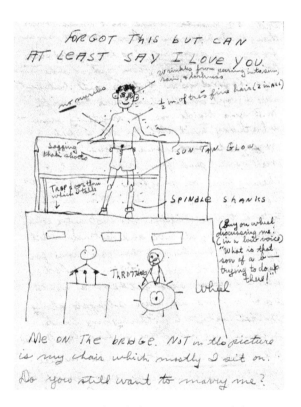

From one of Dad's letters to Mom with his comments in the margin in the scrapbook: *I certainly made life seem much simpler in 1944 – perhaps I was somewhat soft in the head from all the sun and the poor diet.*

*Many of the Liberty ship skippers were afraid to bring their vessels too close to shore. This made it a lot harder for us as the seas were much heavier outside the actual harbors.*

*There was one episode we often laughed about. A particularly nervous, fussy, scared merchant marine captain simply did not want his ship bumped, jostled or scraped in any way. His was a regular cargo vessel—not a Liberty ship. Although the seas were a bit high, Jim made his approach to tie up alongside—a wave brought our ship up and the freighter down. Our bow opened a beautiful gash in the side of the ship from which water poured for hours—like a Giant, urinating . . . it was kind of fun to see the skipper fuss and fume.*

*The Liberty ships that we unloaded were another reason we finally crushed the Japanese. They were manufactured in massive numbers by Henry J. Kaiser. They made so many that they were able to convert some of them to what they called light aircraft carriers. The Liberty ships carried a cargo of about 10,000 tons. Each ship had a small number of Navy personnel on board to "protect" the ship. They usually had a 3' cannon on the stern and as I recall, a few machine guns scattered about.*

*Kaiser had much better luck with the ships than with the automobile he attempted to introduce in later years. Japan had no way they could cope or keep up with this production.*

Kaiser shipyards on the West Coast made about two-thirds of the almost 3,000 Liberty ships built during the war. Kaiser developed an innovative assembly line technique to construct the ships quickly—in as little as two weeks' time—from the parts prefabricated by companies around the United States. These ships actually could be built faster than the enemy could sink them, so the Allied Liberty ship fleet remained strong and well-outfitted throughout the war.

Once LCTs were filled with cargo from the huge ships at sea, they sailed to shore where soldiers unloaded them and then sent the supplies on to their next destination. Dad recalled how tricky it was to approach and land on the beaches: *Once loaded we would proceed to the beach where the Army chaps were waiting. We normally beached on the black and sandy beaches. To help prevent broaching* [a dangerous situation when a ship turns broadside to heavy waves and runs the risk of capsizing], *we would order the anchor dropped 100 to 150 feet from land. This took some timing and skill on our part—otherwise we could be caught 10 or 20 feet from the shore with our anchor mired in coral or sand. We would thus be sitting* [in the shallow water] *as follows* [in the picture below], *at least hopefully.*

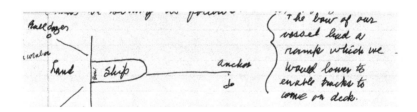

If there was heavy surf, the members of the Army helped keep the LCTs stationary on the beach by using large bulldozers as a counterweight when this equipment was available.

*During the unloading the so-called officer of the* day [Dad or Harnack—he's poking fun at the fact that such regular Joes could be officers] *stayed on watch—to prevent broaching, getting too far on the beach or too far off. There were some treacherous tides which when ebbing could leave you actually stranded on land—obviously not a good situation. Harnack once got us in this situation and we were stuck for five hours. I sent Muriel some of the barnacles that I scraped off the stern which was high and dry.*

This is a photograph of a beach near Hollandia, New Guinea, in 1944 that shows Dad's ship just tucked behind another LCT docked there (see the long arrow on the right pointing to a mostly hidden LCT). This particular beach was one of Dad's favorites since there was no surf, making it easier to navigate and safer from a broaching standpoint.

*After we unloaded, we would use the engines—we had three screws* [propellers, additional engines] *and pulling in the anchor could back off the beach. There was some delicate timing here as it was possible to get the anchor chain tangled up in the screws. You could also get sand in the engines by churning too much. This was bad, of course, and annoyed our machinist mate.*

*It was possible to make the vessel actually go sideways—ahead on port—back on starboard; it used to amaze some of the folks on ships or docks to which we were attempting to come alongside. I believe this was called "crabbing."*

So back and forth, hundreds of times, the LCTs went from sea to shore, carrying a variety of goods: medicine and bandages, bombs and bullets, meal ingredients and rations, cases of cigarettes, liquor, gasoline, toilet paper, personnel and more. The officer of the day watched to make sure the Army crew didn't overload the little ship with supplies returning to the Liberty ships, and to make sure the lines were holding fast. Until areas became more secure, most of these loading and unloading trips took place under cover of night to avoid being hit by enemy fire.

Being assigned to a supply ship came with its own set of perks.

*From the cargo carried in, we were able to keep ourselves well supplied with cigarettes, Army clothing in the form of shirts and underwear and sheets for our beds. We only stole* [commandeered] *bare necessities like toothpaste, shaving cream and razor blades. We never sold any merchandise.*

This tiny vessel would be home to Dad for eighteen long months. He and Skipper Harnack shared the officers' cabin that measured about eighteen feet long by eight feet wide. The remaining twelve men on the crew berthed in a similarly sized compartment on the ship. Here's a sketch Dad drew of his quarters:

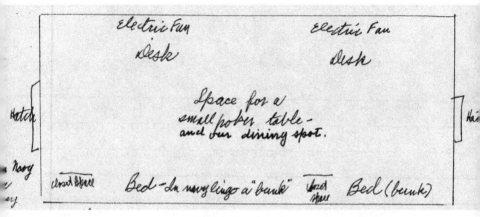

There were no port holes nor were there ever any cool breezes in New Guinea or the Philippines—just wet heat. The humidity was incredibly high and never in my life have I seen such intense downpours of rain. The rain came and went speedily but never cooled anything off. The temperature in the cabin ranged between 85 & 95 but the direct blast of the little General Electric fans made life bearable. We also always had a good supply of cockroaches that actually seemed to be fairly friendly bugs—an occasional shot of DDT helped control the population.

Mold developed rapidly. For example, I stored a pair of my black oxford shoes below deck and after a week they were pure white and, of course, ruined. Florsheim Shoe Company made them for the Navy, and they cost us $4 a pair—over $200 in 1998 if Florsheim is still around. They were really good shoes.

Back in the States, Jim Harnack was an architect by trade, and Dad revealed Jim's artistic flair in his description of Jim's attempts to make that little airless cabin more comfortable. *Jim did one thing that made our cabin more homelike. Rather than having the bottoms of our bunks stretched out in the open (with all our junk showing—shoes, clothes, etc), he ringed them with bed sheets—courtesy of the Army. We painted them a nice deep green and then he put a dandy red border about an inch just above the floor. The same paint that covered our ship—red deck paint undercoating. He let me do the grunt work of painting, but the border was all in his domain. Although Jim was very thin and somewhat shaky, he could draw an almost perfect straight-line sans ruler that I thought to be an odd asset—and a puzzling one.*

*Bathroom facilities* [called "heads"] *were a bit cramped to say the least. There was a room at the stern maybe 8' by 8'—just "aft" of the officers' quarters as they would say in Navy lingo.*

*Everything worked off a hand pump, so you had to bend over slightly, put your foot on a pedal, and pump vigorously to flush the toilet. Sometimes you did get sprayed with some of the toilet water if you pumped too vigorously. The excrement went directly into the ocean.*

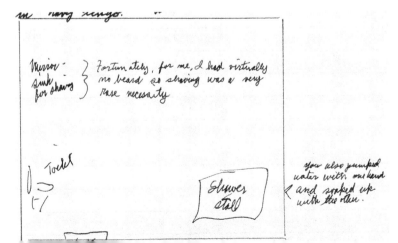

*We did not manufacture our own water, so we had to fill up our lower holds every now and then from either supply ships or various mountain streams. We flung in a few chlorine pills each time we filled up so it's a miracle we didn't all die from some deadly tropical disease—or from the pills.*

I wish I knew where he saw these mountain streams and other things he describes in his journal, but the exact path that Dad traveled during the war is unknowable. While the Navy kept records of every single ship's movements during the war, afterward they deemed LCT records unimportant and destroyed them.

By war's end, over seventy LCTs were lost—from storms, accidents, equipment failure, and in battle. Over a third of the losses occurred near Normandy when storms raged after the D-Day troop landing there. Most LCTs had two crews over the course of the war, so records estimate that a total of about 27,000 men served on board an LCT at some point during the war. Most of the LCT officers and crew wouldn't go on to make careers out of the Navy, so after the war they returned home to resume their civilian lives, leaving their seagoing experiences behind them.

LCTs were hardworking and reliable little ships, carrying tanks, troops, and other vital supplies ashore for the many operations of the war. Some were used as minesweepers while others were equipped with rockets and guns for fighting. Some were clad with armor allowing them to go into particularly dangerous areas such as Normandy.

The LCT was just one of at least twelve different landing craft quickly designed, built, and sent off to carry out their specific set of duties. The details about this one little vessel reveal how remarkably well the Navy responded to the complicated process of developing a wartime fleet. Companies throughout the States ramped up with thousands of American workers pitching in to help build a naval force that could not be beat.

Not much has been written about these small and necessary ships. After the war, the older model LCTs were scrapped, and the Navy redesigned and repurposed many of the newer Mark 6s. Today, one remaining LCT still floats in Bayfield, Wisconsin. Years ago, nostalgic LCT veterans were welcomed by the owner to take a short voyage on this ship, but fewer and fewer LCT veterans are alive to take the journey now. Though the crews may be gone, and the ships might be scuttled, the impact of the LCT during the war should not be forgotten.

*A reunion aboard the LCT in Bayfield, WI.*
*Photo courtesy of Ron Swanson, Editor of the Flotilla Newsletter*

*The only LCT-977 photo that survived the tropical climate.*
*Jim Harnack (L) with Dad (R) on the deck (Middle man is unidentified).*

## CAST OF CHARACTERS ON LCT-977

There were thousands of ships in the United States' fleet during World War II. From the largest such as the battleships and destroyers, to the tiniest of the thousands of amphibious vessels, each ship in the Navy played its own critical role in the Allied effort to win the war. Taking a look at Dad's little supply ship provides a window into the minutiae of planning for every task and assignment in the fleet—both equipment and men.

*Jim Harnack was the Skipper, I was the Executive Officer. We had a crew of 12 but generally it amounted to 16-18 men. This was more properly called "ship's company" in navy lingo. It was not easy to get: 1) a decent camera, 2) film, 3) someone to print the film, 4) Walgreens didn't have any shops out there.*

Navy requirements called for each LCT to have a complement of twelve enlisted men and one officer, but Dad spoke of many "teams" of officers, like his own, working on other landing craft in the South Pacific. In the busiest theaters of war, it made sense to have two officers on board so the men could relieve each other while their ship worked around the clock.

Taking the helm of an LCT during the war was like running a small business. Jim and Dad controlled every aspect of the ship's maintenance, its assignments, and all the men on board. Many in the crew were older than the young officers who had barely dipped a toe into their twenties yet, so it was frequently a challenge for them to maintain discipline among and command respect from the men. LCT officers were fresh out of ninety-day midshipmen training who simply had to find a way to make things work on their own, sometimes bending the rules a little in order to run their vessels smoothly.

Since there was such a small crew on an LCT, it made sense for the men to be capable of performing their shipmates' duties as well as their own. If someone was wounded or killed, another sailor could step in to perform his job to keep the ship operating. The job descriptions of the sailors on these landing craft reflect this overlap of duties. At any given moment, there could be an officer on the conning deck, a helmsman steering the ship, a throttle man controlling the engines, two lookouts, and a fifth man who could relieve any of these stations if necessary.

Everyone shared watches; Jim and Dad worked eight hours on, then eight off. The crew rotated in shifts of four hours in length. Watch standing or watchkeeping is how the Navy refers to how a ship's personnel and duties are divided up so the ship can operate continuously. Twenty-four hours a day, the officers were responsible for navigating the ship safely while their crew watched for enemy activity, made sure all the equipment was working properly, and carried out the ship's assignments.

The Navy meticulously pinned down each man's responsibilities. On every ship in the fleet, each sailor held a "rating" that described a certain set of skills and abilities. For every rating, a specific badge was worn on the left sleeve by all serving in that occupation. "Rate" defines a pay grade. A "non-rate" is someone serving at the lowest pay range—usually a deckhand or seaman. "Rank" is strictly used to designate Navy officers, from the lowest level of Ensign to the highest of Fleet Admiral. The crew of landing craft like Dad's was made up of a mixture of ratings and ranks determined by the responsibilities of the ship.

One of the most important sailors on every LCT was the Boatswain's Mate. He relayed orders from the conn deck and could be given "shifts" as Acting Officer of the Deck. He supervised the painting, cleaning and maintenance of the ship, and if necessary, managed the damage control party response if the ship were attacked and in danger of sinking.

The Skipper kept a daily logbook of the ship's activity that he gave once a month to the Quartermaster, a sailor who primarily acted as a helmsman and signalman when needed (sending and receiving messages). The Quartermaster transcribed the more important items and, with the Skipper's approval, submitted the report to the Group or Flotilla command (in the Pacific, each LCT Flotilla had about thirty-six craft—twelve to a group). After the war, the Navy deemed these logs and reports from smaller ships unimportant to the historical record and they were destroyed.

*The crew seemed to get along with our quartermaster—a young Jewish lad from New York. Quartermaster was a very good rating for an enlisted man. The crew did somehow resent him because he was brighter, much better educated, and certainly more opinionated. There was as far as I can remember, no reference to religion nor did there seem to be any racial animosity or anti-Semitism. Small craft such as ours never had access to church services. Happily, this meant we never had any priests or ministers hanging around.* [Dad was not a religious man.]

The next in the bunch was the Gunner's Mate who cleaned and maintained all the guns and small arms on board the ship and operated the port-side 20mm gun. *I always liked Gunner's Mate second class Schmidt, age 32 from New York. Married but with no children. He had that unique New York accent—unique to us, that is. He was in charge of our two 20-millimeter weapons and various smaller machine guns which were sprinkled about the ship. He served mainly as a seaman—manning the lines etc.—a good and willing sailor.*

*Every time there was an air raid our crew wanted to "open up" as they said. Harnack and I resisted the firing but one dark night in Leyte Gulf, Harnack allowed the crew to "let her go." Of course, all that was hit was air, but it gave the crew a sense of being in the war. Gunner's Mate Schmidt was thoroughly pissed (a no-no word in my day. My aunts Nelly and Julia would have washed out my mouth with soap and water) as they say now because firing the weapons automatically necessitated a lot of cleaning and oiling—a lot of work. I suspect that some of our crewmembers are still boasting about the night we shot down a Jap plane—not at all true.*

LCTs also had a Radioman, although Dad did not mention the person who had this rating on his ship. This sailor received and transmitted all messages for the ship. While not doing this job, he assisted with the anchor while beaching and relieved other sailors standing watch.

Most LCTs had three Seaman, First Class Division personnel. These men were sort of all-purpose sailors—they stood watch, loaded guns, operated the ramps, cleaned, and maintained the ship. In the thirteen months he spent on *LCT-977*, Dad met a number of eccentric seamen.

*I'd say the most memorable character was "Pops" Lannon. He was 39 and from Louisville, Kentucky, and a staunch Democrat which made me like him right away. We could never understand why or how he ever got involved in the armed forces. At 39 he was just too old. He was unmarried, however, and in good physical condition.*

*Late in 1944 we all received large absentee ballots to vote in the presidential election. Although Harnack and I had to censor all the mail, the ballots were sacrosanct. After a couple of weeks passed by, it seemed to us that "Pops" had placed at least four of the ballots* in the outgoing mailbox. I asked him about this, and he blushed a bit but explained that he had always been very active in elections in Louisville—said he was able to vote 27 times for Roosevelt in 1940. He simply stood in for a lot of little old ladies or long dead chaps who he knew would want to vote for FDR. Lannon was a fine sailor and hard worker and certainly had good political sense (though perhaps was not too honorable).

Seaman Burgess was another interesting character. He should never have been allowed to serve in the armed services. He was a young southern lad who never quite followed orders. At some point Burgess began sleeping with a very intimidating machete by his side (a machete is a very large knife used for hacking sugar cane generally—or people.) One night one of the crew woke Burgess and indicated that it was his watch. Burgess responded menacingly, "shut up or I'll cut off your arms."

Once we learned this, we enlisted the aid of a young medical friend, Dr. Orr. He offered to interview Burgess and reported that Burgess was certifiably insane (by his opinion—I would also say very arbitrary) and should be sent home. From time to time, [after he returned home] *Burgess wrote the crew telling them how great civilian life was, but he once stated that he was going to kill those two "motherfuckers" (Navy term) McCurdy and Harnack. Fortunately, he never got to us—at least to me—by 2000, 2001, 2002, 2003, 2004, 2005, 2006.*

Seaman Butts was a young lad who came on board out of the state of West Virginia. He was the kindest and nicest young sailor I ever knew. He did everything he was told to do and then some—always with a cheery smile. He actually could have been *mistaken for Little Abner (I guess it was Lil) a very popular comic strip character of the time. His name was Fred and he was nineteen years old. He never received any mail but did write a few letters to a paper company in West Virginia. Both Harnack and I noted that he described himself as follows: you may not remember me, but I worked there one summer where I was knowed (Fred was not well educated) as "Corner Cutter Butts." The title intrigued us. We thought he was referring to himself as a fellow who took the easy way out—goofed off and cut corners. Fred explained to us that his job was simply cutting corners off boxes as they came down the assembly line—I don't think he ever got a response to his letters.*

Every LCT crew required two Motor Machinist's Mates—one second class and one first class rate (the higher rate given to those with more experience and time on the job). Motormacs, as they were called, were men who were small in size since they worked in the confined space of the engine room. They manned the throttle, maintained and repaired the main engines and other equipment, and stood lookout.

*We were also lucky to have Johnny St. John, our machinist mate second class. He was also very young and kept our diesel engines running which meant we always had lights, refrigeration of a sort, and electric fans that were running. The engine room on our little ship was, of course, below deck. It was almost impossible to move in it—like the tunnel in the movie* The Great Escape—*only worse and hotter.*

Although not mentioned in Dad's journal, a fireman was on the official Navy personnel list for LCTs. This sailor operated the ramp during beaching, inspected equipment in the engine room regularly, transferred fuel when necessary, and stood ready to give first aid to casualties.

Another necessary rating on each LCT was the cook who, with the aid of a seaman, prepared and served the food. He kept the galley clean and in good order, maintained provisions, and kept the Officer in Charge up to speed on what supplies he needed or were on hand. He also cleaned the men's and officers' quarters, showers, and bathrooms. In a pinch he knew how to load and clear jams in the 20mm guns.

*Peeling potatoes on* LCT-1135. *Photo courtesy of Thomas A. Bowman, Jr.—His dad, Thomas A. Bowman, is on the left.*

*We had a wonderful young cook who worked his rear end off for us in a galley that probably ranged from 90 degrees to 110. He tried his best. He was rated "second class" which was a good rating for enlisted men, especially at his tender age.*

As luck would have it, I met a man who served as a cook on an LCT. At age eighteen, John Eskau became a cook's assistant when the original assistant broke his hand in a mishap while handling an anchor. He had no prior experience in the kitchen but quickly learned the ropes from the head cook who in "real" life worked in a tavern.

John told me that the cook's goal was to try to make the best use of whatever he had on hand, no matter how unusual, and to try to keep the crew happy. He was proud of trying to give the men on his ship, from many different cultures, a hot, comforting meal.

Putting the responsibility for the ship's operation on the untested shoulders of 90-Day Wonders was a remarkable thing. The young officers came straight out of the V-12 program and midshipmen school, most without much in the way of work or management experience. They and their men had little or no practical seafaring experience, and most were far away from home for the first time.

Some on their crew had enlisted, revealing a willingness to get involved in the fight. Others had waited to be drafted, showing less enthusiasm for the war effort or, perhaps, dread of service. Many readily followed the young officers' orders, but there were others who challenged the ensigns and grudgingly obeyed their directives.

*Looking back, I think despite our youthful quirks, I at 22 and Jim at 25, keeping our ship running, our crew fed and relatively happy, and most of all, keeping us safe was a remarkable job. I don't think I'm too immodest saying this.*

*The "family" from* LCT-1251—*with their pet monkey.*
*Photo credit and permission: John DeNoma,*
*in memory of Bernard DeNoma, RM2 LCT-725*

So, there it was—a small ship full of men brought together by chance to serve in the South Pacific. Living in close quarters, they got to know each other and became almost like a family.

While the LCT required fewer than twenty men to carry out its work, the larger ships in the American fleet had dozens of officers and hundreds of enlisted sailors. Each vessel, enormous or tiny, was counted on to smoothly carry out its particular and necessary assignment in an organized and disciplined manner. If all went as planned and the enemy was bested, the Navy could indeed say they "ran a tight ship."

# SIDEBAR

"Specifications for LCT Officer and Enlisted Billets" prepared by the Bureau of Naval Personnel, August 1944.

1. Organizing the crew (assigning duties/training) and providing for ship maintenance (inventory of oil, water, gas, etc)
2. Controlling the training, discipline, safety and welfare of the crew (this section includes censoring mail & approving menus)
3. Participating in deck duties involved when the ship is underway (this includes directing everyone to get the ship going, moving, beaching, firing, anchoring, etc)
4. Acquiring and storing all provisions necessary to operate the ship and take care of the men (acquiring things needed from Navy supply bases or, if necessary, from the Army or Marines)
5. Receiving, interpreting, and executing all orders (regardless of the rank of any Army personnel who may be on board)
6. Saving as much of the ship as possible in case of disaster and destroying confidential or restricted material that could get into enemy hands
7. Submitting action reports to the group commander after all engagements

## JOHN ESKAU – Young Man, Big Adventure

The call came over the loudspeaker at the ice-skating rink on December 7, 1941: all *Milwaukee Journal* paperboys were to report immediately to deliver extra editions of the paper.

John Eskau unlaced his skates and scrambled to heed the call to action. Soon enough he would do more than deliver papers. He said, "I was 14½ years old at the time, and two years later I was in the Navy."

Leaving his last year of high school to enlist, John chose the Navy instead of waiting to be drafted on his eighteenth birthday. His older brother, Joe, was already a sailor. Joe lost his hearing in one ear after succumbing to a case of spinal meningitis while at the Great Lakes training base, so he was serving stateside.

After twelve weeks of boot camp, John and 500 other newly minted sailors headed west for embarkation. Crammed on a train for the five- or six-day journey, he shifted uncomfortably in his seat, sleeping while sitting up.

In San Diego, John received further training with weapons, learning to take apart, replace parts, and reassemble guns in a matter of moments. He recalled the gun barrels became so hot during firing practice that the men were forced to take them off and replace them.

Finally, he got onto the water. John learned to maneuver Higgins boats, also called LCVPs, in any kind of weather. One of their similarities to the LCT (on which John would later serve) was the flat front ramp that dropped to unload, in this case, up to thirty-six fully armed combat troops for an invasion. Higgins boats were just thirty-six feet long and eleven feet wide, carrying a regular crew of only four men, two of which manned twin .30 caliber machine guns. The Navy used LCVPs during training exercises to try to determine how many of these tiny boats might be lost in rough seas. Like LCTs, they were difficult to maneuver. While they followed a wave into shore, they also had to be able to back out and turn around without flipping over.

After he completed his training, the Navy scheduled John and the others in his group to head to Iwo Jima for the landings there. However, fate stepped in. Just a day or two after a nice liberty in Los Angeles, he was out on a boat maneuver when he became ill. He wasn't just ill, he came down with scarlet fever, and the illness sent him to the sick bay for three weeks.

After recovering, he and 1,600 other men boarded a troop carrier headed to Hawaii. John doesn't recall how long it took to get there, just that he spent most of the voyage topside in the fresh air. The quarters below were jammed with seasick men, unable to control their bodies because of the rough sea conditions.

Another weird stroke of luck affected John before he left Hawaii. The men were put up in tents while they waited for their orders. During the night, something—John thinks maybe a spider—crawled into his tent and bit him. His leg swelled mightily and he found himself back in the hospital for another week.

Once he was released, he trudged back to the tent city only to find that it was no longer there. He said, "I went back to where I was before and everything was gone. My sea bag was just sitting there all by itself in the field." Obviously, his group had gone on without him.

In early 1945, he finally boarded *Landing Ship, Tank-655* to find the LCT he was assigned to chained right on top of the larger ship's deck. John's job was to man the 20mm guns on *LCT-596*, nicknamed the "Shorthorn" by her crew. The pair of piggyback ships joined a couple of destroyers and other ships and traveled in typical zigzag fashion as part of a convoy headed to Japan.

"When we got to Okinawa, I had never seen so many ships in the water," John marveled. The United States 7th fleet was there en masse. It had formed in the South Pacific and fought in the huge battle of Leyte Gulf before moving on toward Japan.

John's transport ship went in at Buckner Bay to unload Marines and Seabees. Then it delivered John's ship farther in toward Yellow Beach, near the mouth of the Bishi Gawa River on Okinawa. It was near this beach in Buckner Bay where John was stationed for most of his time in the Navy.

A busy Navy supply hub, Buckner Bay buzzed with activity as loads of different ships carried out their tasks. At first, the Navy utilized Higgins boats to carry supplies and troops back and forth to the beaches. After the Seabees enlarged the beach exit, amphibious ships like John's could land right on the beach at high tide. The rest of the fleet's larger ships stayed out to sea, beyond the coral reefs that prevented cargo and other assault ships from getting any closer.

It was in Buckner Bay that John had his first experience with Japanese kamikazes. He leapt to duty, manning one of the ship's guns, and along with others throughout the bay, brought down five of the six enemy planes.

Unlike Dad's experience, John's ship the "Shorthorn" lived up to its hull designation of Landing Ship, Tank and *did* in fact carry tanks. Specifically, the ones equipped with the flamethrowers the Marines used to force the Japanese out of their bunkers.

Like Dad, John's regular crew consisted of about twelve men. His skipper, William Holstein, was just five years older than John and had been a schoolteacher until he was plucked away from his work for midshipmen school.

John's regular assignment eventually changed from gunnery to cook's assistant, replacing a man who injured one of his hands. He and the head cook usually fed the crew in two shifts—six men at a time. He and the lead cook did their best to try to please everyone, although they didn't always share the same tastes in food.

Because John was stationed in the Bay, he and his crewmates

met many friendly local Japanese civilians when they pulled into the beaches. To John, it felt as if these folks had been forgotten by the part of Japan waging the war. So removed from the battles, these locals were going about life as if there was

*John (on the right) with the ship's head cook*

no war, eager to get to know the Americans and perhaps trade fresh fish and produce with them for other supplies.

Once, the commanders ordered John's LCT to pick up some Japanese prisoners of war on a small island nearby called Lejima and transfer them elsewhere. John felt some empathy for the men, particularly one who had a small box around his neck containing a comrade's cremated ashes. This prisoner implored the Americans to take it home to his family.

As John saw it, "The Japanese were just following whoever directed them, the same as the Americans and the other citizens of countries involved. Under command they just did what they were told."

John felt his life in the Navy was very busy and interesting; he knew he had a job to do and never felt too homesick. In many ways, he felt it was a great adventure. He got into some shenanigans when it came to liquor and took every opportunity to explore whenever he got leave. He was barely an adult when the Japanese finally surrendered in August 1945.

He recalled, "All of a sudden the guys were all shooting the guns off and I thought, 'holy cow, what's going on?' I asked someone at headquarters [on the beach] what was happening, and I was told, 'We are discussing peace terms with the Japanese, so shoot them down in a friendly manner.'"

Bullets falling from celebratory shots in Buckner Bay killed six Americans. John was relieved to find out that plans for attacking mainland Japan would now be tabled.

Before finally leaving Buckner Bay, he survived one of the worst typhoons in the area's history that hit after the war ended in October 1945. The storm was ferocious. John's LCT was tied up with about twenty-three others, and the men were told to seek shelter for the night.

During the storm, a larger ship (an LST) got caught on a coral reef, the bottom starting to rip away. The men fought to tie her up next to one of the LCTs. The ships in the bay were banging against each other in winds that exceeded one hundred miles per hour. That night, one of the cables holding the larger vessel snapped, sending the LST and three of the little LCTs loose on the channel and up onto the rocks. It took almost four days after the storm subsided for the tide to become high enough to float those little ships back out to water. John wrote of the storm in a letter home to his mother on October 10th:

> At ten pm we heard an SOS from a navy
> tanker, which was calling for help. She had all her
> anchors out and was drifting towards our channel.
> We could not help her. The typhoon blew itself
> out during the night, and in the morning there

was wreckage all over the harbor. The navy tanker was in the channel lying on its side, and its stern was on top of two army ships, which were all smashed in. They say there are over one hundred men missing from the three ships.

Well ma, I don't know how long it will be before things will be straightened out around here, or when I will receive mail again. Our post office was blown away in the storm. I'll let you know when things settle down. Say hello to the gang and tell them I'm feeling fine.

Because there was no longer a need to invade Japan, a larger ship hooked up John's LCT and towed it through dangerous water full of mines all the way to Korea. A mine cutter worked just ahead of them, but the now-loose mines floated right beside John's LCT. He recalled the men actually reaching out to push them out of the ship's way.

In Inchon, Korea, John stayed aboard his LCT to help deliver supplies to the Army occupation force. All the branches of the military were represented there and assisted the base however possible. John spent a very cold winter on his little uninsulated ship, braving the thirty-foot rises in the tide on numerous trips three miles out to the supply ships and then back to shore.

During John's last four or five months of service, "the Shorthorn" worked in China, hauling troops from Hong Kong. After almost two years overseas, John and about 1,800 other tired sailors finally boarded a cargo ship for home. On the nearly month-long journey, the ship ran out of just about every kind of supply you could think of—a miserable journey John does not remember fondly.

Once he made it back home, he used the GI Bill benefits to enroll at Milwaukee School of Engineering where he trained for his eventual career in Construction, Real Estate, and Development.

He served in the Reserves after the war. One of his buddies had a slew of sisters, and John married the one that seemed the most perfect for him. She was just nineteen years old when they met, John not much older, yet with a lifetime's experiences behind him.

# THE NAVY WAY

It was one thing to get drafted into or enlist in the Navy, yet quite another to get used to a life structured around rigid rules and longstanding traditions. For the most part, the young men who served as sailors and Naval officers just wanted to do their time and return home. This was a time of major adjustment for the boys who left school or work to set sail, and they wouldn't return home without first passing through some universal experiences in the Navy gauntlet.

Dad mentioned a number of Navy protocols and traditions in his journal, and they shed some light on everyday life at sea during WWII. His training in the V-12 and V-7 programs indoctrinated him in the ways of the Navy, preparing him for service, but now he would find out how closely the realities of his assignment lined up with what he had learned.

The Navy's elaborate rules of etiquette dictated how the men and ships interacted with each other in the course of their assignments. One such rule was that no junior member could pass a senior without permission. The junior was required to salute first and wait for the return salute of the senior. Salutes were exchanged between vessels meeting or passing by each other. If a ship wasn't underway and did not have an officer on board, the entire crew had to stand and salute when any officer passed by.

Looser standards were more common on the thousands of little amphibious ships run by 90-Day Wonders. William Baker gives a fine illustration of what was more likely to happen on an LCT in his memoir *The LCT Story.* He recalled that as he approached his ship for the very first time, he snapped to attention and presented himself to Ensign Richard Wilson with a salute and a hearty "Ensign Baker reporting for duty, sir."

Wilson replied, "For God's sake, cut the formality. This is an LCT."

*From "Skill in the Surf," courtesy of Naval History and Heritage Command, Washington, D.C.*

Dad weighed in: *Of course, we had to follow the time-honored custom of requesting permission from the officer of the day when we boarded a larger ship. We wondered what we'd do if the officer of the day told us to get lost. We often did look like a couple of bums, however, so perhaps a refusal might have been in order* [In the tropic heat, Dad and the other men were more likely shirtless and wearing dungarees than their Naval uniforms].

*We were quite thrilled one day while our ship was unloading on the beach. We got a signal from a large ship in the bay. "Commodore X requests permission to come across your vessel." First, we were startled because we had thought that particular rank had been abolished. It was the equivalent of a Brigadier General in the Army. Harnack played the game to the hilt, polished his gold bars, put on a clean shirt and dug a clean hat out of his closet. It was a real skit as he granted permission* [to cross the vessel. This passage shows that Dad and Harnack, like other 90-Day Wonders, were a little more cynical about the discipline of Navy lifers, poking fun at the protocols.]

*The Commodore was accompanied by his aides—two Lieutenant Commanders and four very nervous young Ensigns who were in charge of carrying a vast array of sea bags and other luggage. We realized we saved them all some wet feet and pants—our ramp being down* [the LCT ramp lowered directly onto the beach, so the men avoided wading to shore]. *So much for Navy protocol and Rank Has Its Privilege. They were all part of the Annapolis system which like West Point proudly proclaimed the strict honor system under which they operated.*

There were also etiquette rules that dictated how ships were supposed to interact with each other when out at sea. Dad soon found that these too were often arbitrary in practice.

*In midshipmen school, Jim and I were both fascinated by a course in Seamanship and the various rules in connection with it. This rules book was called* Knights Rules of Seamanship. *We often wondered if some of these rules would actually be applied as a practical matter. One question: [if] we were in a crossing situation with another vessel and had signaled them that we had the right of way, would they accede?*

*We got our answer in Leyte Gulf when, for some reason, a large part of the 7th fleet moved in. It was a massive display of armed might despite the fact that the 7th paled when compared with the 3rd and 5th fleets. There were even some British cruisers. Cruisers, while not as big as battle ships, are huge. I can remember how proud we were that our cruisers were beautifully painted, equipped, and maintained while the British ships were, to say the least, rust buckets. Anyway, we finally got in a crossing situation with one of our cruisers. We had the right of way, gave them the proper signal and they just blew us away—as if we didn't exist—so much for the* Knights Rules of the Road.

The veterans I spoke with expressed their pride in the American naval strength, many recalling the sight of the massive 7th fleet with awe. Ed Knight was an Army medic who headed to battle aboard a ship in this convoy on its way to the Philippines. He estimated that there were over 800 ships in the fleet. His guess was close—there were 738 ships in the fleet for the great battle of Leyte Gulf. Later, Al Exner's ship joined the fleet as it headed to Iwo Jima, and he recalled, "This convoy was so large—400 ships with 80,000 Marines—you could not see how many ships it consisted of even when you went topside."

*From "Skill in the Surf," courtesy of Naval History and Heritage Command, Washington, D.C.*

Every one of these ships traveling across the vast expanse of ocean eventually crossed the equator. It was while doing so that new sailors heading to the South Pacific experienced the traditional Navy ceremony during their first crossing. Following an old custom, "pollywogs," those who had not yet traversed the line, were transformed into shellbacks upon passing through, entering a brotherhood of trusty sailors. Dressed as King Neptune, one Shellback orchestrated the proceedings, often accompanied by a king's court made up of other Shellbacks. Similar to a frat house hazing, the Pollywogs endured a gauntlet of embarrassing contests for the entertainment of the more experienced sailors.

Dad crossed on March 27, 1944, and had this to say: *This [certificate] we got when we crossed the equator. Either going across the 180ᵗʰ meridian or the equator. They beat the hell out of us in the hazing—even now at 69, 70, 71, 72, 73, 74, 75, 76, 77, 78, 79, 80, 81, 82 I can feel the welts on my fanny. In keeping with ancient Navy tradition there was a lot of hazing. My rear end was bright purple from the beatings I received. I did, however, become a Shellback—whatever the hell that is. This gave me the privilege of beating up some innocent rookie who had not previously crossed the equator. This I was never too interested in doing.*

These young men grew up in all parts of the country, and while their backgrounds were different, they would now share many common things as part of the Navy system. There would be only three ways out of the service: the point system, dishonorable discharge, or death. From the day they joined the Navy, the men began accruing the necessary points they would need to earn to finish their service requirement.

*I forgot to mention my trip home in 1945—late June, July, and August.* [Dad received a leave to come home and marry my mom.] *I boarded a brand-new gasoline tanker and headed east. The problem was that the ship had to first unload thousands of gallons of gasoline. I re-traced my journey down the coast of New Guinea, through the Solomon Islands, and then straight toward San Francisco as planned. The ship was diverted to the Panama Canal, however, where some time was spent before catching another ship bound for San Francisco. The whole trip took 66 days that, at the time, seemed like a better way to live than getting killed in the Philippines.*

*It turned out, however, that the war ended abruptly a week before our wedding on 8/23/45. To muster out of the Navy a chap needed points based on months of service and marital status. By marrying after August 15, I lost ten key points that meant I had to return for one more tour of the South Pacific* [to earn the additional points he needed to get out of the Navy]—*via the Philippines, Korea, Okinawa and almost China. I would/could have been out of the service by 9/1/45.*

The armed forces set up the points system, or Advanced Service Rating Score, to determine which soldiers, Marines, airmen, and sailors to send home first. Each man was awarded one point for each month of service whether he was at home or overseas. He earned five additional points for each combat award, such as a campaign star or theater ribbon. If the servicemember had minor children, he received twelve points for each one up to three kids total.

A member of the military could end up serving two to three years in a unit located far from the action; those closer to the action could muster out sooner due to the extra points earned in combat—if he survived. Some service members were rotated home on a different scale, such as pilots who reached a certain number of combat missions.

Many, like Dad, experienced hiccups with the point system. Al Exner served in the European theater but didn't earn enough points to leave the Navy, so he was sent to the South Pacific for another tour that included the invasions at Iwo Jima and Okinawa. Although he had accumulated almost twice as many points as he needed after those offensives to go home, when the war ended he continued serving because his rating was considered essential to the wind-down.

After fourteen months at sea, just before his marriage, Dad received a promotion to Lieutenant Junior Grade. My parents spent the last part of their honeymoon on the train to San Diego, California, blushing every time they returned to their berth from the applause of the other passengers as they walked by. Mom returned home alone when Dad headed back to the South Pacific to serve another nine months as an officer on a larger ship transporting luckier soldiers and sailors back home.

In all, Dad spent almost three years on active duty before he was finally honorably discharged.

Sometimes sailors received less than honorable discharges. Blue discharges, also known as "blue tickets" (because they were printed on blue paper), were often used to discharge homosexual personnel from the military. They were also disproportionally given to African Americans—during the war black Americans received about a quarter of all blue discharges while making up only about six percent of the armed forces. Those who were presented with a blue ticket were unable to receive GI Bill benefits and faced difficulty reacclimating into society or finding jobs because of the associated stigma.

When Congress first started working on the GI Bill, the American Legion expressed concern that blue tickets were being given for trivial or unreasonable reasons. Legion members argued that some people, through no fault of their own, simply did not have the aptitude to serve, and that their lives would be unnecessarily and negatively impacted by the dishonorable discharge. The House Committee on Military Affairs took on the issue and declared that those receiving blue discharges were being treated the same as if they had received dishonorable discharges, calling it "a squeeze play between the war department and the veterans' administration." Even though the committee suggested reforms, it wasn't until the summer of 1947 that the blue discharge designation was discontinued.

The rarest of all was the dishonorable discharge, given for the most serious offenses committed during service. These could include murder, rape, desertion, or other serious crimes.

Of all the ways to leave the military, the saddest and most final way to leave was to die while serving. Over 416,000 American troops lost their lives in WWII, the deadliest conflict the world has ever seen.

It wasn't always practical to transport the bodies home, so fallen sailors and Marines were sometimes buried at sea. First, any government-issued items were removed from the dead and passed on for use by others. Then the ship's crew laundered the deceased's clothing, converted any foreign money in their possession to U.S. currency, and placed these items (along with their dog tags and other personal belongings) in a package to be sent to the next of kin.

Al Exner witnessed only one such ceremony while serving on the USS *Lubbock*, and it followed many of the typical Navy protocols for burials at sea. The unfortunate young man fought in the battle at Iwo Jima where he was struck and pierced all the way through his body by a mortar shell. Arriving on the *Lubbock* for treatment, Al could see there was volcanic ash throughout the inside of the Marine's body, and he knew that with such mortal injuries there would be no way to save him. In moments of lucidity, the injured man screamed out streams of obscenities about the Japanese while the ship's medical crew tried to comfort him. Al, a religious man, prayed to God that the young man would be forgiven for the things he was saying while in such pain and terror.

After the suffering Marine died, the crew placed a five-inch .38 shell between his legs, and then sewed his body into a blue shroud so it would not be visible in the water. A chaplain spoke words in his honor. As his body slid off the board feet first into the water, the ship made a slight curve to avoid his body being caught in any of the propellers.

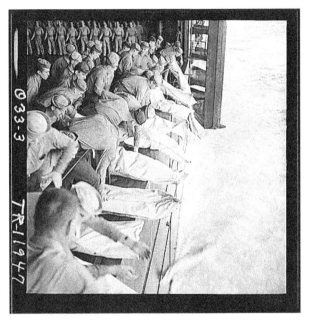

*Photo courtesy: National Archives 80-G-468912*

Though Al did not mention all the details of this burial, typically an American flag covered the corpse with the union placed near the head and left shoulder. All officers and men who were not on duty were called to services with these words broadcast on the ship's loudspeaker, "All hands bury the dead." Someone might play the somber notes of "Taps" followed by a volley of three shots ringing out in the air in honor of the fallen man.

For a brief moment, the ship's flag flickered as it was lowered and then quickly raised back up. A crewmember recorded the longitude and latitude of the burial, and along with the flag that had draped the body, this notation was sent to the next of kin.

It is a relief that my grandmother never received such a package or a telegram delivering terrible news. Back home she joined millions of other women paying tribute to their sons by hanging a service flag in her window. Also known as a "blue star banner" or "son in service flag," these eight-by-fourteen-inch banners hung facing outward to show passersby that a family member was off at war. Each star represented a single relative, with room for up to five on each banner. If a loved one died in service, a slightly smaller gold star was sewn over the blue star nearest the top of the flag. This tradition continues today; Gold Star Banners are proudly hung in recognition of and honor to the men and women who gave the ultimate sacrifice to this country.

*This was the blue star banner my grandma hung in the window for Dad. You should note that he pasted it into the scrapbook upside down—the fringe would have been on the bottom.*

The last Naval tradition Dad took part in before he finally mustered out of the Navy was to take home a piece of the flag that flew above the deck on his final assignment aboard the USS-148.

*I believe this was my piece of the ensign (ensign is ship's flag) from my last Navy gig—the USS-148 Landing Craft Medium. This is apparently a Naval custom to cut things up when a ship is decommissioned.*

*This is the piece of flag Dad kept from his final ship as it was decommissioned.*

Over time, the American Navy adopted the English term "ensign" for both the flag and the first rank of young officers. The word wraps up Dad's war experience in a single neat bow. He began his long adventure as a newly minted Ensign in the United States Navy with his star and stripe on his sleeve, and ended it taking home his own piece of an "ensign" to keep forever secured on the last page of his scrapbook.

## FORCES COMBINED
## YET ALSO CONFLICTED

Before the attack on Pearl Harbor, our government was ill-equipped to take on a war on multiple fronts that would need ground, air, and naval forces directed competently by agencies back home. General George Marshall, Roosevelt's Chief of Staff, and Harry Stimson, Secretary of War, reorganized the War Department under the War Powers Act of 1941 into three distinct and independent branches: the Army Ground Forces, the Army Air Forces, and the Army Service Forces.

To house the growing War Department under one roof, the Army's Construction Bureau began work building the Pentagon building in September 1941. After the attack on Pearl Harbor, the work intensified, with crews sometimes working around the clock in a rush to finish the construction. The monstrous building rose in just sixteen months, with some employees moving in before the structure was fully completed on January 15, 1943. If there was ever a time for the various divisions of the War Department to work in concert, it was at that moment. It wouldn't be until after the war that the Army, Navy, and Air Force were all brought together permanently into the Department of Defense.

As with any undertaking, the collaboration between the

Army, Navy, Air Force, and Marines didn't take place without conflict. As with any difficult undertaking involving millions of people, tensions invariably flared up as the roles were defined.

During the course of his three years at sea, Dad interacted with sailors and officers of many different rates and ranks in the Navy. He also came into regular contact with folks serving in the other branches of the military when their assignments overlapped. His journal is full of anecdotes about these interactions, and they help to illustrate the complicated organizational structure of the war machine. These entries also illuminate the cast of characters, both honorable and not, and that the delicate balance between the various personnel was not always maintained.

Dad found his place in this newly organized defense department as a young man of just twenty-two, thrust into the role of officer and leader of men on his small landing craft. The first thing he discovered, echoed by many veterans, was that the larger the ship the stricter the protocols. With the LCT being one of the smallest vessels in the fleet, there were no career Naval officers on board to show Dad how to do things "the Navy way." This was both a blessing and a curse. He and the other LCT officers did their best, using what they learned from training and manuals, as well as flying by the seat of their pants. Most tried to lead with dedication and discipline to support the war effort with honor, but of course there were exceptions, as Dad recalled in his journal.

*There was another LCT . . . ensign in our group by the name of Bill B-----. He ran a sloppy ship and was a real fuck-off. (Excuse the Navy jargon). He realized early on that by keeping his ship at a low performance level, it would not be called on to perform any difficult or unusual tasks. He used to define this problem as just "tuffsky shitsky" (about the extent of his vocabulary). While his ship was laid up (non-operative), chaps such as Harnack and the LCT-977 (us) got his work assignments.*

*Bill's ship did carry in some cargo and it was his custom to steal certain highly prized items—like Air Force safety glasses (just an example). These he could and did sell for a small profit. The word was that he had once allowed a Filipino father on board. The father was pimping for his young daughter—too commune.* [Unfortunately, many young women suffered the trials and pain of war, too.] *I never said that the generation that saved the world wasn't crude.*

When the war began, the entire Navy consisted of about 300,000 members; now that same number represented the number of officers needed to lead a wartime naval force that eventually grew to almost 3.25 million strong. In their work, Dad and Jim Harnack found that it takes all kinds of people to run the Navy.

At one point they came across two peers on a similar-sized vessel called a PT boat. Patrol torpedo boats were small, very fast, and made of mahogany. The Navy used them for scouting and harassing enemy forces by disrupting their supply routes. According to the National WWII Database, PT crews were similar to LCT crews in both size and composition, known to be informal and even undisciplined at times, able scavengers who found whatever goods they needed to bolster their supplies.

Dad recalls how PT boats became famous back home: *Early*

*in 1942 to boost morale on the home front, the armed forces issued propaganda films through newsreels. They were shown in movie theaters along with the movie. An early favorite was shots of our brave and bold sailors hurtling themselves in small wooden boats in heavy seas. The vessels were PT boats equipped with torpedoes to be aimed at and possibly hit and sink "Jap" ships (the boats had 2 Ensigns and a crew of 10-12). The newsreels never showed any of the sunken ships, however. Long after the war, there was a movie "PT Boat 109" a future President, Jack Kennedy, was featured as played by actor Cliff Robertson. Kennedy was pictured not only as a hero but one helluva swimmer.*

*While working on Noemfoor Island in August of 1944, we encountered our first and only PT boat. Two disconsolate officers had sent out an S.O.S using signal flags and being the only other Navy ship in the area, we were sent out to rescue them. It seems their engine or perhaps engines had conked out and they had run down the batteries trying to re-start them. They were just bobbing about in the ocean. We towed them into the beach.*

*One of the officers was a bookish type chap who had been an anthropologies/naturalist at the University of Chicago. He was not the dashing hero type at all. In fact, he confided in us that he would have given his left testicle (or perhaps it was the right) if he could have had duty on a ship such as ours. He also said he couldn't believe the bugs, the specimens, and the near Stone Age natives that he could have studied in the jungles of New Guinea.*

Another 90-Day Wonder, this officer was much like Dad and Jim, a studious type out of his element but doing his best to support the war effort. However, others they met spoke of

PT personnel that lacked the character and morals expected of Navy leadership.

*On my trip home, a fellow passenger was a Navy warrant officer from a supply ship that supplied the PT Boats with food, clothes, guns, and torpedoes. To put it mildly, in Navy language, he said the PT Boat skippers were, in general, just a lot of cocky, useless motherfuckers. He further added that "they and their torpedoes couldn't hit a bull in the ass with a spade." He said the crews often mishandled the alcohol that was to be used to power a little engine which propelled each torpedo. They apparently would dilute the alcohol, drink it, get drunk and then not properly replace it. Our passenger was a crusty Mustang so perhaps he exaggerated. Thereafter, my image of PT boat heroism was completely destroyed.*

Mustang is a slang term used to refer to someone who came into the Navy and served as an enlisted man before finally receiving the rank of commissioned officer. The commission came with much better pay and retirement benefits. In Dad's opinion, he feared that Mustangs would never be accepted as equal by any of the proud young Ensigns who had graduated from the military academies.

Dad and Jim Harnack frequently encountered Merchant Marines in the course of their assignments. The Merchant Marines was a collection of non-naval ships that delivered goods and passengers. It had existed, though in smaller numbers, prior to the war. Men serving on Merchant Marine ships were civilian volunteers without military standing or government benefits.

The Merchant Marines were willing to hire African Americans who could sign on to any position that they were qualified for. In fact, over 24,000 African American men served in the Merchant Marines during the war. Although some shipping companies hired by the U.S. government in this capacity required the crews to be segregated, others did not, and the mixed-race crews became known as "checkerboards."

*African American Merchant Marines*
*Photo courtesy National Archives 111-SC-180663*

The early years of the war, in particular 1942, were extremely dangerous for the Merchant Marines, as German U-boats sunk dozens of ships sailing without Navy protection in U.S. waters. To fill the need for Mariners during the war, some shipping companies lowered their standards for hiring which gave American civilians the stereotypical impression that the new hires were drunks, thieves, and brawlers. Nevertheless, these very brave young Merchant Marines carried out the vital task of delivering goods and soldiers to battle while suffering an estimated 9,000 casualties in the process.

*The skipper on the gasoline tanker on which I rode home was a proper old-fashioned sea dog—Merchant Marine. He sometimes joined us at the captain's table for breakfast and regaled us with his past feats as a sailor who never expected to earn his present salary—$15,000 a year. In fact, he felt at $15,000 he was "stealing."* As civilian employees, the Merchant Mariners did make a fine salary, with bonuses given for work in the more dangerous areas of the war.

*Since the ships were privately owned, the personnel were paid on a very beneficial basis for them. The officers were members of the Merchant Marine so that an officer of the same rank as I received the same pay as I. He would then get substantial pay boosts every time the ship got into a zone closer to the war. Officers on some of the watches would get time and a half and the double time pay for certain hours. An officer with rank equal to mine could earn between 12 and 15 thousand dollars a year—lots and lots of money in those days. They were exempt from the armed forces and always got much better food than we did.*

What Dad fails to mention here is that the Mariners received no benefits from the government even though they paid income taxes on what they earned while at sea. As William Geroux points out in his article titled "World War II Shows Why We Need the Merchant Marine," "If their ships were torpedoed, they stopped getting paid the moment they hit the water. They were off the clock when swimming for their lives." These men never received veteran status either, and although they were in the sea trenches along with their fellow Americans, they are not included for remembrance on Memorial Day.

Merchant Mariners had a reputation among Navy leaders for scoffing at military discipline and failing to fall in line when ordered. Dad continued with his recollection of the Merchant Marine skipper from the gasoline tanker: *We the passengers who had been away from the States for a long time were thrilled when the cook offered us fresh eggs for breakfast—a rare treat. The skipper declined the eggs pointing out that they had been out to sea for three weeks at which point there was no such thing as a fresh egg.*

*He was a fearless and competent sailor. He demonstrated this in Hollandia, New Guinea. On our way up the coast in 1944 we encountered a Liberty Ship captain who refused to tie up at one of the few piers in New Guinea without benefit of tugboat assistance. The captain was obviously a boob, afraid of his bosses and maybe just scared. Our old sea dog was in a hurry to "pump" gas and head home. Within five minutes he had us safely alongside the pier—no problem.*

Another group of unsung heroes in the Navy were the Seabees—the nickname for the Naval **C**onstruction **B**attalions. Dad said, *I never thought the Navy Seabees got enough credit for their war efforts. In general, they seemed to be older Navy guys and they worked their butts off building docks, piers, air strips, running all sorts of mechanical gadgets. They were part of a dying breed of chaps who can and do fix anything, wordlessly and with great efficiency.*

As early as 1940, the government hired groups of civilian contractors to build bases in the South Pacific after the Navy became convinced that infrastructure would be needed there in the event that the United States became part of the conflict. However, by international law, civilians can't fight back against enemy attack. Additionally, once the United States entered the war, the construction workers already working under government contract were too few in number to meet the demands for the numerous bases and landing strips that would be needed.

The Navy decided to form a special organization that could both build facilities and defend themselves at the same time—the Naval Construction Battalions. Highly skilled tradesmen, such as carpenters, electricians, and plumbers, made up these battalions. These men put their creativity to use and made do with whatever materials they had (or didn't have) on hand. By the end of the war, over 300,000 men proudly served as Seabees, supporting the efforts of all branches of the military.

*Seabees building a Quonset hut in Guadalcanal*
*Photo courtesy: National Archives 80-G-38217*

While many people and organizations composed this vast and complex military network, tensions and rivalries between the branches were bound to arise.

As noted previously, prior to the war an average of 425 Ensigns graduated from the Naval Academy at Annapolis, Maryland, after four years of training. During wartime, thousands of Ensigns were suddenly coming out of the Midshipmen V-7 training program after just three months.

*Neither Jim nor I had much respect for regular Navy personnel, their protocol, and their formality. Any Annapolis ensigns that we encountered avoided us like the plague. They had the "ring" on one of their fingers that in their minds designated them as kings of the road. My group of Ensigns were called "feather merchants" and of course, were ignored by the average Annapolis graduate—we were very often a lot smarter but to them just "90-day wonders." They discounted the fact that most of us had attended much better educational institutions (better than West Point and Annapolis, that is).*

*One thing that often bothered me was the intense rivalry between the Army and the Navy. I sometimes wondered who we were fighting—the NIPS or the Army. (We called the Japanese NIPS then—when we tired of called them Japs.) The rivalry I believe was and still is fostered at the jock level—football. That seems stupid to me being a non-jock of course.*

*As a rule, we were assigned by the flotilla commander to help the Army unload cargo. At the same time, we were instructed never to do anything for the Army that we construed as being unsafe for our ship. That is in tying up alongside, or going down channels we knew were bad, etc. This often resulted in wars of words between us and various unloading Army officers.*

*I was always very happy that I chose the Navy. It just seemed more civilized. Of course, I would never have chosen the Marines or either of the Air Force groups.*

As I've mentioned before, Dad wasn't a particularly physical or imposing man, and most definitely did not like confrontation. I can only assume here that he didn't think he possessed the strength or fearlessness to be closer to the thick of battle.

Dad's LCT once caught a ride on top of a larger vessel, and it was there that he and Jim joined some Air Force personnel who were already on board.

*We loved it during our trip from New Guinea to the Philippines; we got a free ride inside an LSD—Landing Ship Dock. This was a vessel normally used to repair various ships. They filled their deck with water; we sailed in (after they dropped their rear gate, of course. I think they carried 3 LCTs), they drained the water and there we sat for a nice, comfortable ride.* [I would have loved to see that.]

*I kind of looked at the Air Force pilots, the ones we met, as being overly arrogant. The pilots were just different than we were— perhaps more fearless and I suppose, braver. They certainly did a great job in general. Harnack and I were just miffed at these guys who came on board the LSD. They completely ignored us and as fellow officers in a different branch, they should have been civil and at least faked being sociable.*

Was the War Department a well-oiled machine? Probably not entirely. But it did manage to help pull off the biggest victory of the twentieth century. We can only imagine what the world would look like today if these soldiers and sailors, officers and grunts, medics and cooks, and all the rest hadn't put aside their differences to join forces and wipe out the Axis.

## SECTION TWO: SETTLING IN

Over the course of the World War II years, almost sixteen million Americans left their familiar lives back home to go out in the world to serve. After just weeks or months of preparation, these new sailors, soldiers, Marines, and pilots left behind the relative free choice of their former lives to enter the strict codes and discipline of the military. What would happen next was out of their hands.

The phrase "comrade in arms" reflects how most who served felt a sense of brotherhood with their fellow sailors and soldiers, people who stood side by side with them working through the same difficulties for their shared purpose. These new "families" forged during war were made up of the bonds of shared experience and hardship, joy and sorrow. Underlying every effort lay the constant threat and thrum of sudden danger and its horrors.

And yet, they still woke up in the morning hungry for a meal, sought the protection of friendships with their mates, and longed for loved ones back home. Life in the war zone would require shifting into a new norm—taking on each day's assignments and accepting the tedium that often came with them.

Making the best of their new reality.

# FEEDING THE FORCE

*In general, we dined on Army K or C rations—the C rations were better. At least 10 days a month we had fresh food—meat, butter, eggs, etc. The other 20 days we ate a lot of standard Army food although we always had supplies of flour, coffee, and a lot better quality of canned stuff than the Army had. We drank enormous quantities of coffee from Army canteen cups using evaporated milk as our cream. We always had large bags of coffee beans in our hold.*

*Our meals were brought to us* [the officers] *breakfast, lunch, and dinner. One of the crewmembers did the carrying. Jim and I did not wait in line. We ate in our own cabin.*

This struck me as a mundane entry in the journal, until I began thinking about the logistical nightmare of feeding millions of servicemen all over the world for years on end.

One complication was that the war was raging in wildly varied climates: The South Pacific's steamy heat, Europe's seasonal conditions, and North Africa's deserts. The packaged food had to withstand long-distance shipping and then remain unspoiled in storage as it waited for further delivery. Troops experienced different conditions depending on their assignments and location—they could be isolated on ships, dug deep into foxholes, camped out in tents, or in vast wide-open country. If they lacked direct access to supplies, they had to carry their food rations along with them, adding to the weight of their packs. On a base or a ship, a cook stood ready to feed as many as hundreds of men at a time, or as few as a handful.

Wartime shortages of meal components posed another challenge for the United States Army Quartermater's office as it developed the food program. The stated goal was that all American soldiers "deserved to be fed the best food available in the best and most appetizing form within the realm of reasonable possibility particularly . . . troops in combat." This was no easy feat.

"Food for Fighters," an old war reel put out by the Office of War Information, shows that the Army started with a scientific approach to the meals. They studied the enemies' foods to determine how to give our men a leg up with more vitamins so they could fight more efficiently. Over a lively and patriotic soundtrack, the propaganda in the movie claims that with all the technology the Army was developing to feed our men, "no one on earth need suffer from malnutrition or hunger" after the war's end.

One of the first rations developed was called the Field Ration D—a small and portable item intended to provide a combat soldier with one day's 1,800-calorie requirement in an emergency situation. A D-Ration consisted of three 4-oz chocolate bars manufactured by the Hershey Chocolate Company. To call the universally disliked, bitter bars "chocolate" was a great stretch. To meet the calorie requirement, the folks at Hershey reduced the sugar, mixed in oat flour to keep the bars from melting, and added vitamins. The resulting pasty mixture couldn't even be poured like normal chocolate but was pressed into the molds. In fact, the bars were so dense that some soldiers shaved slices off the side of the bar in lieu of biting into it.

The bar's flavor was less important than its nutritional value. In fact, they purposely tasted unappetizing to keep soldiers from eating them at will instead of eating for the goal of keeping a soldier alive in a dire pinch. The Army made the mistake of releasing the bars for general consumption before informing the troops of their true emergency ration purpose. One taste turned most soldiers off for life.

For regular meal consumption, the Quartermaster developed Army K- and C-Rations, the latter being more palatable. C-Rations typically consisted of three cans of a meat and vegetable mixture, three cans of bread-type items, and one accessory pack. Here's an example of an early C-Ration:

- Package of biscuits (usually soy-based)
- Package of graham crackers
- Package of sugar tablets
- Three cans of meat
- Fruit bar, chocolate bar, caramels
- Powdered coffee, bouillon, lemon drink
- Chewing gum
- Nine cigarettes and matches
- Package of toilet paper
- Can opener

(Later packs also contained a spoon, a halazone water purification tablet, and salt tablets to ease heat exhaustion.)

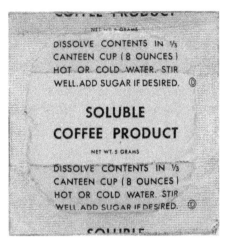

*Dad sent these wrappers home
to go in the scrapbook*

While the C-Ration succeeded in meeting all the nutritional needs, it came up short in other ways. Meat components were tough to acquire and produce in the vast quantities needed. Complaints flew in from the field about the monotony of the flavors, a problem the Quartermaster couldn't solve until troops first consumed the stockpiles of unpopular items. To make matters worse, much to their dismay, men coming off the front lines for a few days' respite were often fed the exact same rations in the mess halls.

C-Rations were also heavy—sometimes over three pounds per meal. It was hard to be a mobile, nimble soldier with a pack full of cumbersome and bulky cans.

In 1942, with paratroopers needing lighter packs for combat and assault missions, the Army released a modification in the form of the first K-Rations. These meals contained a small can of meat or cheese, biscuits, powdered beverages, and candy. Once again, toilet paper and cigarettes were included. A snippet of beige toilet paper is pasted into Dad's scrapbook with a notation from Mom calling it "Johnnie Paper."

The Cracker Jack Company, along with The H.J. Heinz Company and Patten Food Products, were the main packagers of K-Rations for the Army Quartermaster. Workers first boxed the canned meat and cheese products in the K-Ration individually, then placed them together with the other items in a plastic bag that could later be reused to keep other possessions dry, such as letters or photographs. Employees placed the completed meal in a plain cardboard box and dipped it twice in wax to make it waterproof. The final step of assembly was to put each plain box into another slightly larger one with a colorful label designating the meal as breakfast, dinner, or supper, so soldiers could easily select the right meal.

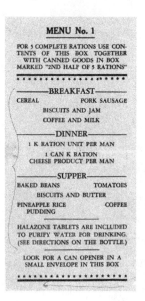

**MENU No. 1**

FOR 5 COMPLETE RATIONS USE CONTENTS OF THIS BOX TOGETHER WITH CANNED GOODS IN BOX MARKED "2ND HALF OF 5 RATIONS"

————BREAKFAST————
CEREAL                    PORK SAUSAGE
     BISCUITS AND JAM
     COFFEE AND MILK

————DINNER————
     1 K RATION UNIT PER MAN
        1 CAN K RATION
     CHEESE PRODUCT PER MAN

————SUPPER————
BAKED BEANS              TOMATOES
     BISCUITS AND BUTTER
PINEAPPLE RICE            COFFEE
     PUDDING

HALAZONE TABLETS ARE INCLUDED TO PURIFY WATER FOR DRINKING. (SEE DIRECTIONS ON THE BOTTLE.)

LOOK FOR A CAN OPENER IN A SMALL ENVELOPE IN THIS BOX

Dad taped a typical menu from a K-Ration into his scrapbook and added the comments that "*all of this marvelous 'cuisine' came in one small Cracker Jack box*" and that it was "*all good for people who wanted to lose weight.*"

Although K-Rations were intended for just a few days' sustenance under battle conditions, many soldiers ate them for days or weeks at a time. Sometimes they were simply the easiest meals to distribute. During peak production in 1944, over 105 million K-Rations made their way to our troops. Use of K-Rations tapered off near the end of the war when the Quartermaster developed better C-Rations, and in 1948, the Army discontinued production of K-Rations altogether, distributing the remaining rations to non-military feeding programs abroad.

Patrick Henry Post No. 33 American Legion New Castle, Ky. Best wishes from the men of 17 and 18

Made In U. S. A.

Produced and assembled in the States, both C- and K-Rations sometimes included well wishes from Americans working on the assembly lines.

The candy industry is one example of how some lucky American businesses were kept afloat by producing items for troop meals during the war years. Even though sugar was rationed back home, sailors and soldiers might find a stick of Wrigley's chewing gun or a hard candy in their meals. Hershey and Mars developed and manufactured M&M's for exclusive sale to the military. The multi-colored coated candies could withstand long-distance travel and heat to arrive in the hands of our GIs and sailors, well representing the company slogan of "Melts in your mouth, not in your hand."

Not every meal for our servicemembers came from a box. The armed forces made valiant efforts to keep our troops supplied with food and life's other necessities wherever they were stationed. However, depending on a servicemember's proximity to various supply channels, this could be a hit-or-miss proposition. Military bases and supply ships sprinkled throughout the South Pacific were likely the best sources for food items.

*We did not have much access to any Navy supply ships. The Supply ship was called a "tender." We had one which we rarely found.* In theory, tenders cruised about the sea loaded with food and necessities for other ships and bases in the area. It's a mystery how little ships like Dad's received their food supplies, but it appears that it depended on geographical location, timing, and luck. The Pacific theater of war stretched over 3,000 miles, so for ships not assigned to a large flotilla, finding a tender was like finding a needle in a haystack.

John Eskau, cook's assistant on *LCT-596,* spent much of the war anchored in Buckner Bay near Okinawa so he was lucky to have a tender conveniently located nearby to serve all the ships there.

Common canned items included fruit, vegetables, and juices as well as canned meat such as Spam. The cooks used sugar, flour, coffee, and yeast every day, although the heat wrought havoc with these staples. Al Exner remembered eating bread filled with weevils in the mess hall and said he later watched the crew throw sack after sack of bug-infested flour into the ocean. Even the candy and snacks sold in the ship's store were regularly full of worms.

*John Eskau showing me a photo of him and other cooks*

The constant flow of dehydrated and powdered items demoralized the sailors. Food processing companies diced the dried potatoes into little cubes, several of which my father sent home for Mom to neatly paste into the scrapbook. Cooks found that even after soaking, they barely passed as mashed potatoes.

Patricia B. Mitchell's article "WWII Navy Food Remembered" features the story of Lanier Anderson, Jr. who was assigned to a destroyer escort. He was once sailing with a small British group of four warships in the South Pacific that had been issued some of the American potatoes. Several nights after the delivery of the spuds, Anderson was on watch and received a visual message from one of the British ships. It read: "Those potatoes you gave us: we have tried boiling, frying, and stewing them. How can they be prepared for eating?" There would be no help forthcoming from Anderson whose own cooks had already failed to make them edible.

Eggs and milk also came in powdered form. The guys choked down the eggs at breakfast by drenching them in plenty of ketchup. In a nod to their tender age, sailors found that fresh milk was one of the things they missed most about home.

Dad remembered: *Our problem was refrigeration. We had a 10 cubic foot General Electric Refrigerator so the food (fresh) lasted maybe a week. Harnack and I discovered that butter rots from the outside in. We would take a pound of butter and shave it down a bit—whittling off all the grunge. We used to spread this on crackers for a late-night snack, along with our canteen of coffee—coffee in the loosest sense of the word.*

Refrigerated ships, nicknamed "reefers," delivered fresh food throughout the South Pacific. There were only ten such vessels up and running before 1944 when several more new ones were delivered—hardly enough to supply the troops in such a vast ocean. Although many more reefer ships were ordered, building them was such a slow and difficult process that most never made it out to sea before the war's end.

Al Exner served a short stint on a reefer after the USS *Lubbock* broke down and was in for repairs. He joined the twenty-man crew already assigned to the little floating grocery. After being underfed for so long, he ate freely of the cheeses and fresh food on the ship, ending up with terrible digestive troubles all the way to his next stop in Manila.

Sometimes the little LCTs received a large quantity of a particular item which created a vexing problem for the cooks. John Eskau and the head cook once traded 300 pounds of hamburger to the Army for liquor and other supplies. They had no such luck when a huge order of mutton from Australia fell into their laps—the two men scratched their heads trying to figure out what to make of this meat neither had ever seen before.

Throughout the South Pacific, American bases sprung up and became staging and supply areas for the forces in the area. If the LCT crews made a stop nearby, they were able to requisition supplies there.

Ron Swanson, editor of *The Flotilla* newsletter whom I contacted frequently while researching LCTs, once emailed a story about his father Doug Swanson to me. Doug, a young sailor on an LCT, went ashore with a requisition order from his skipper. He and another crewmember reported to the big freezer unit at the base and showed their papers to the armed guard. While his friend waited outside with the guard, Swanson went in to gather the things on the list. On the way out he noticed a beautiful ring of frozen bologna hanging on a shelf—probably slated for an officer. He quickly grabbed the sausage and stuffed it down the front of his shirt, concealing it by holding the other boxes to his chest. The guard checked off the three or four boxes, and Swanson and his friend went on their way. As soon as they got out of the guard's sight, Swanson threw down the boxes and yanked out the sausage that by then had "burned" a white circle on his chest. Back on the ship, his skipper laughed and took it in stride and the crew enjoyed a fine meal that night.

Some veterans forged relationships with local natives in an effort to improve their diet by trading canned goods for fish and eggs. Because John Eskau's LCT was parked just offshore in Japan, he became friendly with local fishermen and farmers. John told me, "They were not the real enemy, they were real people. They hated the 'Japs' too because they were treated like second-class citizens by them." His new Japanese friends even invited John and some crewmates to a party on land. After their hosts sternly told the young Americans to mind their manners and respect the ladies, they spent the evening eating, drinking, and thoroughly enjoying themselves. Had they gotten wind of it, the Navy brass would surely have frowned on this evening of fraternizing with the enemy.

Another source of food was directly underneath their ships and some cooks learned to take advantage of the bounty of the ocean. One LCT cook had a line trailing behind his ship as it entered the Bismarck Sea near New Guinea, yelling with delight when a blue marlin took the bait and tugged. He became a hero to all aboard as that 100-pound fish supplied an unexpected and delightful savory meal.

On the LCTs, cooks rose to the occasion and did their jobs very well under challenging conditions in tiny and extremely hot galleys. Most of them, like John, tried their best to keep all the men on the ship well fed and happy, even though their age and cultural differences made it tough going at times. It was sometimes an accomplishment to figure out how to make a meal out of the ingredients available at any given moment.

Cooks with baking skills aboard ships were a rarity and much in demand. Some felt good at the basics of meal preparation but drew the line at baking. Others had received more training or came from pre-war food industry careers. When he wrote his journal many years after the war, Dad still recalled how fine his cook was and extolled the virtues of his bread and cakes.

When interviewed for *The Flotilla*, LCT cook Bill Miller recalled: "We not only had to cook, but also bake bread and all the other things a baker was required to do onboard an LST or larger warship. I am glad to have attended cook and baker school for four months at the Navy Pier in Chicago, right after boot camp at Great Lakes. It was a good learning experience. It takes a lot of bread to feed a crew of twelve men and two officers."

He went on: "The skipper came up to me one day and said, 'Cookie, we are having officers come aboard for inspection, would you make some of those jelly cinnamon rolls and place them on the galley table?' When the officers arrived, they ate a couple of the rolls, inspected my galley and gave me good marks. I was always able to butter up the crew and skipper by baking something."

Lots of cooks on these little ships came in for a good deal of ribbing. It was rumored that amphibian vessels got the dregs of boot camp—that if a man had an aptitude for nothing else, he was sent off to learn to cook. These guys were shoved into a galley to prepare meals for twelve men from a cookbook where ingredients (if they could even be found) were measured to feed one hundred. One skipper remarked, "That's ok, I'm not sure my cook can read anyway!"

As for Dad, one upside to working on a supply ship was that if he and his crew were tasked with delivering something, they could at least pinch a little for themselves when necessary.

Two years into his stint with the Navy, my skinny father received a thirty-day leave in the summer of 1945 and traveled home to marry my mother. The journey itself was remarkable for its zigs and zags, taking him an unbelievable sixty-six days to reach his destination (during which the Americans dropped the atomic bombs on Japan.)

My parents often joked that Dad weighed less than Mom on their wedding day. Nonetheless, the looks on their young faces show how happy my parents were to be reunited and married.

After their wedding, Dad had to go back overseas—his post-war assignment was to bring soldiers home from the South Pacific. He once remarked that the Army loaded the transport ship with excellent food for the men in a small gesture of thanks for their service. Alas, most of the soldiers spent their whole journey doubled over, suffering from seasickness, unable to enjoy the wonderful spread of food onboard.

By the time Dad was home for good, his lack of sufficient nutrition while away was painfully evident. *On the whole I had a restful summer recovering from my loss of weight in the tropics. I believe I was about 130 pounds upon my return and 6'1/2" tall at the time. I've lost a lot of tallness since then but gained a lot of weight.*

Many veterans grew nostalgic telling me about how their mothers fixed them favorite meals upon their return. Others spoke of how they relished drinking fresh milk and eating things like crisp salads. John told me that to this day, he never eats ice cream without feeling grateful for making it back home.

Facing real hunger was no joke for our fighting men. Sometimes out of desperation, men stole food. Al Exner worried he might not be fed the whole way home at war's end, so to be sure he had something to eat, he swiped six cans of sardines from the galley.

Al received a new uniform in San Francisco on his way home after the war. He wryly told me he was a little thin through the middle after almost two years away. Years later, knowing he could never fit into that uniform again, a neighbor cut it up and used the fabric to sew little jackets for Al's children.

On his transport train home from the west coast, Al

volunteered in the mess car, mostly hoping to end up with something to eat for himself. The lieutenant commander in charge of the train had two boxer pups with him on the journey. He ordered Al to bring him a few steaks. Fetching the steaks quickly, the gaunt young sailor thought that he might actually be offered one. Instead, he was shocked to see the commander chop up the steaks and feed them to the dogs.

The saddest food story I heard came from Army medic Ed Knight, who endured months and months of grinding combat in the Philippines. He remembered often fighting for three weeks at a time, never even being able to take off his shoes or have a clean change of clothes. Finally, with great relief, the Army would pull the guys back from the front and give them a hot meal.

Ed lost many of his friends during battles, including a good friend he called Helton. The Army had set up a temporary area to treat the wounded near a battle site on the road from Manila to the mountains. Helton was in a truck driving out to collect the wounded when it was shelled and he was killed.

His battered body was brought back to the triage area and neatly covered with a blanket. Later, a traumatized Ed watched in disbelief as an infantryman nonchalantly used Helton's covered body as a table, sitting down to open his C-Rations. Over seventy years later, Ed's voice still cracked as he told me the horror he felt when that soldier reached across his friend's body to offer him a bite of his lunch.

# SMOKE 'EM IF YOU GOT 'EM

The "war book," as it came to be called in our family, was the big scrapbook we loved to pore over when we were kids. Inside it were all kinds of foreign and interesting things, from a time long before we were even a thought in our parents' heads.

Curiously, taped to one of the pages is a flattened, empty package of Lucky Strike cigarettes. Why on earth did Mom and Dad decide to save that?

While today we live in a country with very few places to light up, not that long ago, smoking was commonplace. At the end of the 20$^{th}$ century, people could still smoke at work, in restaurants and bars, and up until 1990, on airplanes. The dangers of inhaling tobacco smoke were not well known until the 1960s, when the Surgeon General's Office first added a warning on the label of every pack of smokes.

Back in the 1940s, glamorous movie stars lit each other's cigarettes on screen, and even the President smoked. When Dad tucked that souvenir pack of Lucky Strikes aside for safekeeping in 1944, the President was Franklin Delano Roosevelt, known for wearing a jaunty hat and clasping a loaded cigarette holder between his teeth.

In his retirement Dad wrote, *I am not defending cigarette*

*smoking, but it was what most people did during the war. This was an era when doctors still had ashtrays in their offices so smoking was considered a proper custom. The cigarette folks wanted us all to learn to smoke—and we did in the forties.*

*Here is the empty pack Dad sent home to Mom, with her notes below it.*

The story behind this green Lucky Strike package is one of both American wartime ingenuity and marketing savvy. The green and gold dyes used in the brand's packaging contained copper and chromium, costly materials in great demand for the war effort. To skirt around this problem, the American Tobacco Company decided to change the package's paper from green to white, all while keeping the well-known red bull's-eye in the center.

The real genius was in how the company marketed the new white packaging. The switch was first explained as a reaction to complaints from women that the original green color clashed with their carefully chosen and fashionable outfits.

Then, the company rolled out a patriotic advertising campaign, "Lucky Strike green has gone to war," launched just as the invasion of North Africa began. Most of the remaining green packs of Lucky Strikes found their way overseas to the soldiers. It wasn't long before a link formed in the minds of folks back home between the original green packaging and the green of Army uniforms. Voila!—sales of Lucky Strikes shot up thirty-eight percent in 1942.

Apparently, Dad saw through these marketing ploys: *In early 1942, Lucky Strike, aiming for the female market, changed its package to a cleaner, more attractive white. Part of their giant ad campaign was 'Lucky Strike Green has gone to war.' This was a crock and meant that we got a lot of old cigarettes—those of us who were overseas. The "green" never came back.*

*We stole our cigarettes from the cargo we hauled—Chesterfields for me and Philip Morris for Jim Harnack—our Skipper. There was never a "ship's store" to buy this sort of thing, at least not for us.*

Some of the veterans I spoke with who were also assigned to small ships like Dad's lucked out because they were part of a flotilla, or group of ships, that included a supply ship. Those men recalled receiving one carton of cigarettes (ten packs of twenty) per month as a ration. Additionally, men assigned to larger ships had access to the ship's store where they could buy extra packs whenever they were available.

Ed Knight remembered that in the Army, when the troops were lucky enough to receive them, cigarettes came in small round metal tins about the size of a can of peanuts. He explained to me that the can had a very snug lid designed to keep out the jungle humidity. Each container held about forty cigarettes that were usually shared among the men in the unit before having a chance to rot in the heat.

There was another way that those serving got their tobacco fix—delivered right inside their meal kits. Dad said, *"Each little box of K-Ration food came equipped with four 20 Grand cigarettes or four Wings cigarettes plus four matches—just to get the youngsters hooked on tobacco, I suppose."*

I couldn't pin down exactly *why* the Quartermaster General decided to include cigarettes in these ration meals, but I found some suppositions about it. Beginning in WWI, soldiers turned to cigarettes as a way to briefly calm their minds. *The New York Times* weighed in at the time saying that smoking was a way "to lighten the inevitable hardships of war." We know that a lot of men smoked in the 1940s, so maybe providing them with cigarettes was simply an attempt to boost troop morale.

Cigarette companies were not averse to cultivating this notion, offering to supply free cigarettes to the troops. In advertisements, they encouraged families back home to send smokes to their loved ones, resulting in positive benefits to their bottom lines. The cigarette manufacturers definitely lobbied the government to include cigarettes in the rations, insisting that they were an essential item.

On a more human level, smoking gave the men something to do when they were bored or stressed. In fact, the phrase "smoke 'em if you got 'em" originated during WWII. An officer would say this to his men when it was okay for everyone to stand at ease or take a break. Of course, those breaks went smoke-free for many soldiers unable to get their hands on a cigarette.

Complaints from the soldiers and sailors in the South Pacific about the short supply of smokes were common. Many wrote into *Yank*—the weekly Army newspaper—to express their irritation. Dad cut out one of these articles and Mom dutifully pasted it into the scrapbook.

In the article, Sgt. John L. Kulsick (representing nineteen other GIs too) wrote in from Dutch New Guinea to say, "Why is it that for the past two months we have been issued Japanese cigarettes instead of American brands? Is there any justifiable excuse for keeping American cigarettes in bases . . . and pushing these salvaged weeds onto us?"

Dad, who also happened to be in New Guinea, wrote about this very topic in his journal, saying: *There was, for example, a general in New Guinea who hated cigarettes. Despite a good supply of American brands and despite the fact that all other needed supplies had been sent to the beach, he refused to allow the Army*

"Jap Cigarrette"

*to unload the American brands of cigarettes. He said, "The soldiers can smoke the cigarettes seized from Japanese supplies." The latter were like poison. The Japanese had their own class system, so their officers got a much better grade of tobacco—they* [the Japanese cigarettes] *too were poison.*

Most agreed that the Japanese cigarettes tasted terrible. Private Robert Vitorich succinctly described this in an excerpt of his letter to *Yank*. He said that when smoked, the Japanese cigarettes "taste like a dry herring burnt between two pine boards." The newspaper included this illustration:

Just imagine the quantities of Japanese smokes that ended up in American hands by way of battles won or Japanese supply ships captured. Numerous soldiers and sailors, not just my father, were addicted to smoking and found themselves stuck with the commandeered cigarettes as they went about their business in the Pacific. It seems ironic that while we supplied cigarettes to our men to keep morale up, we also likely depended on our enemy's resources to provide this small comfort.

While Dad enjoyed his wartime cigarettes like almost everyone else, he wasn't much for the disdain non-smokers directed their way. He commented, *There was talk at the time*

*Drawing from* The Yank *accompanying Private Vitorich's letter.*

*that General Doug MacArthur, safely sitting in Australia, hated people who smoked cigarettes. Doug was a bit hypocritical. He always held a pipe in hand.*

Even the Red Cross included packs of cigarettes in the care packages for prisoners of war. This organization, dedicated to saving lives, was unwittingly providing people with a health hazard. During the war, the United States assembled an astounding twenty-seven million care packages, which were shipped to a neutral country such as Switzerland then sent on to the POW camps.

The prisoners in the camps often pooled and shared the food items in the packages but saved the smokes to use as currency. The guys could use them to bribe German guards or to trade with their comrades for other items they needed. Even non-smokers used their cigarette rations as a means to trade. Although he didn't smoke, John Eskau received his monthly issue of one carton of cigarettes, dreaming about what he could use them to barter for. On top of his list was liquor. John and his friends had Army contacts with access to booze, so it made for an easy trade.

In Germany, the Nazis had a love/hate relationship with smoking during the war years. A Nazi doctor was one of the first in the world to link cigarette smoking to lung cancer. Dr. Karl Astel determined that as the popularity of smoking grew in the 1930s, so did the incidence of lung disease. The Nazis launched an anti-smoking campaign that included distributing pamphlets about the dangers of smoking, banning tobacco advertising, and limiting who and where people could smoke. However, they didn't outlaw tobacco altogether—the taxes raised from it created vital revenue stream for Hitler.

As the German defeat approached, more and more citizens started using cigarettes as currency, the value averaging about fifty cents each—a huge amount at the time since a pack of twenty sold for about twelve cents back in the States.

Some believe that cigarettes may have played a big role in saving Germany's post-war economy. Part of the Marshall Plan, devised to help repair war-torn Europe, included shipping over 200 million American cigarettes to Germany. Based on the street value of a cigarette there at the time, that's over $100,000,000— an astronomical sum in the late 1940s (*and* now). There is no doubt that the Marshall Plan had a tremendous and positive economic impact on American tobacco farmers and manufacturers.

When the war finally ended, it seemed that a generation of Americans had become addicted to smoking. The GIs, sailors, and officers received their cigarettes free of charge and returned stateside to continue their habit. Those nervously waiting at home smoked to relieve the stress of a frightening, massive, and faraway war. Some estimates say that by 1949, half the men and over a third of women in America smoked.

This statistic included my mom and dad. I was the youngest of five kids in my family, and before I was a thought in my parents' heads, they kept their stash of Chesterfields (unfiltered of course) above the oven. My older brother Bob snuck one once and after smoking it became a non-smoker for life. By the time I was born in 1962, my parents had both kicked the habit.

Even though the war machine had fueled his addiction for years, Dad was finally able to quit for good.

They also subjected the family to secondhand smoke on lengthy road trips, opening just the tiny, triangular windows near the dashboard in the station wagon to let the smoke escape. Bob and Pat, ensconced (sans seatbelts) in the rear-facing seat in the back of the car, escaped the worst of the fumes.

All of my siblings share a singular memory, however—the image of Dad reclined on the couch in a curling haze of smoke, a little tin-topped, plaid beanbag ashtray resting squarely on top of his chest.

When I was real poor, real young and real slim. In 2002 I'm still poor, real fat and real old. I see a cigarette in my right hand. I gave up cigarettes in 1962.

Jean    aug 1950    Bob

# BOYS AND THE BOOZE

The formal definition of the word "vice" in the dictionary is "a moral failing or bad habit. Traditional examples of *vice* include drinking alcohol, smoking tobacco, and gambling in card games." Many soldiers and sailors smoked up a storm during the war, and I soon discovered that most were also "guilty" of these other vices too.

Dad brought up the topic of drinking in his journal: *We were very fortunate that we never had any easy access to hard liquor. It would have been very easy to become addicted. Of course, in those days there were no other types of drugs readily available. I guess those were a gift of the rebellious 70's and the age of affluence in the 80's and 90's.*

The Navy was completely "dry" during the WWII years, meaning that no alcohol could be procured for drinking on any vessel or in any Navy yard. Historically, this wasn't always the case; in 1794, the United States Navy adopted the British tradition of giving each sailor a ration of rum every day. At that time, those who were underage or didn't drink were paid a little bit more in wages to make up for the skipped liquor ration.

In 1914, Secretary of the Navy Josephus Daniels issued General Order No. 99 that called for the complete ban of alcohol. A teetotaler from North Carolina, Daniels was really unpopular with many folks in the Navy who thought that by making the Navy dry he was also making it "soft."

Twenty years later, the Navy took an informal poll of its officers to determine whether or not to lift or alter the ban. They overwhelmingly voted to maintain the ban but did change the policy to allow liquor on shore at officers' clubs and stores. So, in theory, liquor wasn't allowed on board ships during the war years.

In practice, only the medical officer or captain of the ship had access to medicinal booze. Either might "prescribe" a drink if a sailor went through a particularly frightening or stressful experience. Others, like Admiral Eugene Fluckey of the submarine USS *Barb,* sometimes allowed the crew to have a beer or two just because living in close quarters under dangerous conditions took such a toll on the men.

As you'll recall on board the USS *Lubbock,* Al Exner and his shipmates offered little bottles of whiskey to each of the Marines heading to the beach for the invasion of Iwo Jima. That little bit of liquor might calm an injured man's pain while he waited for a medic to reach him.

Editor Ron Swanson shared the story of Ralph Avery in the newsletter *The Flotilla.* On D-Day in Normandy, Avery waited nervously on his LCT for the landing to commence. He later recalled, "On board, we were just waiting and wondering if the guns would work, if there would be enough ammunition . . . Everybody was scared, you know, nervous. We knew it wasn't going to be good. Before the invasion, a case of Johnny Walker Red Label was brought on board. I never had any of it, but we all knew it was there and no one would have been denied if they had asked for a drink. I think with the amount of tension and the adrenaline, I could have finished a bottle and not even felt it."

Many veterans remember getting a ration of booze, but of course this depended on their access to supply ships. Doug Swanson on *LCT-8* told his son, Ron, that he routinely received a ration of six beers and six cans of Coke every month. He wasn't much of a drinker, so he would hide his beers. When the others on his ship had run through theirs, usually in just a few days, he would then go ahead and sell or trade each of his beers for two cans of Coke.

Back home, the United States Department of Agriculture ordered that brewers set aside fifteen percent of their production to be sent to the troops. Many of these American cans of beer were painted a drab olive color to camouflage them from enemy aircraft.

Al Exner was at sea for very long periods of time but remembers getting off the ship at Cebu Island in the Philippines for an afternoon of swimming and football on the beach. The officers on the *Lubbock* issued each man two beers and a sandwich—thoroughly enjoyed by all.

The Army was also dry during WWII, again in theory. The Canteen Act of 1901 prohibited the sale of any "intoxicating" liquor at any place the Army conducted its business. What's funny about this is that beer and wine weren't considered intoxicating and could be sold or consumed at any post if allowed by the commander. Army vet Ed Knight recalled that while still serving after the war's end near Japan, the Army issued several bottles of beer and two pints of wine per week to each man.

These stories about small liquor rations contrasted with others I heard about the constant transport of huge quantities of liquor during the war. Where could all this booze have been going? Some of it was traveling the globe to officers' clubs. Dad had some experience with these: *As soon as most areas were fairly safe, the Navy set up officers' clubs. These weren't really clubs since all a chap could do was get drunk. For a nominal sum, maybe $1 or $2, you joined the "club." You bought a coupon book entitling you to drinks—usually whiskey and lemon juice—but lots of ice. The drinks were a dime. I believe you could also get a beer. I never saw such an arrangement for enlisted men nor were they allowed to enter the so-called "Officers' Clubs."*

*I met a friend on the beach in Finschhafen, New Guinea, and proceeded to drink five whiskey and lemon juice drinks in about a half hour. Since the clubs were only open for 30 to 60 minutes (a day), you had to drink like mad to use up your quota. In the heat—like 100 degrees, 100 percent humidity and because I never drank before, I got rather sick. The friend I met was Ensign Bob Howington, a lad from Freeport, Ill—quite a chance meeting considering how big the world is.*

*Officers' club on Espiritu Santo, New Hebrides*
*Photo courtesy: National Archives ACES-88-21*

There are plenty of stories about the unfortunate results of combining young men inexperienced with drinking and sudden access to booze, several of which I found in interviews with veterans featured in issues of *The Flotilla*. In one, LCT Skipper Don Corwin said, "One of my worst experiences was when we had transported several barrels of wine. I left [the ship] to get orders and was gone some time. When I returned there was hardly a sober crew member aboard. The men were so inebriated that we were unable to get underway."

In another story, the hold of the Landing Ship, Tank that transported both Skipper Darold Beckman and his LCT to their assignment was loaded with cases of beer. He recalled, "Seaman Campbell, at one hundred ten pounds, was the smallest crew member. He seldom spoke to me, but among the crew he was constantly telling comic talks about his adventures around Philadelphia. He made no secret of his love for alcohol and he cried pitifully that he was sailing for weeks across the Pacific among thousands of cases of beer and couldn't get a drink. Later, stumbling upon a cache of Japanese sake in a New Guinea jungle, he became intoxicated, while the rest of the crew spit out the salty brew as undrinkable."

On another similar ride, Charles K. Brown found that the LST's tank deck was loaded to the brim with beer and whiskey. The whiskey was in the middle of the cargo compartment with beer stacked all around it and on top of it. He concluded that the higher-ups either wanted to surround the highly flammable whiskey with a natural fire extinguisher (beer) or they wanted to make sure all the whiskey made it to its destination.

This was a very real worry for those in charge, as many stories about delivering booze ended up with some of it going "missing." The sailors often stole liquor from the Army supplies they handled even though these shipments were regularly under guard.

Corwin recalled, "On one memorable occasion one of our flotilla was given a load of hard liquor to take ashore. On the front of the load were three or four army men with guns to prevent looting. As it was late in the day when we hit the beach they decided to unload in the morning. That night a number of rafts paddled around the stern and liberated a significant number of cases."

John Eskau, still a teenager while serving as a cook on an LCT, thought his whole experience in the war was an adventure. He told me with a glint in his eye how he and his friends once "sort of shifted 100 cases or so of beer into our cargo hold." John met these friends, Army cargo loaders, who also enjoyed a drink or two. They would unload a set number of cases of liquor from a large ship's cargo hold, save half for themselves, and slip the other half to their friends, some like John serving on ships in the harbor. When the higher-ups in the Army demanded to know where the commandeered liquor had gone, the loaders placed the blame elsewhere, saying that the Merchant Marines had stolen them.

John was also nearly caught up in some very real trouble caused by liquor. He had a few days of leave and another sailor asked if he would like to help out on another ship headed to Shanghai to pick up a load of liquor. He had never been to China, so he said, "Why not?" When they arrived at their destination, twenty-nine military police swarmed the ship. The skipper of the ship was arrested for suspicion of selling booze on the black market.

It is remarkable how these sailors often said they "liberated" the booze when speaking of stealing it. On *LCT-730*, Edward Jensen remembers when he and several crew members took some beer from a shipment destined for an officers' club and hid it from the Army officers inside one of the bulkhead compartments on their ship. They quickly painted the bolts, closing the doors shut. The paint dried so fast in the Pacific heat that the Army found nothing amiss on the ship and never recovered the lost beer.

Back on *LCT-1150*, Skipper Beckman recalled, "Late one day Fleming [the signalman] received an order to move a cargo of beer from a Liberty ship to shore. Before the LCT beached and MPs came aboard to guard the merchandise, six hundred cases of beer had mysteriously vanished into the tank under the crew's quarters. I was informed ex post facto. To keep me quiet, Rookstool traded three cases for a Simmons mattress for my use, hoping I would not put the crew on report."

Even Dad's crew had devious moments, although he and Skipper Harnack did follow the orders to keep their ship dry. *Occasionally our crewmembers stole some beer from the cargo we unloaded. This was an effort full of futility—unless you like your beer served at 85 to 90 degrees temperature. We just did not possess a proper system of refrigeration.*

The proverb "necessity is the mother of invention" rang true for many servicemen trying to get their hands on some booze during the war. If the Navy was dry, and they couldn't steal any liquor, they'd just have to make it themselves.

And make it they did.

*Thanksgiving picnic and dinner at Submarine Net-tending base, Espiritu Santo. Photo courtesy: National Archives CURT 556*

On *LCT-804*, ship's cook Bill Miller set to work concocting his own wine. He said, "We had an extra-large quantity of fruit, so I found a large container and mixed in the fruit with sugar, yeast, and water and allowed it to ferment for several days. I then bottled the concoction in Coca-Cola bottles. The skipper was not aware of my scheme. Well, one day I gave one of the crew a bottle which he promptly took up to the gun tub to drink. As he came down to the deck, he ran into the skipper who asked him what was the matter. He told Skipper that he had drank some of Cookie's wine and felt sick. I thought sure I would catch hell for that, but the skipper tried one himself and said he liked it and to keep up the good work. Soon after I was given a rating of Ship's Cook Second Class!"

Seabees, members of the Navy's construction battalion, were also renowned for making their own alcohol. A former Seabee told author Eric M. Bergerud about his makeshift distillery: "Every Seabee outfit built stills. I made raisin-jack in five and ten-gallon batches. You would get a gallon can of raisins and put them in a five-gallon can. You would then fill it with distilled water and add some yeast. Then in goes five pounds of sugar. Put a stopper in with a rubber hose which you stick in another can of water so it wouldn't smell. You didn't want a nosy CO or master of arms (Navy Military Police) to find it. We'd hide it in foxholes. In about twenty days it was ready. Sometimes it was pretty strong, sometimes the batch didn't work out. Depended upon the weather or something. One batch was outstanding. I filled a soup bowl full, drank it down and in twenty minutes I could barely walk. Good stuff."

Back home in the States, many distilleries supported the war effort by transitioning their production from whiskey and other liquors to industrial alcohol. In Kentucky alone, during a two-year span from 1942 to 1944, its fifty-seven distilleries made 244 million gallons of industrial alcohol—about three times more than normal peacetime production.

This industrial alcohol, or ethyl alcohol, was used to make a substance called Buna-S, a necessary ingredient for making synthetic rubber for tires, gas masks, hoses, and life vests. Most importantly, this grain alcohol was made into fuel. Added to gasoline, it boosted the octane level enough so it could power the high-performance engines in American fighter planes, and later, increasingly replaced kerosene as the propellant used to launch torpedoes.

It dawned on the men handling the torpedoes that they were in the unique position to sneak small quantities of the pure grain alcohol to accumulate in secret stashes. Soldiers created a new cocktail, aptly named "torpedo juice" during WWII. They mixed two parts of ethyl alcohol to three parts of whatever juice was available, usually pineapple, orange, or grapefruit.

Industrial alcohol was clear, 190-proof (compared to 80- or 90-proof store-bought alcohol) and was very flammable. One veteran described his first swallow of torpedo juice as "an electrifying and jolting experience—sort of like being kicked by a mule." He went on to say that he didn't exactly enjoy the experience, but drinking it seemed to be the manly thing to do. Besides, he said, at least he had the satisfaction of "beating the system."

Once the higher-ups in the Navy got an inkling of what was going on, they began adding something called croton oil to the fuel alcohol to keep the sailors from drinking it. It colored the alcohol, and even if consumed in very small quantities, produced miserable adverse reactions, such as burning sensations, vomiting, and intense diarrhea.

On one submarine, the USS *Gudgeon*, the fuel came on board in five-gallon jugs that the crew then poured into huge fifty-gallon storage tanks making them too heavy to steal. Guards assigned to watch these tanks sometimes turned a blind eye and allowed some of the alcohol to be siphoned off and go missing.

Once on shore for leave, the submariners would take their bounty of stolen fuel and improvise stills in order to extract the croton oil. The process began by slowly heating the alcohol in a one-gallon pot to the temperature at which it could evaporate. Then, they covered the pot with something cold, like a plate of ice, so the alcohol would begin to condense. In an hour or two, the men could drain this condensed alcohol into a cup, and it would no longer have any trace of the dreaded croton oil. Talk about patience.

Thirsty fellows on leave often set up stills in hotel bathtubs just in case they exploded—which, of course, they did. According to Mike Ostlund's book *Find 'Em, Chase 'Em, Sink 'Em: The Mysterious Loss of the WWII Submarine USS Gudgeon,* one such incident happened at the famous Royal Hawaiian Hotel on Waikiki Beach. In 1942, the Navy leased the hotel so its members could use it during their leaves for rest and relaxation. In Ostlund's book, crewmember George Seiler recalled how some of his unlucky crewmates set up a still in their hotel bathtub that suddenly blew up. By the time firefighters finally fought the alcohol-fueled blaze back, it had destroyed part of the interior of the hotel. The amateur distillers were not charged with any crimes, but they all ended up pitching in to pay for the damage.

Clever men looked for a safer way to get that croton oil out of the industrial alcohol. There are accounts of sailors trying to use bread to do it. The theory was that if a man sliced the ends off a loaf of bread and then slowly poured the liquid through it like a filter, he might trap the offensive oil inside. I could find no proof that this method actually worked.

Meanwhile around the world, other countries involved in the conflict found ways to get the occasional morale booster cocktail to the members of their military. In the early 1940s, Stalin ordered every Russian soldier (numbering upwards of twenty-eight million) to be given one glass of vodka per day. Wehrmacht soldiers commonly enjoyed a Jägermeister or two on the front lines.

It wasn't just the Americans who were interested in a little drinking. The record is full of stories about wartime imbibing from many of the other countries involved in the conflict. While rice sanctioning in Japan caused sake production to drop by eighty percent during the war, the country's servicemembers received a ration of sake on important days such as the emperor's birthday. The British fleet had "brewing boats" that produced up to 250 barrels of beer per week at sea, destined for the South Pacific to provide English soldiers with their beer rations.

Of course, American men serving in WWII had more important things on their minds than procuring their next drop of alcohol. But for many, drinking was a common part of everyday life before the war, and it continued to play a part during this dark period in human history.

During the war, a stiff drink could help dull feelings of stress, loneliness, or fear. Alcohol could be used to help ease pain when no other medication was readily available. Sharing a drink created camaraderie between men living together under unrelenting stressful conditions.

While many of the anecdotes in this chapter are funny, the effect of alcohol on those who served in the war was also profound. There is a sense of desperation in these tales; these young men sought any comfort they could find. I wonder if their drinking to excess was just a sign of their relative youth and inexperience with liquor, or if it was a reaction to the stress they felt from being under constant threat.

After the war, many WWII veterans experienced the symptoms of post-traumatic stress disorder, a clinical diagnosis that wouldn't be known until after the Vietnam War. Many returning soldiers and sailors turned to heavy drinking to numb their grief, night terrors, survivor's guilt, and depression.

Veterans from the WWII generation chose to grin and bear their "shellshock." They didn't talk about their experiences and decided to go on with their lives through sheer force of will, even if adjusting to civilian life seemed an impossible goal. Hundreds of thousands returned without visible scars yet were plagued by all they had witnessed. For several years after the war's end, veterans hospitals throughout American still took care of men experiencing psychiatric wounds, with very few doctors trained to help them work through their pain.

Divorce rates doubled in the years after the war, demonstrating the negative effects of the veterans' trauma on their families. In 2010, a study in California revealed that WWII veterans committed suicide four times as often as men their age who had not fought in the war. As the years went by and the idea of PTSD became more accepted, some aging veterans began to seek therapy for their symptoms, finally finding the relief they so deserved.

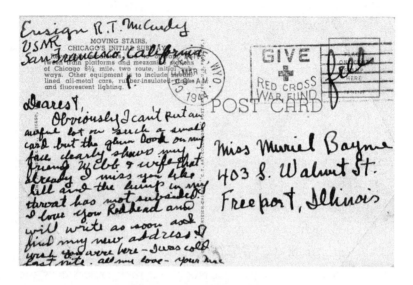

## THE TIES THAT BIND
### How V-Mail Kept Love Alive During WWII

*Dearest, obviously I can't put an awful lot on such a small card but the glum look on my face clearly shows my friend Webb and his wife that already I miss you like hell and the lump in my throat has not subsided. I love you Redhead and will write as soon as I find my new address. I wish you were here—I was cold last night. All my love –Your Mac*

My dad was off to war, but not before dropping this postcard in the mailbox on February 11, 1944. Soon after, he joined a thousand or more other sailors at the dockyard in San Francisco, scrambling up the gangplank to board the USS *Ommaney Bay,* his ride to the South Pacific. Letters and postcards would have to be enough to keep the love alive with his girl back home in Illinois.

In contrast to today's near-instant communication with people around the world, during the uncertain times of WWII, people had to rely on the handwritten word to stay connected. Dad's girl Muriel, my mom, tucked many of Dad's letters into their treasured wartime scrapbook.

*My Darling. Here it is Aug. 19 and I have only penned 13 notes to you since the first—not to say the least but partly our latest move is to blame. We got word of it at the last second on the 16th so for 2 days and 2 nites we were busy underway at sea. It was plenty rough the first night out with several of the crew getting seasick and some more claiming attacks of indigestion, which I doubt. However, these guys like to act salty—they aren't.*

During the war years, letters provided a critical link to keep relationships strong as couples and families were separated, often for long periods of time—in my father's case, almost three years total. Hearing from home boosted the lonely American soldiers' and sailors' morale, making them feel more connected to life at home. Conversely, each note from the front reassured those back home that, at least for the time being, their loved one was okay.

In one letter Dad wrote to Mom, he tries to convince her about the importance of receiving mail by pointing out how jealous he feels of others' mail calls: *I can see you aren't too sure what letters from home mean. One kid here who writes dopey, asinine, stereotyped love letters gets about 15 big thick love letters each mail call from his girl written in bright red ink which I practically am dying to sneak a look at.*

My mom picked up her pen along with millions of other

people, and before long billions of wartime letters and packages clogged up the delivery system and slowed it down.

*The armed forces encouraged us not to request packages from home—the sheer bulk of which would hinder the all-out war effort. At any rate packages would take weeks to reach us and were frequently stolen in transit. Harnack once received a package of marzipan candy (he loved that) and another time a package of fudge from his mother. Needless to say, the two candies after several months in the hold of a cargo ship, in 100 degree plus temperatures, arrived in a somewhat disheveled condition. Jim ate all the marzipan and I tested one chunk of fudge just to be sociable.*

Finding space to transport the bulky mailbags was a major concern, especially from stateside to the front. Large ships handled the mail's weight, but they were slow and easy targets for enemy attack. Planes were faster but had less room for cargo and ran the risk of being shot down. It was critical that mail not take up space better used to deliver food, medicine, and equipment to the troops.

During the Great War of 1914-1918 (now known as WWI), the Post Office Department learned a tough lesson that if mail was lost or delivered slowly, it damaged American morale. As early as 1938, the department began devising a better plan to supplement regular mail should the need arise again in a time of crisis. Part of this plan included embracing British microfilm technology. In a collaboration, the War and Navy departments introduced "V…-Mail" in 1942 (the three dots and one dash is the letter V's Morse code symbol).

The process for using V-Mail couldn't have been easier. If

Mom wanted to send a letter from Freeport, she picked up the pre-printed 8½-by-11-inch form from either the local post office or a neighborhood store. The two-sided piece was both stationery and envelope—after composing her letter, she simply folded it up, sealed the edges, addressed it (to and from addresses were on both sides of the form), and dropped it in the mailbox.

In the United States, the post office sent the V-Mail to one of three processing facilities. From there, the War and Navy departments took over with the help of the Eastman Kodak Company—a huge manufacturer of cameras and film. The letters were unsealed, censored if necessary, and run one at a time through a machine called a Recordak that photographed each letter onto 16mm film. It was critical that the address directly above the message was clearly and accurately written because only this side of the sheet was filmed. The address on the outer side of the form directed mail to the first sorting location as the letters began their journey. Since the forms were all the same size, unlike regular mail and packages, the V-Mail letters could be quickly processed and sent on their way.

The resulting single, 100-foot roll of film containing 1,700 individual letters went into a metal canister for delivery. The space saving was dramatic—compared to the twenty-two mail sacks needed to hold 150,000 V-Mail letters in paper, now just one sack could hold that same number of microfilmed letters.

V-Mail had several advantages over regular mail. For one, it got there faster. Before V-Mail, a letter might take a month or more to reach its destination but now could arrive in twelve days or less. Moreover, the War Department guaranteed V-Mail delivery. The postmaster saved the original letters, including their serial numbers, until the airplane delivering the microfilm arrived safely. If a plane went down, mail handlers could re-film the original letters and send them again.

On the other side of the world, the process was reversed, printing out the photographs for delivery. Only after printing the film did workers finally destroy the originals. Mail handlers folded the final product, now about one-fourth the original size, in half and placed them in a tan-colored envelope for delivery.

Ed Knight gave me one of these envelopes from a letter he received. To me it seemed so tiny, measuring just 4½ by 5½ inches total. Ed speculated that the armed forces chose the tan color because it was cheap to produce and easy to camouflage on the battlefield.

Luckily my mother had good penmanship, because a clear hand was critical to the V-Mail process. The postmaster encouraged people to use dark, highly visible ink and to write as legibly as possible. Once the image was reduced, the letter itself and the addresses became more difficult to read. If the address couldn't be deciphered, delivery of the letter might be delayed indefinitely.

As I looked at my parents' letters written so long ago, I barely recognized my father's twenty-two-year-old penmanship. It was boyish, loopy, and full of flourishes. By the time I arrived in 1962, his writing had morphed into a tight, leaning, and scratchy hand. Years later while retired, he scrawled his WWII journal in nearly illegible longhand on page after page of lined notebook paper.

Those in the military were granted permission to send first-class mail, including V-Mail, at no charge. They were instructed to write the word "free" where the stamp would normally go, followed by their name, rank, and service branch.

Along the margin on one page of the scrapbook, just beside a letter taped there, Dad scratched: *It appears as if the armed forces didn't have to pay for postage. I could have handled the penny for a one-cent stamp, however. It's interesting to note that the post office folks accepted on blind faith the written-in 'free.'*

The military post offices censored all mail, V-Mail or otherwise, as it passed through the military post offices to make sure no confidential information was divulged. For example, unit locations or activities might be blacked or even cut out of the letter. All parties knew their letters would be read and accepted the loss of privacy as a reality of wartime.

Officers censored the mail of enlisted men in their unit, stamping and initialing the finished piece. A sailor who didn't get along well with a superior could request a "blue envelope" in order to forward his letter to a different, perhaps more unbiased censor. This person certified that the letter didn't contain any confidential information, sealed it up, and sent it on its way.

On little *LCT-977*, Dad and Skipper Harnack censored their crew's mail. They looked for any information that might be valuable to the enemy, such as the strength of troop divisions and the locations of U.S. fleets and armies. "Loose lips sink ships" became a common mantra during the war, showing up on propaganda posters stateside. Officers also kept an eye out for signs of plummeting morale, or that the men were losing the will to fight—both huge factors that would impede the American goal of winning the war.

The job of censoring the mail must have been a thankless one. It was up to Dad and Jim to review the letters of their crew and use a razor to remove any content that concerned them.

Here is a photo of one of the razors Dad used to slice up his crew's letters, removing any offending sentences, as well as a stamp he initialed. Crewmembers shared letters they received from family with Dad, showing him how they felt about his censoring responsibilities.

*It's this razor which has caused statements like this to be brought to me by the crew. I quote from one of their return letters, "and who is that dirty, rotten, son of a b… who censors your mails" or "that guy RTM ought to be nailed to a cross."*

Commonly, officers censored their own mail. Superiors placed faith in them that they wouldn't give away any key information in their letters. Everyone proceeded with the knowledge that as the mail went along on its way, it would pass through bases or larger ships and could be randomly checked at any point.

Even though they knew their letters could be censored down the line, officers often revealed more than they should have in their own mail. Maybe they took their chances knowing it was unlikely to be censored or were just careless or cavalier in the writing. One letter of Dad's clearly violates some rules (although it IS wonderful to get a glimpse of his surroundings): *My new home is a little farther north in New Guinea—pretty much the same as ever. One novelty here though is the fact that one airstrip is almost on the beach so the in and out coming P-40's zoom right out over us. Several are parked nearby on some coral where they made forced landing. Coral is more widespread than I've ever seen— sound like an old hand but in five months, I've seen plenty. The whole island is surrounded with it, so in order for LCT's to beach they made a jetty over the coral. It makes quite a pretty picture too. The road is yellow gravel and goes very prettily over a hill into the jungles. At low tide the coral is everywhere so I imagine cat eyes and shells flourish. I read in* Newsweek *that Marines in the Solomon's sell cat eye necklaces for $50 so perhaps I better get busy.*

In his book *The LCT Story*, William D. Baker recalls that

often a fellow officer would just initial in the middle of the censor stamp without actually reading the letters. Even so, Baker was careful about what he wrote in his letters home. He usually left out stories of drinking or gambling—things he knew his family would disapprove of.

Baker sent home 209 letters in just over a year's time that his mother carefully saved. In one of them, he talked about the types of letters he saw while censoring his crew's correspondence: 1) to the family with the main theme that all is well, 2) to the wife with gushy, romantic words, 3) to the girlfriend in a flirtatious manner, and 4) to the buddy with a tough, profane tone.

Dad weighed in on this topic fifty years later in his journal: *It seems odd now to see letters written in pen and ink. Of course, I pledged eternal love and all that. I believe I successfully deep-sixed most of my poetic heart-felt love letters. They wouldn't wear well as prose, but they certainly were well meant. Deep-sixed, by the way, is a nautical expression meaning 'I flung it overboard.' I did have nice firm handwriting—and was also long on bullshit.*

Most servicemen, including my dad, carefully avoided saying anything that would cause their loved ones to worry. Every veteran I interviewed agreed. Ed Knight endured some horrifying experiences in the Philippines, but his letters always said, "I'm fine, doing the best I can, miss you all," and the like.

Every day, Dad lived under the threat of constant danger: from the enemy, from handling bombs and other dangerous materials, from tropical diseases and more, and yet he never mentioned these things in his letters home. *I, being a kind and lighthearted lad, never once wrote home expressing fears or threats of death or any of those sorts of things. I wanted to spare Mom, Dad, Aunt Nelly, and Muriel any needless worry. I passed this same lighthearted kind of information on to my brothers and their families. These are things I never mentioned in my letters home. I could list dozens of additional disasters—like the Japanese Kamikaze pilots late in our stay in the Philippines—that could have happened but I've made my point.*

The postmaster discouraged people stateside from enclosing loose items and photos in V-Mail since these things held up the system and often jammed the machines. Eventually, the War Department decided that it was okay to enclose photos of babies born after the father left for the war or of children still under one year old. During processing, technicians placed the snapshots (that could include the mother) in the upper left corner of the V-Mail so they wouldn't bend when they folded the piece for delivery.

It's a mystery to me why the mail handlers in the South Pacific allowed Dad to so regularly send items home to Mom for the scrapbook, particularly items that could have given the flotilla's location away. *By the way—in censoring the crew's mail I inadvertently picked up a few bits of Jap invasion money. Here are some. The large notes are on pretty good paper too as you will notice. Also, I'm sending an Aussie coin—I don't believe I ever did before. Now you have something for the book from every place.*

In addition to the problem of loose items, another predicament for those processing V-Mail stateside was that many women sealed their letters with a kiss, leaving behind a lipstick impression. Over time, the lipstick built up in the Kodak machinery, damaging the microfilm and in turn affecting the printed letters. Post office employees nicknamed this well-meant yet irritating problem born from love the "scarlet scourge."

Occasionally, the postmaster delivered full-sized V-Mail sheets "as is" because in that moment it was either faster to do so or because of a lack of nearby processing equipment. In the scrapbook, Dad points out a particular V-Mail letter delivered to Mom in its original full-size state by regular mail (now enlarged, framed, and hanging in my house.) Damaged forms like this one couldn't pass through the machines.

*Note that Dad censored his own letter here*

None of the examples of V-Mail taped into Dad's scrapbook were letters he received from Mom. In the forward to his book *War Letters: Extraordinary Correspondence from American Wars,* Andrew Carroll says that very few notes from the home front survived because it was impractical for servicemembers living under difficult and cramped conditions to clog their limited personal storage space with letters.

Carroll pointed out that sadly, many WWII letters that *were* saved bear the stamp "return to sender" because the soldier, sailor, or airman had died before the note arrived overseas. In a grim flipside, due to delays in mail delivery, sometimes a letter from a soldier arrived back home in the weeks after the War Department notified the family of his demise.

Back in the States, propaganda posters with slogans such as "The next best thing to a leave—is a letter" or "V-Mail is Speed Mail—You write, he'll fight" encouraged people to send letters. The Red Cross even got involved, imploring people to write frequently and to stay positive in their letters, avoiding any sad or discouraging news that might dampen the soldiers' morale.

Despite the propaganda, some letters delivered an unhappy blow to the recipients. Sometimes a wife or girlfriend broke off a relationship in writing. Many couples, separated by thousands of miles, found that absence did not necessarily make their hearts grow fonder. Some were on shaky ground before the war separated them. For others, the anxiety, distance, and loneliness were just too hard to take.

During WWII, these notes came to be known as "Dear John" letters. Some people think the name came about because

John was a common name at the time, such as in the legal use of "John Doe." Others attribute it to a popular radio program called "Dear John" that aired from 1933 to 1944. Each episode began and ended with star Irene Rich writing a letter to her Dear John.

Every man dreaded receiving one.

In his book, Carroll includes a Dear John letter sent to Seaman Sylvan "Sol" Summers. For some unknown reason, Sol saved this letter although he shared the fact that his crewmates regularly gathered their Dear John letters in a pile, lit them on fire, and tossed the ashes into the ocean.

Others couldn't so easily brush off the pain these letters caused. Al Exner told me the story of a crewmate who received a Dear John letter. Shortly after he got it, he came to the ship's sickbay where Al worked, curled up into a ball, and within days, passed away from sadness. Al called it "broken heart syndrome"—a type of heart attack triggered by the despair of losing a loved one.

I couldn't believe what he was saying, but it turns out to be true. Known as stress-induced cardiomyopathy, its onset is the result of hearing terrible or shocking news. With this condition, a barrage of stress hormones brings on chest pain, shortness of breath, and a change in the heart's rhythm. It is very rare to die of broken heart syndrome, but it *is* possible.

Luckily for Dad, my mother never penned a Dear John letter. In fact, she saved many of the notes and V-Mails she received from him along with the bits of memorabilia he sent to her. When I read these missives and the words of love they contain, I get a glimpse of what their young relationship was like. Family lore has it that from his temporary home in the South Pacific he even proposed marriage in a letter, but if so, it was never saved.

At the end of his first eighteen months of service, Dad finally earned a short trip home. After receiving the papers giving him permission for the leave during which he would marry my mom, he dashed off an excited note to her—my very favorite one of the bunch: *I've got 'em today! Should be home in 30 to 35 days. Mom says you "announced" so good luck on the pile of showers you ought to have. I'm the happiest guy in the world, look out. I love you. Call Ma and tell her the great news.*

*All my love, Bob*

# BOREDOM + INGENUITY = FUN

Sailors, soldiers, Marines, and airmen became like family, growing close while serving in tight quarters under tense conditions. They teased each other, assigned nicknames, laughed, talked, learned everyone's "tics," and talked some more. Moments of intense threat could be followed by hours or days of pure monotony and boredom as they carried out their assignments, working toward earning enough points to go back home.

Dad describes how they spent their time together: *There were no movies, no radio, nor did we have access to any appliance that might provide us with music. Of course, in those days no one had television.*

*We spent a lot of time chatting with our crew—getting their views on life. Sometimes it could be very frustrating, when discussing personnel on various athletic teams, to come up with a forgotten name—and nowhere to go to get an answer. For example, in the late 30's the University of Pittsburgh had some really powerful football teams. Jim Harnack, being from Pittsburgh,* [he was born there October 14, 1919] *would bring up some names in let's say the Pittsburgh University backfield of 1938. Biggie Goldberg we both knew—Dick Cassiano we both knew. Then the question would arise—who replaced Cassiano at halfback when he graduated? I believe we finally decided it was a chap named Stebbins—but who really cares now? Nor should we have cared then, it just helped pass the time.*

Dad and Jim Harnack, Ensign and Skipper, and their little crew on *LCT-977* had plenty of time to do absolutely nothing while they waited for their ship to be loaded and unloaded, over and over again. *Once I was actively assigned to a ship, we had a lot of time to do nothing but read or write as we waited for our little ship to be loaded from supply ships and then unloaded on the beach by army personnel.*

*Obviously, "fighting a war" also involved lots of sitting around. This is another indication of how much time we had to kill while waiting to be loaded and unloaded. This could take many hours— perhaps all night. Actually, Seinfeld and crew believed they invented a show about "nothing." They should have been in New Guinea— on an LCT. We wrote a lot of letters during our "waiting" time, talked a lot of trivia, and played as much poker as we could arrange.*

*Jim and I entertained each other in a variety of ways. One caper involved the number of letters we each received from our respective girlfriends in the month of June 1944. One could say that we were easily amused. Our mail arrived maybe twice a month in large bundles, so it all had to be sorted out by postmark date. I always thought I received a lot more mail from Mom* [he's referring to Muriel, not his mother] *than Jim got from his friend Ruth. I set up some bar type graphs for the month—Jim was red, I was blue. Startling enough Jim killed me in numbers. It turned out that Mom was vacationing in Lake Delavan with a group of friends. I still*

*have the graph—kept it as a joke. Grandma Mabel* [a nickname he
gave to Muriel's mother] *never thought it was funny. Jim Harnack
and I did.*

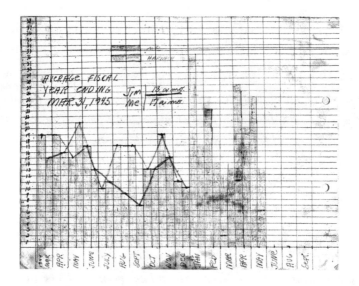

*There were virtually no books to read, crossword puzzles to
solve, word jumbles to unscramble or cryptograms to de-code. There
were hardly any magazines or newspapers while overseas. Once in a
great while we received a copy of Stars and Stripes—an Army paper.
While I was returning home in 1945 someone unearthed a copy of
Bram Stoker's "Dracula." It became an unbelievable hot item. At
least 10 of us took turns reading it.*

Dad and his crew suffered from a lack of reading material,
but in the larger Navy world, access to books depended more
on what type of ship a sailor served on—and luck. There was
a monumental effort back home to get books into the hands
of our fighting force. The American Library Association, along

with the Red Cross and United Service Organization (USO), put together the Victory Book Campaign of the early 1940s. Americans donated over eighteen million books, and over half of those were in good enough condition to be sent to war-torn areas of the world. In the field, men came to temporary library tents or checked out books from military trucks roving the countryside, filled to the brim with books.

Posters graced the walls of American libraries stating that when the Japanese and Germans burned books and destroyed libraries, they waged war on the American culture. Franklin D. Roosevelt wrote, "In this war, we know, books are weapons."

In the Navy, most large ships such as battleships, destroyers, and aircraft carriers had libraries of their own. The number of books contained in these floating libraries directly correlated to the number of people aboard the vessel, so a large ship might have as many as 2,000 books to enjoy.

The government provided millions of small, easy-to-carry books to the military. Although paperbacks existed before the war, their production exploded after the war when the men returned and clamored for more of what they had become used to.

*Photo Courtesy: National Archives 165-L2-43-1917*

Al Exner worked as a medical surgical technician and spent a lot of free time reading medical textbooks to stave off the boredom. He's not sure, but he thinks his favorite was titled *Legal Medicine and Toxicology*, written by Dr. Halperin, Chief Medical Examiner of New York City. For Al, trying to find out why people were killed from certain injuries was like a mystery story.

John Eskau happily received books from home, although this happened only occasionally. On the other hand, Ed Knight served deep in the jungle and didn't have books, and if he had, they would never have survived the humidity and rot surrounding him in his foxholes.

If they didn't have books, many sailors instead passed the time playing cards.

Easy to carry, and guaranteed to provide a moment's diversion, decks of cards were everywhere during the war. Most veterans recall playing Hearts or poker—on Al's ship the men who played called it "Payday Poker," since they bet on their future earnings. He also remembered quite a few men playing craps on the ship, and that they made out quite well on that too. Al told me he abstained from gambling because he was too busy trying to send money home to his mother.

Many a pocket on all fronts of the war contained a deck of Bicycle playing cards. Teaming up with the British and American intelligence agencies, this company secretly designed a very special deck of cards that later became known as the "Map Deck." These decks made their way to POWs in detention camps in Germany by way of care packages allowed by the Geneva Convention.

All playing cards are made of two layers of paper fused together, but in these decks, maps of secret escape routes were sealed between these layers. The hope was that these maps might help Allied prisoners of war find their way to safety. Once soaked in water, the cards' layers could be pulled apart revealing the maps hidden inside. These decks were considered so top secret that even Bicycle Playing Cards doesn't know how many of these decks were manufactured or how many survived the war.

In the fifteen months they spent together, Dad and Jim Harnack became best of friends. Jim was a young man with a wonderful sense of humor and an unusual and memorable laugh. Dad recalled of his friend, *Jim was a practical joker and always a perfectionist at what he did. When an unsuspecting victim fell for one of the tricks, he would be greeted with his spectacular laugh—adding to the embarrassment. He was an architect* [with a degree from Carnegie Institute of Technology] *and also an artist (and an observer of people). Jim also decorated the bulkhead (that's a wall) over his desk with a gadget called a "fathometer." It was a clock-like thing allegedly capable of measuring the depth of the water beneath our ship. I'd say that 7 out of 10 people fell for this gag—until somewhat lamely they realized the absurdity—again the laughter.*

*The earlier reference to poker reminds me of an adventure we had one night with a couple of strangers who we lured into our game. They were reluctant from the very beginning. Generally, we played cards with three or four friends from neighboring ships. They were accustomed to the erratic behavior of Jim and his occasional outbursts of hysterical laughter. I fed Jim the straight lines—he provided the routine. We really startled the strangers and sent them back to their ship with a lot less money than they had at the onset. We never saw them again despite a diligent search—you don't discard people who lose* [at cards]. *About three weeks later our friend Keith Bailey from* LCT-981 *told us that he had bumped into a couple of Ensigns who asked if he knew a pair of Ensigns from the* LCT-977. *They were sure we were both completely crazy—especially the guy with the laugh.*

*One day Jim decided we should have a dead man's poker hand painted on our little table. He knew the suits of the two pair but was beside himself trying to determine the nature of the fifth card.*

To give some background before Dad goes on, the story of the dead man's hand goes all the way back to the late 1800s and is central in the tale of Wild Bill Hickok's murder. He was shot to death over a poker hand in a saloon in Deadwood, South Dakota. There is no definitive proof of the hand he was holding at the time of his death, but legend has it that there were two pairs—aces and eights—and an undetermined fifth card.

*He asked around—wrote his parents and girlfriend. The latter researched the matter at the Carnegie Tech Library to no avail. No one seemed to know. Finally, out of desperation, he chose the queen of hearts—because it was colorful. The picture was laid out thusly* (here Dad scrawled a little drawing of the aces and eights fanned out along with the queen). *He drew them on the table painting them with thick and shiny red, black, and white paint. They were so beautifully done that nine out of ten visitors would reach out to pick them up. Their failure to do so would be greeted with the usual guffaws.*

While Dad and Jim seemed to make the most of any opportunity they had for a little fun, their job could still be monotonous and boring. They looked to anyone they met in the course of carrying out their assignments for a little human interaction.

*Some of the unloading parties—both Army and Navy had interesting personnel with whom we could "shoot the breeze" as they said in 1944 and 1945. There were often a few hucksters in each group—"fuckoffs" we called them. They were often engaged in merchandising of some sort—watch repairs, developing camera snaps, or just buying goods from us.*

Jim and Dad became friends with other young men working in the same flotilla, or assigned to the bases, ships, or ports they served. Officers' clubs, set up once locations were more secure, became places where the officers assigned to LCTs in the area would gather for conversation, cards, and a quick drink or two.

*We had a friend, Dr. Orr, who was perhaps 28. He was the chap instrumental in enabling us to unload Seaman Burgess (Burgess being the young man with the machete who I mentioned earlier). He must have had some real problems himself but being young ourselves, we didn't realize this. He was fixated on dirty limericks that were in vogue at the time. The good doctor would recite his newest one and my fellow officer, Harnack would laugh hysterically. Dr. Orr would then ask Harnack if he had any new creations—Jim always did come up with one.*

*Thank God I can only remember the following: "There once was a girl from Diaz, who had a dress that was cut on the bias. She had a little loop, through which she could poop, and catch a piece of ass once or twias. (Jim had a certain musicality about himself.) I never have been one to tell a dirty story. I think today, January 30, 2000, 2001, 2002, 2003, 2004, 2005, 2006, 2007 you could probably recite this on regular TV prime time.*

Since Dad was a bit of an introvert, reading his warm recollections of his friend in his journal both surprised and touched me deeply. I was heartened to discover that someone understood his quirky sense of humor and really had his back during that lonely time.

*Jim and I escaped boredom by engaging in our frivolous and trivial "psychological" studies that gave us something other than ourselves to think about. For example: as a student of architecture Jim was subjected to a boring class in drawing. He said that as a rule the class was poorly attended except for the day that a live model came in to pose in the nude. The seats were full. This gave us some hours of discussion on why there is the male obsession with peering at naked women—even fairly scrawny models.*

*We also attacked this from the standpoint of the model. According to Jim she arrived and coyly and modestly undressed behind some screens before letting it all hang out. I think these nutty conversations helped keep us on a fairly even keel. I think our senses of humor saved us.*

The men appreciated music of any kind. In C.K. Brown Jr.'s article for *The Flotilla* "Charlie Brown Goes to War," he described how after his dad's LCT transported some office equipment, they suddenly had a phonograph and some records to perk up the ship's atmosphere. According to him, "the photograph may have been in exchange for services rendered or maybe a moonlight requisition, that part of the story is lost to the sands of time."

*Harnack loved song lyrics—often chanted tunes from the Mikado. One day his girlfriend, by letter of course, mentioned a movie of the early forties and a song "The Trolley Song"—"clang, clang, clang went the trolley, ding, ding, ding went the bell." Jim almost lost it trying to reconstruct the actual melody. Fortunately, after some weeks, the girlfriend sent him a page of notes. Jim mastered the tune and it became part of his routine at various poker games. For a man who still can't sing a scale, I was most impressed.*

On the other side of the world, James Baker, author of *The LCT Story*, wrote home to his sister from his LCT in the Mediterranean that he "finally heard 'Trolly [sic] Car' sung by a gal at a USO show. She also sang 'Don't Fence Me In,' which is supposed to be pretty popular right now, but which we haven't heard before. The show gave us a lot of laughs and was just what we needed because yesterday it seemed like the whole navy was against me."

One beautiful product of the home front was the USO, or United Service Organizations for National Defense, an amazing coalition of public and private entities devoted to providing a "home away from home" experience for servicemembers. Typically, the government provided the locations and funding, while local groups provided the volunteers and entertainment. Organizations of various faiths cooperated fully in this undertaking, and everyone was welcome no matter the venue. It should be noted, however, that while the USO policy welcomed all races, in all-white communities the organization did not press for integration.

The USO set up more than 3,000 clubs that became places for servicemembers and families to socialize, dance, and enjoy themselves. While no two clubs offered the same activities, the list of possibilities contained hundreds of items—sports and table games, glee clubs and movies, sewing classes, and day care. Charming, young, wholesome women volunteered to become Junior Hostesses, whose jobs were to dance and talk with the servicemen at these clubs.

The most well-known service of the USO was its Camp Show program. Funded by the USO but run by professionals in the entertainment industry, Camp Show troupes took the show on the road on tours that lasted anywhere from three weeks to six months. From 1941 to 1945, over 1.7 million people saw at least one USO Camp Show.

Some groups consisted of very large collectives of performers and celebrities that presented shows at military bases in the US. Others focused on entertaining soldiers recovering in military hospitals, sometimes by arranging for artists to draw portraits of the injured men to send on to their families.

The most famous circuit of all was called the Foxhole Circuit that took shows overseas to all the major combat areas. By the end of the war, over 7,000 performers had traveled overseas as part of this circuit to boost morale, including popular stars of the time such as Al Jolson, Mickey Rooney, Judy Garland, and Marlene Dietrich.

The most notable and dedicated performer in the Foxhole Circuit was comedian Bob Hope. He loved to record his weekly radio broadcasts at military bases or outposts, the audience full of servicemen. He took a troupe to the combat areas in North Africa and Italy in 1943 and followed that up with a trip to the South Pacific the next year.

Ed Knight once saw Mr. Hope and his show right at the water's edge somewhere near the Philippines. He remembered how the men climbed the palm trees for a better view of the show. Ed was most impressed that Mr. Hope lived just like the other guys on the base, taking his shower right out in the open like all the soldiers did—a "regular guy."

According to *The Flotillla*, Richard Kerr from *LCT-1049* saw a Bob Hope show that he enjoyed immensely while training on Kauai, Hawaii. He recalled a particularly funny joke that Hope liked doing to describe a salute. "He said, 'You bring your hand up like it is full of honey and put it down like it is full of horse manure.' This brought roaring laughter from everyone."

American entertainers got behind the effort to boost the morale of the troops at home and overseas, often at their own peril. Bob Hope had several very close calls, namely in Palermo, Italy, when German bombs took out the area surrounding his hotel. Twenty-eight performers died while on USO tours, most the result of plane crashes. Glenn Miller, leader of a famous big band swing orchestra, performed for soldiers over 800 times with his Army Air Force Band. He died in a plane crash over the English Channel, on his way to Paris to perform a show for troops after the liberation of the city. Back home, the famous actress Carole Lombard died when her plane crashed on its way back from a trip she took to sell war bonds.

*Bob Hope entertaining a group of mostly patients at a hospital in New Caledonia. Photo courtesy: National Archives 111-SC-193734*

Al Exner saw a USO production of *Oklahoma!* on the beach put on by a very small troupe of performers. There was a torrential downpour that day, but the actors and audience paid it no mind. Rudimentary benches made of coconut logs were laid out in rows on the sand for makeshift seating, and Al and his shipmates settled in to see the show. Everyone was soaked through but completely happy. Al was so grateful just to have a little bit of entertainment.

If the performers themselves couldn't be where the men were, the armed forces tried their best to bring the next best thing. Many Army and Naval bases on land set up outdoor movie theaters, showing Hollywood films under the stars on makeshift screens. On larger ships, lucky sailors sometimes saw an occasional movie screening right on the deck of the ship.

But mostly, the guys created their own forms of entertainment. The vets who fought in the South Pacific had fond memories of time spent on the beaches there in quiet moments. Many remember swimming, playing catch on the beach, collecting seashells, stringing volleyball nets between trees, or just relaxing under a shady tree.

Al Exner described a beach in New Guinea where he saw land crabs "that were so big they looked like rocks that would suddenly sprout legs" and of spiders "as big as your hand" coming down from the trees.

On the beach, Al met a native man strong enough to crack open coconuts in a snap and offer the halves filled with coconut water to Al and his crewmates. The native wore a fantastic boar's tusk bracelet that Al coveted and went on to acquire by trading his Navy shirt for it. It's one of Al's favorite souvenirs from the war—worth the price of replacing his shirt from the ship's store.

In between Ed Knight's many horrifying and arduous missions in the Army, he and his friends took the opportunity to find some respite and rejuvenation at the beach. He told me they would wet down their cot's fitted sheets and run down the beach with the fabric against the wind, thereby filling it with air. After quickly tying the ends together, they could then use the balloon they created as a floating device. As long as the men kept the fabric wet, they were able to bob and float leisurely among the waves.

The military branches sometimes gave leave to their men so they could take a day or two off to explore the local communities.

John Eskau was an avid skater and had, in fact, heard about the bombing of Pearl Harbor while ice-skating with friends. Once during a leave in China, he scrambled onto a rickshaw and after insisting that he didn't want to go to a "cathouse" [a brothel], convinced the driver to take him to a roller rink. After a long ride all the way across town, the driver unceremoniously dropped him off at the front door of a nondescript building containing a rink. John stepped inside and came upon a schoolteacher and her young students who gaped at him in

*Ed Knight (center) on the beach with two buddies*

surprise as he laced on some skates. He joined the group and had a wonderful time, showing them the American tradition of "crack the whip."

Back on the LCTs, it was up to the skippers to watch for signs of crew fatigue or distress. Imagine these young officers, sent out to do a job they were only minimally trained to do, tasked with keeping their crew's morale up in the midst of so much uncertainty and tedium, none of them knowing when they might finally return stateside.

Dad recalled: *Neither of us ever let ourselves get visibly depressed, as did many of our fellow officers. Many of the crew did become discouraged about their sad state of affairs—deservedly so. They had a much tougher job trying to maintain their sanity than did the officers.*

*When Harnack and I departed for home in June of 1945, we took separate ships. We saw each other only once after that, corresponded once a year until 1953, and that was that. It was like the final episode of M.A.S.H when Hawkeye Pierce and BJ Hunnicutt split up. They talked briefly about getting together, wives and all, realized the improbability of that and then as Hawkeye Pierce said, "Let's face it, we'll never see each other again." Jim and I didn't shed any tears, but we had been very close for . . . months. We were good friends.*

Jim returned from the war and spent a year working as a draftsman for a large firm in New Jersey and eventually decided to go off on his own. He was former president of the State of New Jersey American Institute of Architects. He married his girlfriend, Ruth, and they remained happily wed for sixty-seven years. When I found out that Jim died on August 21, 2013, the obituary stated that Ruth was still alive.

I decided to send a copy of Dad's journal to her, thinking that she might enjoy hearing the tales he told of his and Jim's friendship during the war. Several weeks later, I received a note from her that read: "I have spent hours fascinated with your note, and your father's war-time observations. Presently, both my attic and downstairs doors are locked, without keys on the premises to prevent me suffering from accidents. When it becomes possible for me to search through a huge collection of books and photograph albums, I will let you know if Jim had a camera in the Pacific. Thank you so much for sharing."

I never heard from her again.

Many WWII veterans forged strong bonds with the men they served alongside, attending reunions in the decades after the war. Only they could understand and share what it was like to live through that defining time of their young lives together, the moments never to be forgotten.

# WASH.DRY.FOLD.REPEAT – Sailor Style

Everyday life goes on, even when fighting a war. Sailors still get up each morning and put their pants on, one leg at a time. But how does one find a way to wash those pants when one is off at sea?

Imagine how hard it would be to keep a uniform up to snuff under the challenging conditions of war. A colossal mountain of laundry comes to mind after considering that millions of Americans served in the Navy.

The tale of wartime laundry began in boot camp, where the Navy issued each man all the pieces of his uniform from underwear to overcoat. White clothing for summer, with blue taking its turn during the cooler seasons—a moot point in the hot South Pacific. Each sailor received a stencil with his last name and first initial, or in some cases, last name and service number. He went to work filling in the letters using India ink to mark every single piece of clothing—even his socks. When finished, he hung the clothes on a wash line or laid them carefully on the grass to dry.

The sailors-in-training learned to pack everything they owned in one canvas sea bag, following a strict procedure for doing so. Each item of clothing was rolled up so tightly it looked like a small salami—maybe one and a half inches around. Foot-long cords with crimped metal tips were tied in square knots on either end of the cylinder to secure it. One bonus of correctly rolling the clothing was that it was pressed in the process. A well-packed sea bag could contain a fellow's whole wardrobe and blanket if it was loaded properly, so the men underwent countless drills until they had the entire process down pat.

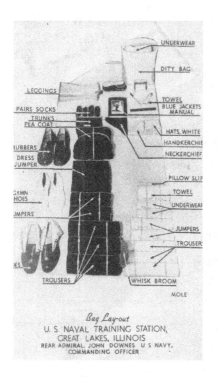

Bag Lay-out
U. S. NAVAL TRAINING STATION,
GREAT LAKES, ILLINOIS
REAR ADMIRAL, JOHN DOWNES  U S NAVY,
COMMANDING OFFICER

For most new seamen, their ship assignment came by luck of the draw—the type of vessel a sailor was assigned to determined how he would later take care of his dirty clothes.

The larger ships in the United States' fleet had their own laundry facilities right on board. For that matter, many also had their own stores, post offices, tailor shops, barbershops, and even cigar lockers. The sailors serving on such vessels placed their carefully labeled clothing in a bag and sent it to the laundry for washing—as easy as that.

However, men like Dad serving on the smallest ships in the Navy had none of these luxuries and had to make do on their own. Demonstrating a hefty dose of ingenuity, the crews on the little LCTs took care of all their chores, including the wash.

Slow-going LCTs were designed to operate along the shoreline with a range of only about 500 miles. Even so, some began their journey by following orders to travel all the way from Pearl Harbor to the South Pacific on their own power as part of a larger fleet of ships.

On one such long journey, an LCT crew improvised laundry duty by tying their clothes together with a rope and hurling it over the side. As the ship's propeller moved and churned the water, the ocean did all the work. The men then hauled up the line and laid the clothes out to dry on the deck. To some degree, they were clean, although I can imagine how stiff the salt-encrusted fabric must have felt.

More often, larger, faster ships delivered LCTs overseas—either in three separate pieces or fully assembled on their decks. In his memoir featured in *The Flotilla*, LCT skipper Darold Beckman recalled seeing his LCT briefly in New York before it was taken apart, the pieces of the craft divided between two different vessels for transport. While waiting in town to disembark, someone recommended he buy a washing machine in order to make his life a lot easier once he got overseas. He took the suggestion to heart, and days later, the new appliance was carefully stowed away with the bow of his future ship when he and part of his crew sailed. His electrician kept that well-used machine in good repair throughout the ship's whole tour of duty.

Of course, most LCT crews weren't lucky enough to have their own washing machine. Ordinarily, they would gather on the deck and begin by filling a large basin with water arduously pumped from their storage tanks—there was no running water aboard ship. Then, using cakes of soap and washboards, the men would do their best to give the clothes a thorough washing before hanging them on a line to dry. Protocols were looser on the LCTs and the men preferred to wear their work clothes instead of their Naval uniforms, often going shirtless to get some relief from the blistering heat.

Operating near the shore gave the sailors and officers the advantage of access to the native islanders, who in many cases were willing to do the men's laundry for them. Dad recounted, *From time to time we hired Filipino women to clean and press our clothes. Everything came back in beautiful shape. The Navy suggested this was a very bad practice since the water used by the women could be infested with parasites called "flukes." They might enter your body through the pores and generally head for your liver on which they might dine for years. Liver flukes went to the liver and heart flukes went to the heart—according to the Navy. It also was supposed to take years to develop—at age 86 I guess I'm safe—at least from the flukes. Although Seaman Burgess may still be out there somewhere waiting to kill us. We reluctantly fired our laundresses.*

Al Exner also hired a Filipino woman to take care of his sailor whites. He recalled that they came back just perfect, "the whites as white as snow." He would meet this tiny woman at the gate to the Navy base where she took his soiled clothing and the soap he provided. Al thought she probably did the laundry in the river, which helps confirm why the Navy brass likely frowned on the native washing practices.

A typical sailor's uniform included a one square yard piece of black silk to be tied as a scarf around the neck. Al's developed a small hole in the knot from being tied the exact same way every day. He knew he would have to replace it soon, so he decided to give it to his Filipino washwoman. She wished to wash it for him at no charge, but he told her, "No, you should be paid!" She was delighted to receive the scarf, along with the soap that she kept for herself, and later made herself a skirt out of the fabric.

Prior to his time in the South Pacific, Al spent a very intense tour serving in the surgery ward at Netley Hospital in England. A man who sterilized the surgical equipment there ran a laundry operation on the side. Al paid him just fifty cents per week to take care of all his dirty clothing.

Across the ocean in the Mediterranean, another LCT officer dropped off his laundry with an old Sicilian lady who clapped her hands and smiled whenever he came through her doorway. Like Al, William Baker contributed the soap. He and his laundress would count each piece of clothing as it came and went and agreed to the usual form of payment, two packs of cigarettes. Baker's washwoman always said "hello" as he was leaving, so he would quizzically answer "hello" and walk out. It wasn't until later that Baker learned that "ciao" means both hello and goodbye in Italian. She had cheerfully assumed that the English word worked the same way.

I never gave a moment's thought about how laundry was done during WWII until I read the passage in Dad's journal. When researching the topic, I found it was another example of how these resourceful young men found ways to get any and all mundane tasks completed. These stories paint a marvelous contrast between the laundry methods themselves and the all-too familiar wartime pictures of smiling young men in sailor whites and officer blues.

*Dad is at the top in newly-issued sailor whites*
*(traded for officer dress blues soon after)*

# SECTION THREE: HARSH REALITY

Millions of civilians became members of the military and settled into their new lifestyles overseas, participating in the worldwide effort to defeat the Axis. In previous sections, we saw how these people adjusted, trying to find ways to live a "glass half full" existence in the midst of horrific warfare. However, it was a constant struggle for those serving to remain optimistic with the ever-present threat of danger surrounding them.

Most Americans never dreamed of the vicious and unspeakable things the enemy would do to achieve their goal of world domination. Stateside, people sat in darkened theaters and looked on in horror at the newsreels of the concentration camp liberations. In the winter and spring of 1945, as Soviet and American teams entered the camps where six million people had been killed, they not only discovered starving prisoners covered in dirt and excrement, but the evidence of the unspeakable medical experiments that had taken place. Imagine coming upon huge caches of teeth containing fillings, tons and tons of human hair, and hundreds of thousands of pieces of clothing never to be worn again by the owners.

General Eisenhower, Supreme Commander of the Allied forces in Europe, walked through the Ohrdruf Camp (one of the first to be liberated) and later wrote in his book *Crusade in Europe:*

> I have never felt able to describe my emotional reactions when I first came face to face with indisputable evidence of Nazi brutality and ruthless disregard of every shred of decency. Up to that time I had known about it only generally or through secondary sources. I am certain, however, that I have never at any other time experienced an equal sense of shock. I visited every nook and cranny of the camp because I felt it my duty to be in a position from then on to testify at firsthand about these things in case there ever grew up at home the belief or the assumption that "the stories of Nazi brutality were just propaganda."

Eisenhower immediately requested that American and British newspaper editors and photographers come at once and record the truth for all to see. He ordered nearby German citizens to walk through the camps in order to witness the actions their leader had wrought in Germany's name. American soldiers also toured the camps so they could see for themselves the evil they were fighting, the resulting images left to haunt these veterans for the rest of their lives.

On the other side of the globe in the South Pacific, Americans battled with another Axis foe whose tactics had never before been seen. From the Bataan Death March to the Japanese kamikaze suicide pilots, it seemed that the Japanese willingness to commit crimes against humanity knew no bounds. Following orders, Japanese soldiers raped, mutilated, and massacred hundreds of thousands of civilians in an evil attempt to dominate the region. In Manila alone, it is estimated that over 100,000 civilians fell victim to this unfathomable cruelty. In China, the despicable Japanese Unit 731 used citizens in macabre medical and chemical experiments, such as seeing how much pressure a human body could take before it exploded.

To be sure, there was no mercy for Americans in uniform. American prisoners of war routinely endured starvation, beatings, and death marches and became targets for bayonet practice. Fighting the tenacious Japanese in their pillboxes, tunnels, and trenches became a struggle to the death—their enemy's code of honor did not allow for a shameful surrender.

Every veteran I interviewed supported the decision to drop the atomic bombs—after seeing the lengths this enemy was willing to go, the bombings seemed to be the only way to stop them once and for all.

Dad had some thoughts on this in his journal, decades after the war's end.

*I have to admit that it was somewhat of a thrill to receive my mustering out letter even though it was a canned one. It gave me a sense of accomplishment even though in later years the Japanese and Germans have become known in some circles as the victims. For example, one of Julia's junior high school teachers actually preached to impressionable young twelve-year-olds about our inhumanity in dropping the atomic bombs, leveling Dresden Germany and the rest of Germany. I remember calling the young woman's principal asking him to have her turn down her rhetoric. He didn't—apparently the woman had tenure.*

*I think you had to be there to be qualified to render . . . opinions* [unless you were there, you had no right to judge] . . . *The Germans especially and the Japanese to a degree deserved some sort of retribution. After all, give or take a few million, there were 25 to 45 million deaths due to the war in the period 1939-1945— all of those deaths were absolutely unnecessary. They were caused because Germany and Japan wanted to dominate the World. I can still remember newsreels in 1937-1939 (before the war) depicting hundreds of thousands of German citizens screaming their approval in major German cities as Hitler proclaimed (English translation) "Germany over all." This was before Germany started the war.*

*The Japanese actually believed their Emperor was a god. He got off scott free. Hanging him would have been impossible for the Japanese to bear. Japanese atrocities before and during the war were at least as bad as those committed by the Germans.*

*A bit of my philosophy. The hated "Japs" as we called them in 1944, had hopes of taking over Australia as well as Southern New Guinea. They never made it to Australia nor did they last too long in New Guinea. The quality of their bills* [currency] *was quite good. They made crap for equipment, garbage for rations, and couldn't even make good cigarettes. They were very skilled, however, in creating mindless beasts and fanatics both in the armed forces and on the home front. It's* ~~1999, 2000, 2001, 2002, 2003, 2004, 2005,~~ *2006 written and crossed now, and I'm still fighting WWII.*

The Allies were up against true evil.

It is difficult to pin down the exact number of deaths

worldwide caused by World War II. The National WWII Museum provides a number of 60 million with an asterisk that states, "Worldwide casualty estimates vary widely in several sources. The number of civilian deaths in China alone might well be more than 50,000,000." As Dad wrote in his journal, every single one of these deaths was unnecessary.

# DANGER LIES IN WAIT

*I have never been one to talk about the rigors of the war, the fear of death, etc. and was very fortunate that I never experienced even approximately the chaos of earlier landings in New Guinea, Guadalcanal, Tacloban—and so on. Even so, death was everywhere.*

By the numbers, a gig in the Navy was a far safer prospect than serving in the other branches of the military. Over four million people contributed to the United States naval effort during the war with just over 62,000 losing their lives. Dad's assignment to a landing craft supply ship and not a destroyer, battleship, or minesweeper (ships that were all bigger and easier targets) would be a major stroke of luck for our family. Since little ships like Dad's swarmed into the harbors with supplies only after the invasions that had secured American footholds on land, they were rarely in the thick of battle themselves.

Dad arrived at Buna, Papua New Guinea, to report for his assignment under Skipper Jim Harnack on *LCT-977* in the spring of 1944. *At Buna the war really came home to me. The beach was still a mess from the earlier invasion and except for a scraggly outpost of Australian troops, there was no sign of life. We did stumble upon a small and neat cemetery covered with white crosses. They belonged mostly to Army lads from Wisconsin and*

*Michigan—I think probably the 32ⁿᵈ division. It was very sad and very scary to realize that after about 16 months of war in the Pacific, we had only advanced 60 miles up the coast of New Guinea. Even at 22, our hearts went out to the poor dead soldiers and their families.*

The Battle at Buna lasted a grueling 117 days beginning in November 1942. At Buna, the Japanese desire to win at any cost shocked the Allied troops who came face to face with the tenacious enemy already dug deeply into the jungle landscape in bunkers.

At the end of the battle, America suffered devastating losses—620 men died and over two thousand more were injured. The great majority of these men belonged to the 32ⁿᵈ Infantry known as the Red Arrow Division. Because so many members of the Red Arrow Division came from Wisconsin, the city of Milwaukee commemorated the division's bravery, naming a beautiful park downtown after it.

Dad arrived in the aftermath and stood ready to supply the fragile toehold on land that the Allies had gained.

*Our first assignment was the invasion of a tiny island off the coast of New Guinea called Wakde. We landed on little Wakde Island on D-Day and there supplied the chaps on the 12-mile stretch with supplies. We never realized how close we were to the Japanese. Harnack*

**It's a Crazy War Up**

WAKDE, DUTCH NEW GUINEA—All the line of the American-held Wakde tor it was a damn crazy war, For a m fanatic and well-supplied Jap infantry s to drive the task force back into the P: The Japs were jungle-wise and determine they continuously threatened a break th For a month, the small force charged with ing the mainland flank of Wakde drome, re seized by the Americans, had a tough assign Fighting along the narrow 12-mile beach was the bloody, nerve-snapping type that t night hours into jungle hell illuminated by muzzle flashes while yells of attacking wounded Japs echoed among the ironwood Then the arrival of reinforcing troops the "patrol all day and guard or fight all r routine the force had followed for three breaking weeks. American casualties wer a fraction of the 1,911 Japs killed and P Heart awards were few. When he could sit back and think, N Leonard Sweeney of Olyphant, Pa., summ up: "Sometimes it isn't the down paymen *and I took a casual walk inland one day. There seemed to be a tiny road parallel to the beach. We noted a sign "Minefield." Thus ended our walk.*

Dad and the other inexperienced new members of the Navy had good luck on their sides as they escaped injury or battle, but often they were responsible for their own close calls.

*It was along the coast off Wakde Island that Harnack and I were put in for the Silver Star—some kind of Navy medal for bravery. It was on a beautiful moonlit night and Jim and I were transporting a young army lieutenant and 20 of his charges for a landing on the beach (this was not an invasion—*[they were]*. . . just rejoining their company.) We were sitting on the conn deck of the ship having a very learned discussion about the size, shape, and clarity of the crescent-shaped moon.*

*Suddenly all hell broke loose. The sky all around us was illuminated with all sorts of tracer bullets from machine guns on the shore.*

At this point, the American forces occupying the shoreline shot at anything that moved, the bullets pinging on the sides of the little ship.

*Jim turned on our signal light which was like a broad searchlight and I leapt down on the stern displaying the American Flag* [in the light]. *Fortunately for us, the shots were from so-called "friendly fire."*

*I'm sure had they been Japanese guns we would have been mincemeat (especially me). Needless to say, the army lieutenant requested an overnight stay. Our flotilla commander thought that we should have some sort of award for bravery and he submitted the necessary papers to the Navy brass. We got no award—friendly fire doesn't count. (Actually in our early 20's, Jim and I could have cared less about medals. In fact, we thought the whole episode was a big joke. I still do in 1999, 2002, 2003, 2004, 2005, 2006, 2007).*

Although LCTs were rarely directly involved in combat, it would be naïve to think they weren't under the constant threat of danger. Seventy-one of these little vessels sank or were otherwise lost during the war. As Dad will describe, plenty of things could kill a non-combatant on a supply carrier like his.

*LCT-977 was stationed for a few weeks on Noemfoor Island which is at the northern end of New Guinea—almost exactly on the equator. One day, while we were anchored just off the beach, an army bomber flew over and "inadvertently" its bomb doors opened and a couple of 100-pound bombs dropped within a hundred yards of us. Our crew was furious to say the least. That night in censoring the mail, we had to cut out a lot of complaints about the incident— not good for morale on the home front. I like to think it was an accident, but it could have been fatal for our doughty [fearless, dauntless] crew—and, of course, me. We were the only Navy ship on the island. Looking back, perhaps the young airman actually thought we were an enemy patrol boat. Probably this answers our own chaps trying to kill us as the crew said. I believe they referred to the fliers as "mother fuckers."*

*We often unloaded 1000, 500, and 100-pound bombs for*

*the Army Air Force. It made us very nervous when sometimes the
unloaders dumped the bombs rather vigorously from the cargo
net—hitting our deck and making a lot of noise. Harnack used to
complain that it woke him up from his naps. Jim slept a lot and as
I said earlier, he had a great sense of humor.*

*One Army Lieutenant assured us that the bombs could not
explode without detonator caps being attached. One day in Leyte
Gulf, having discharged a rather large load of 100-pound bombs,
we were surprised to hear a lot of explosions inland. The word
got back to us that some of the "harmless" bombs from our load
had dropped from the truck and blew up part of an ammunition
dump—it could have been us.*

John Eskau's LCT once picked up a Japanese bomb to
transfer it to another ship for delivery to Pearl Harbor. The
bomb itself was carefully crated, but the Merchant Marine who
tried to hoist it up and off of the LCT accidentally dropped it
back onto the little ship's deck, destroying the crate. The crew of
the LCT decided to wrap the bomb with a heavy net, thinking
that it could be lifted to the other ship in that manner. John
actually laughed out loud as he told me that the Merchant
Marine proceeded to drop the bomb, net and all, two more
times before finally hauling it off the LCT and aboard his ship.

William Baker wrote to his parents, "The closest call for our
ship occurred when a stray shell splashed into the water and
exploded alongside a cargo ship loaded with ammunition just
after we had pulled away from that ship. Our tank deck was
stacked high with ammunition."

Vast quantities of gasoline and other types of fuel constantly surrounded the men serving on supply ships. If not fueling the ships, cranes, planes, and other machinery in the area, it might be piled up waiting for delivery for future use inland. John Eskau told me that one of the most dangerous things they did was simply refueling their own ship. Dad echoed this statement and added:

*We used to haul large drums of hi octane gas in "leak proof" cans. It used to bother us that despite "leak proof" we could always smell gasoline and we were all heavy smokers, lighting up and snuffing butts—would have made one helluva bonfire—or explosion.*

*Drums of gasoline being unloaded from an LCT on the beach.*
*Photo courtesy: National Archives 80-G-53830*

Japanese planes regularly flew over the decks of the little LCTs while they worked. Mercifully, the Japanese considered most LCTs too small to be significant targets. After the Battle of Leyte Gulf in October 1944 through the end of the war, Japanese kamikaze suicide planes were a prevailing threat to the U.S. fleet, sinking dozens of ships and damaging hundreds of others. Dad recalled seeing many kamikazes late in his stay in the Philippines, and he had some strong opinions about them too. *These pilots were another good example of the pathetic lack of knowhow and skill on the Japanese side. The quality of their equipment* [aircraft] *was poor and by 1945 most of their decent pilots had been killed.*

John Eskau had his own tale about kamikazes, but the telling also demonstrates his and other sailors' inexperience and hair-trigger responses to the enemy. John's ship went in to Buckner Bay near Okinawa to unload Marines and Seabees there. "We had pulled in and as we backed out, another ship pulled in and six kamikazes came swooping in." Americans on ships all over the bay fired at the Japanese, including John manning the 20mm gun on his LCT. The group was able to shoot down five of the six planes.

The larger ship, a Landing Ship, Tank that pulled in after John's LCT had pulled away, was now a sitting duck in the middle of the bay, other American ships on either side. The sixth Japanese plane turned toward the LST, flying level with the water as it aimed to strike. John and other Americans cried out to "cease fire," knowing that because of the position of the plane between the surrounding American ships, firing at it would cause crossfire. Many kept firing anyway to a tragic result. In the attempt to stop the kamikaze that struck the LST, killing three in its engine room, friendly fire from other ships injured or killed about fifty-one men on the LST's deck.

For every man, there was no escaping the reality of the threat of danger that permeated their everyday lives during the war. Though Dad didn't dwell on this in his journal, one incident brought this home for Dad in a profound and sad way. *Even so, death was everywhere. There was a young ensign, for example, in the Leyte Gulf in the Philippines. We had been there several weeks when the ensign—McCormick, by name, arrived right out of training. On his second day he tied his LCT alongside a Liberty ship to take on cargo.* [While loading cargo] *the ship was struck by a Japanese Kamikaze pilot. They brought the young ensign to a hospital, still alive but legless and armless. Fortunately for him, I feel, his second day in the Philippines was his last. He died not knowing what hit him. I remembered the ensign from college—he had a nickname like mine and sat next to me for a semester in a course called Public Utilities (at Wisconsin—actually a very boring course).*

This was close to home. McCormick, like Dad, was just another student in college swept into the war, but then he ended up getting killed. Dad's flotilla group was nearby that December day when this tragic event happened—it could have just as easily been his misfortune as the other young ensign's.

One of the first *Flotilla* newsletters I received in the mail contained the full story about the death of Ensign McCormick—the very same man Dad described in his journal. As I read the article that told the story from a different perspective, I couldn't help but wonder at the coincidence of it.

The Liberty ship Dad mentioned was the SS *Marcus Daly*, and it was tied up to another ship because of severe bow damage from an earlier Japanese attack. Ensign McCormick's *LCT-1075* was alongside loading cargo. This time three Japanese fighter planes, or "Zekes" as the Allies called them, attacked the *Marcus Daly* once more. One kamikaze dove toward the bridge of the larger ship, angling down and across the ship, first snapping off its cargo boom, then destroying the gun tub and taking out the side lifeboats. The Zeke finally veered into the unlucky LCT where it exploded, setting the little ship on fire.

There were many other LCTs in the area at the time, and they frantically fired anti-aircraft guns during the attack. Some reported that the diving plane was a kamikaze, although this was never confirmed. As told in Dad's story, on *LCT-1075*, Ensign James McCormick was fatally wounded. The ship's other officer, Ensign Darrel Maxwell, was listed as missing in action, presumed dead. LCTs in the area picked up the other survivors (although several online sources report the loss of the entire crew), as well as two men from the *Marcus Daly* who had jumped overboard to avoid being struck by the diving plane.

On nearby *LCT-1071*, the officer in charge, Joseph Herrington, was a very close friend of Ensign McCormick. According to *The Flotilla*, he had even attended McCormick's wedding in San Francisco just before he was posted on his own ship. He wrote a letter to Jim's widow Vivianne, and in her response, she said the family had no news regarding her husband's death other than what was contained in the original telegram.

In her letter she said: "Dear Joe, I received your letter yesterday and I'm afraid I'll never be able to tell you how much it meant to me. Thank you very much. You see, your letter is the only word I've had about Jim since the telegram. We received it on January 3rd and it was very brief, saying only that Jim had died of wounds received in action and that he had been buried on Allied territory pending cessation of hostilities. It didn't say where or when or anything else! Naturally it was a terrible shock to all of us because I thought that he was comparatively safe and in the New Guinea area."

As I read her letter excerpted in *The Flotilla*, my heart sank as I realized this family received word of the death over three weeks after it happened. They had blithely carried on during the holiday season, thinking Jim was safe. My mother probably did the same back in Freeport, Illinois—sure that Dad was mostly out of harm's way on his supply ship.

Imagine living under the constant anxiety and stress brought on by war, danger lurking around every corner —and to do so at such tender ages. Dad chose to stay mum about any worries he had, instead choosing to do his best to reassure my mother, his parents, and other friends and relatives back home.

*These are things I never mentioned in my letters home. I, being a kind and lighthearted lad, never once wrote home expressing fears or threats of death or any of those sorts of things. I could list dozens of additional disasters that could have happened, but I've made my point.*

I think he *did* make his point. Many young men opted to join the Navy over the Army, Air Force, or Marines thinking it would be a way to avoid facing combat. None of these options guaranteed a young man's escape from the perils of war.

Over 700 American naval vessels sank or were otherwise destroyed during the war and over 1,500 Merchant Marine ships like the ones Dad loaded and unloaded were lost. On damaged ships that managed to stay afloat, scores of sailors and officers suffered injuries or died in the chaos of the attack. Others in the Navy were felled by accident or illness in the course of just doing their jobs.

The lucky ones came home.

# ED KNIGHT – Brave Army Medic

"My desire is that generations to come might see that our freedoms have come at great costs—costs to those who lost their lives defending it, to the many who lost limbs and were crippled for life, to those who lost loved ones, and to those like me who were neither wounded nor killed but harbor bad memories."

These are the words of Edwin Hershal Knight, spoken to me some seventy years after his service in the Army during World War II. While some of the details faded in his memory, others were so profound that they had indelibly and permanently imprinted in his mind. Since we talked in 2015, Ed has passed away, but his story will not be lost.

Ed grew up on a small farm in Dallas County, Arkansas, a "poor farm boy" for whom a penny was a valuable coin. As a teenager during the Depression years of the 1930s, he looked for any legitimate means to make some spending money, including collecting scrap metal from around the farm to sell. At the time, the Japanese government was buying it up, and it wasn't until later that Ed realized that some of the metal he scrounged probably ended up in the planes and ships used to attack Pearl Harbor.

In fall 1941, at the age of eighteen, Ed entered Arkansas Polytechnic College in Russellville. Soon after, the Japanese attack in Hawaii drew the United States into the war. Ed recalled, "America rallied behind our President because we were in danger of losing our free, democratic society through the action of these two evil forces. We had no alternative but to fight."

About seven months later, Ed received his draft notice from the Army, or as he called it, his "congratulatory letter," ordering him to report on May 26, 1943. Although he had two years of college under his belt, enough to pursue the role of commissioned officer, he decided instead to enter the service as a private. He heard commissioned officers of the time mockingly referred to as "90-Day Wonders" and the idea of being the butt of a joke didn't appeal to him.

He traveled by coal-powered military train to Camp Roberts in California to begin sixteen weeks of basic training. Over the course of the four-day trip, the men on the train opened every window because of the heat, only to usher in the heavy smoke and soot of the engine.

After the first three weeks of training, he received a weeklong furlough, borrowing $100 from the Red Cross so he could come

*Here is Ed during his furlough with a young relative, George Edwin (Grady Knight's son)*

back home. After that brief respite, he went back to California to a succession of different camps where he crawled under machine-gun fire, threw grenades, practiced using his rifle with targets, and sharpened his combat skills. He had no idea where he would be sent, but it began to dawn on him that odds are it wouldn't be good.

On December 10, 1943, he joined 6,000 other Army troops on a huge ship that sailed underneath the Golden Gate Bridge—the last he would see of America for three Christmases, he recalled wistfully.

After two weeks at sea, the ship made landfall in New Caledonia, an island east of Australia. The troops were there to replace soldiers from the 43rd Infantry Division killed or wounded fighting the Japanese on the Solomon and Marshall Islands. He recalled, "I spent my first Christmas overseas in New Caledonia. There were no celebrations, no Christmas lights, no gifts exchanged, no cards and letters received. There was only homesickness without close friends to sympathize. As time slowly passed, I thought about what lay ahead, would there even be a next Christmas?"

The conditions grew worse; first a bout of diarrhea spread throughout the entire camp, and then the men endured a typhoon. Heeding the warnings of the storm's approach, they securely anchored their twenty-cot tent. After midnight, gusts of wind rocked and eventually pulled down the tent and scattered the cots. Late the following morning, the soldiers rounded up their belongings, set up another tent, and counted their blessings that no one had been seriously injured.

In New Caledonia, Ed received his assignment. The medical detachment of the 43rd Infantry Division needed volunteer replacements. Ed told me, "One day someone approached my group of men and asked if anyone wanted to volunteer. No one raised their hand, so the man pointed straight at me and said, 'Now you are a medic.'" Authorities randomly selected several others to join Ed in this role.

Since these "volunteers" had no prior medical experience, the Army shipped them off to New Zealand to learn first aid. Ed spent the next four months training. His home was a tent encampment set up on a former racetrack in the small country village of Pukekohe, surrounded by beautiful verdant hills dotted with hundreds of grazing sheep and colorful dairy cows. He recalled playing football during off-hours and enjoying a wonderful diet that included lamb chops and ice cream. He laughed while telling me that even though he had reached the highest weight of his entire life in Pukekohe, his waist measurement was the smallest he would ever see.

When they completed their training, the new medics again boarded a ship—destination unknown. Two weeks later, they anchored in New Guinea where the 43rd Division was to replace the 25th that had been fighting in the jungles there for several months. The 25th had made some headway, so it was a relatively quiet war zone by this point. For the next six months, instead of treating the wounded, Ed gave medical attention to soldiers with physical problems such as the painful skin lesions caused by "jungle rot"—a common ailment in the tropics.

The soldiers set up tents in a coconut grove that ran parallel to the Pacific Ocean. Often the large nuts fell, first hitting the cloth roof of the tent with a bang and later providing a tasty snack. The men constructed a washbasin out of a steel helmet placed on a homemade rack made with poles cut from the jungle and nailed to a palm tree. When shaving or washing, they were always alert, watching for falling coconuts dropping from forty feet above. For bathing, there was a fifty-five-gallon drum placed on top of a rack with a showerhead attached, the water constantly warm from the equatorial heat. Mosquitoes and rats posed the biggest threat during this period in Ed's service.

The medics had time for recreational activities while living near the jungle. They swam and played volleyball using a net strung between two palm trees. They played cards. Occasionally they would watch a black-and-white movie projected onto a bed sheet as they sat on coconut logs.

Life in the tropics required ingenuity. "I remember learning to cool our bottled Cokes by placing them in a steel helmet filled with gasoline. With a car pump, we pumped air into the liquid. This caused the gasoline to evaporate and cooled the drinks somewhat," recalled Ed.

Just before Christmas 1944, the men learned they would be leaving the island soon and to be ready at short notice to pack up their gear. Ed recalled, "Christmas Day, my second Christmas overseas, passed without any great celebration. We did, however, have a good meal prepared and were able to share candy and cookies that had been sent from our American homes weeks before. Even though some was melted and moldy, it was quite a treat in this jungle setting that lacked the atmosphere of a joyous

Christmas under the equator stars. Unfortunately, some of our Christmas gifts didn't arrive until March of the following year in another country where we were sent."

*This was the 169ᵗʰ medical detachment, 43ʳᵈ Infantry Division.*
*Ed is on the far left with his arm over his knee. Several of these men were killed.*

Ed and the others made their way to catch their ride to the next assignment. Amphibious ships nicknamed "gators" landed on the water's edge to collect the soldiers, then lifted their ramps to head out toward the waiting troop transport ships. The sea was rough, with six-to-eight-foot swells, and the men, unaccustomed to the water, soon grew seasick. When they finally reached the anchored ship, many of them were too ill to climb the twenty-foot Jacob's ladder to the ship, so the Navy dropped down nets and hoisted them up onto the deck. The waves barely affected the mammoth troop carrier they boarded and soon the men felt much better.

Ship leadership assigned Ed's group to "holes" on the various decks where the men would sleep, cots stacked four deep—a couple hundred troops in each compartment. During the darkness of night, all light was shaded out as the ship sailed under blackout conditions to avoid enemy detection. Even the light of cigarettes and matches was not allowed on the outer decks. Minesweepers attached to the sides of the ship could be heard scraping the hull throughout the night. Air conditioning and fans were turned off in an effort to keep enemy submarines from detecting their presence, so the 169th medical detachment sweltered below deck while sleeping, usually without clothes.

Each night, additional ships joined the convoy that Ed soon learned was heading to Luzon for the invasion at Lingayen Gulf. By the time they reached the Philippines, there may have been 800 or more ships all told. Ed was in awe of the sight, saying, "As we continued to sail along slowly at about fifteen knots, other ships were joining our convoy until ships could be seen in every direction—forward, backward, and on both sides— until they faded into the horizon. It was amazing to see ships an equal distance apart sailing together as one unit, and after sailing through the night to awake the next morning to see the ships in the same formation."

Ed's unit commander called him and the other medics into a room to be issued supplies, and he packed his large backpack as full as he could. As the days passed, the normal laughter and fun turned to quiet anticipation and nervous concern for what lay ahead. Ed wondered what the enemy would be like and how he would react to them, and also worried that his attention to the wounded and dying would be insufficient.

Very early in the morning of landing day, January 9, 1945, Ed polished off a large breakfast of beefsteak and eggs, the high-energy meal meant to prepare him for the long day ahead. While he was eating, the convoy's battleships shelled the beachhead and the ship's anti-aircraft guns fired at the Japanese Zeros flying overhead. After eating breakfast, Ed swung his loaded backpack and the small folding shovel he would later need to dig foxholes onto his back, donned his steel helmet, and slung his carbine rifle over his shoulder. He was as ready to go as he'd ever be.

Ed's group would face many months of grim fighting in the Philippines. The Japanese had already dug deeply into hiding places in the hills, ready to face the Americans and bracing to hold back the invasion. For the first few days after its arrival, his division encountered little resistance as it moved into the foothills. Each night the men worked in pairs to dig their foxholes for sleeping, taking turns with digging and keeping watch. But before long the machine guns and shelling began in earnest. "You'd fight for three weeks and never take off your shoes or clothes. Every three, four, five weeks or so, the Army pulled the guys back if they could to give them a hot meal," Ed recalled.

There are events that are impossible to "un-see," and Ed witnessed more than his fair share of those in the Philippines. For one, the sight of a young infantryman running down the hill for help, shot through his femoral artery, blood gushing out with every heartbeat. He lost so much blood by the time he reached Ed that Ed was unable to find a vein in which to inject a supply of plasma. A physician nearby also failed, and he and Ed watched the young man gasp his last breath. Ed lamented, "The soldier could have saved his own life by applying a towel tourniquet from his pack, but instead lost his self-control and ran."

Or the time Ed found himself climbing up a steep incline of ash inside the dormant volcano Mount Pinatubo, dodging bullets while attempting to drive the Japanese out of the huge crater. He provided cover for a GI who approached an enemy foxhole, watching as the solider fired into the hole, pulling the lone survivor out only to shoot him point-blank in the forehead. Ed spoke dully to me when he said, "This is what war leads men to do."

Later that same day as night approached, it was time to once again dig in for the night. Ed felt like an exhausted hamster on a wheel. While working, he heard a bullet zing by his ear and land with a thud, knowing immediately that it had hit a soldier nearby. He rushed over to try to help the man whose blood streamed from a bullet hole in his back and chest. Ed's training set in—he covered both holes with Vaseline and cellophane from his backpack to prevent the possibility of suffocation. As he injected two pints of plasma, he thought that the soldier was slipping away. In reality, the man was in a state of extreme shock, but still told Ed that he had killed nine "Japs" that day and was still not scared of them.

Shock and trauma occurred every day. Army leaders dispatched Ed and the other medics to an area where American troops had set the village's huts on fire, killing more than fifty Japanese, and then had piled the dead and set them on fire as well. As Ed looked for any troops in need of aid, he encountered a young soldier, blank with shock, still sitting in his foxhole after an encounter with a Japanese soldier the night before. It seemed his enemy had tumbled into the infantryman's foxhole, and when the American realized who it was, he decided to play dead. The Japanese searched him, took his canteen (a major commodity in the tropic heat) and climbed out of the foxhole. The young man's decision to play dead had been a wise one, but in all the eight months Ed battled through Luzon, he had never seen a person as white from shock.

It was several weeks after landing at Lingayen Gulf that Ed had one of his most terrifying experiences. His infantry unit was on the offensive, set to intercept the Japanese along a sixty-mile highway that ran all the way from Manila to the mountain resort area of Baguio. Ed's group had stopped at a place where a narrow dirt country road intersected the paved highway at an angle— almost like the letter "Y." Another narrow road crossed a rice field, connecting the other two in a pattern that now resembled an "A."

All infantrymen stationed themselves in two-man holes to keep watch alternately, so it was in the triangle the roads formed that Ed and his medic partner began to dig their foxhole for the night. Before they could finish, artillery shells started pounding the troops south of the little crossroad. The two men dropped their shovels and administered to the wounded until things quieted down, returning just before dark to finish digging their shallow berth.

At about one in the morning, Ed saw the silhouette of a Japanese soldier about twenty-five yards away, who shouted what sounded like "shoo-go, shoo-go" as he threw up a flare to temporarily light up the sky. In this brief illumination, Ed saw two Japanese soldiers walking toward the paved highway before disappearing into the darkness.

Lying awake in his foxhole for the next several hours, Ed eventually heard the movement of dozens of enemy troops approaching on foot up the dirt road, followed at a distance by some very slow-moving trucks. Ed remembered, "I listened to hundreds of men passing by, coughing and sneezing and talking quietly. I frantically tried to pull out handfuls of the muddy soil beneath me to make my foxhole deeper and further hide my location."

As the enemy walked by just a few feet above him on the dirt road, a rat scurried into the foxhole and squirreled into Ed's armpit. What to do? Should he squeeze his arm to kill the rat or wait? Before he was forced to decide, U.S. troops met the enemy on the northern perimeter of the road where an enormous fight commenced.

In the noise and chaos of this moment, the rat decided on its own to leave the foxhole, but the real enemy still surrounded Ed. By daylight, the Japanese trucks rambled right above where Ed concealed himself in his little ditch. Suddenly, an American gun one hundred yards to his north began firing 35mm shells point-blank at the trucks, sending the Japanese occupants jumping off on the opposite side of the dirt road. Ed could hear the moaning of the injured, and he could see their rifle bayonets sticking up above the ditch across the road.

He held the handle of a grenade, pulled the pin, and threw—anxiously waiting for five seconds until it exploded. He knew that five seconds was long enough for the enemy to catch it and throw it back, injuring or killing the one who threw it. At this same moment, the Japanese could be readying their own version of a grenade, striking them on their helmets to detonate and throwing them before they nearly instantaneously exploded.

Soon one of the trucks burst into flames, the intense heat forcing Ed and his foxhole buddy into a scramble to get away from it. They crawled north through the adjacent foxholes, finding two other pairs of medics lying dead in successive foxholes. When they reached the area where the two roads joined, they sprinted across the paved highway and jumped into a large ditch, dodging the Japanese artillery surrounding them. Shouts of "medic, medic" came from all around the adjacent field. The two men ran out to aid the wounded, and shrapnel soon hit Ed's buddy. After Ed administered first aid to his friend, he realized that although he had been missed, the shrapnel put some holes through the side pocket of his fatigues.

When Ed finally returned to the large ditch, about ten feet wide by six feet deep, an Army chaplain jumped in beside him, hit by a bullet while crossing the highway. Before Ed could load all the wounded on a first aid truck, an artillery shell came in, tearing slabs of flesh from the poor chaplain's legs and arms. Ed didn't have any bandages large enough to cover these wounds. The chaplain called out, "I can't die, I can't die," but there was nothing Ed or anyone else could do for him.

Sometime later, as Ed sat dazed in the trench from the relentless pressure of the past night, a shell landed ten or twelve feet away, hitting two soldiers sitting there. Ed knew when one of the men's eyes popped right out of his head that a concussion killed him instantly. The other lay wounded by shrapnel and plaintively called for Ed to bandage his wounds and get him transported to a medical station.

By mid-morning, things had quieted down, the biggest evidence of the battle an American tank that had suffered a hit and was ablaze, still sending billows of smoke hundreds of feet in the air. An infantry first sergeant told Ed that he and most of the other Americans ran out of ammunition and that he had resorted to beating a Japanese soldier to death with his shovel.

Ed and the other survivors were soon loaded up in trucks and taken to a safe area for a few days of rest and hot meals before their next conflict.

The battle at the intersection had been a bloody one; over 600 Japanese soldiers died and 130 Americans were wounded or killed. Ed finished this story saying, "I believe that six of those killed were medics. God spared my life for a purpose."

The Americans used napalm flamethrowers, mortars, tanks, automatic rifles, machine guns, and grenades in the epic fight to take Hill 355. They also used hand-to-hand combat for much of the fighting. In either case, the battle created scores of injuries for Ed and the other medics to treat. During the ensuing days, many others grew ill with malaria, diarrhea, and hepatitis because of the abundance of flies and mosquitoes.

But by this point in the war, the Japanese had lost a lot of planes, so the Army was not quite as concerned about keeping their camp areas in darkness. They utilized artificial moonlight, searchlights shown into the clouds to reflect the light and illuminate the area below so they could see what was going on and watch for any Japanese soldiers who might try to infiltrate the area. Once the searchlight was cut off, commanding officers warned Ed and the others never to crawl out of their foxholes to urinate or defecate because they ordered other Americans on watch to shoot anything that moved. That was how individual foxholes became private toilets.

Ed helped thousands of men during the two years he served as a medic, and some remained in his memory decades later.

Ed told me the story of one good-humored man he cared for. An artillery shell hit this soldier while he was tucked into his foxhole, the blast blowing off his leg. The injured man, though weak, applied his own tourniquet made out of a towel while he waited for help to arrive. This probably saved his life. With a sigh, Ed said to me, "Ninety-nine percent of the people I came across would not have had the presence of mind to do that and would have died."

After Ed gave the injured man three pints of plasma, his patient said something that Ed would never forget. His voice now stronger, he said, "Well, when I get my new leg, I am going to have to learn to jitterbug all over again."

As the Philippine Islands Campaign wound down, Ed and his division made preparations to head to the invasion of Borneo, what is now Malaysia. But it was not to be. On August 16, 1945, while on a training mission, the word came belatedly to Ed that the Americans dropped an atomic bomb on Hiroshima, thereby bringing the war with Japan near its close. Everyone was overjoyed at the news, but no real celebration took place. Ed and the other men were just too exhausted to react.

Soon he boarded yet another ship on a seven-day voyage to Japan, where he spent the remainder of his days in service. Along the way, his transport ship encountered a typhoon at sea with twenty-foot waves that caused much seasickness among the men and the pet monkeys that some of the troops had brought on board. As the ship approached Japan, the monkey owners were ordered to throw the monkeys overboard because Japan would not accept them.

"We docked in Yokohama, a seaport in southeast Honshu, in central Japan. As we arose after our first night's sleep, we observed that Mt. Fuji, the highest mountain in Japan, was white with new snow that we had not observed the day before. It was a beautiful sight."

Surprisingly, Ed told me that the Japanese people had a friendly attitude toward the American troops. They were ecstatic that the war had ended and even invited the men into their homes for meals. Ed recalled, "Isn't it amazing how you can be fighting the Japs one month and be eating in their homes as friends the following?"

When I asked him what his assignment was during this time,

Ed sheepishly told me that his job was to hand out condoms to all the servicemen!

Unfortunately, during his four months in Japan, Ed succumbed to malaria. After all the battles he had survived, mosquitos almost took him down. After a week's time, the doctors finally got the fever under control, but he would continue taking medicine to fight the disease for many months.

At last he earned enough discharge points to be released from the Army; he traveled two weeks by sea to California, then on to Camp Chaffee in Arkansas to finish the discharge process. While at Camp Chaffee, he met a man named Bob Madden originally from New York State. As they talked, they realized they were heading to the same place. When Ed explained that his destination was his sister Julia's house on Woodruff Avenue, the man laughed and said he was also going there to meet his wife, Edyth, who was staying there with her sister. Bob met Edyth while she served in the Women's Army Auxiliary Corps. It was in that moment that they realized they were brothers-in-law—Ed had not yet heard of their marriage.

A week later, Ed headed home to the Pine Cove community near Sparkman, Arkansas, to see his parents. He lived with his brother for a summer before enrolling in college in the fall at the University of Arkansas. He echoed the sentiment of other veterans, claiming that the GI Bill was the greatest thing related to war that happened to him. He earned both his bachelor's and master's degrees by taking advantage of this program for veterans.

Ed enjoyed a long and successful career as a schoolteacher

and principal in both Arkansas and New Jersey, moving back to Little Rock to retire. While teaching in 1948, Ed met and married his wife Doris, a math teacher, who remained by his side until his dying day. They delighted in their three children and the many grandchildren and great-grandchildren that followed.

He thought often of the men he patched up and sent away for further medical assistance. Ed quietly said, "I had no idea what became of any of them, and only hoped that in some small way I made a real difference in their lives."

Ed told me he wondered why many of his military buddies were killed and yet he was fortunate to come back alive. For this he had no explanation. His faith guided him and he believed that he was here for a purpose. In parting at the end of our last conversation, he reminded me that our liberties have come at a great cost, saying, "May we always thank God for those who have fought that we might enjoy the freedoms that we enjoy and too often take for granted."

## "MEDIC, MEDIC!" – From Injury To Recovery

Ed was just one of thousands of newly trained medics who saw the horrors of war firsthand yet disregarded their own safety to treat the injuries of their fallen brothers. Medics, along with thousands of doctors, surgeons, and nurses, battled against the never-ending stream of incoming wounded, sick, and dying. To win the war with the fewest casualties possible, the United States would need to develop and rely on a complex combination of medical innovations, logistical strategies, evacuation and treatment systems, and determination.

Many a survivor owes a debt of gratitude to the incredible life-saving efforts of medical personnel, scientists, and military medics. Working with limited supplies, technology, and access to sterile environments, their achievements were remarkable—98 of every 100 wounded men recovered from their injuries compared to the 90 who survived such odds in WWI.

Though not trained in the medical profession, many unit leaders and Navy skippers also played a key role in the everyday efforts to keep our servicemembers healthy and ready for duty. Dad weighed in: *We were lucky that none of us came down with any serious ailments—a simple emergency appendectomy would have been almost impossible for us to obtain. I acted as the ship's doctor and dentist and psychologist, so ailments were treated with APC tablets (a pill containing aspirin, Phenacetin, and Caffeine. Phenacetin was one of the first anti-inflammatory drugs), toothaches through a bottle of oil of cloves. The oil did ease the pain and stalled the inevitable extraction. In the tropics there didn't seem to be a lot of common colds, so colds were no problem. Luckily, we were young, fairly strong, and very fortuitously, disaster never struck the USS LCT-977.*

The medical departments of the Army and Navy were responsible for our servicemembers' health and wellbeing from the minute they entered the service, had their physical and received their vaccinations, to the moment when they finally returned home from their tour of duty.

The size and scope of these two departments ramped up dramatically once the United States entered the war. They grappled with how to plan for building new facilities, to finding and training the additional personnel to fill those spaces. With millions of Americans joining the fight, it would be a necessity to come up with the means to treat the wounded wherever they fell.

The Surgeon General not only advised the Secretary of War and the Chief of Staff, but also oversaw the entire complex of medical departments: everything from dental care, veterinary care of military animals, and the sanitation of remote surgeries to hospital dieticians, physical therapists, and the pharmacy corps.

Creating this system was a vast undertaking and treating battle-wounded servicemen would be the priority. Millions of soldiers, sailors, and Marines who weren't injured in the fighting were often on their own to deal with tropical diseases and other day-to-day maladies that came up.

*There were a lot of doctors and nurses who did great jobs but not in my area. There was no access to medical help when I was on the LCT—about 13 months nor on the LSM for the balance. I did not see a dentist for 36 months nor a doctor—not too good.*

*There were lots of tropical diseases wherever the GIs went and all one needed to contract the disease was a simple bite from an infected mosquito. I had a friend in Madison who as late as 1948 was still having occasional attacks (the high fever apparently recurred. I can't remember whether it was the male or female mosquito that did the damage). Around Leyte Gulf and Samar there was a lot of elephantiasis. This was caused by an infestation of worms and played hell with a chap's legs and genitals. This made us nervous.*

Dad and Skipper Harnack took care of the men on their little ship to the best of their ability. Flukes, schistosomiasis, elephantiasis, and jungle rot were just a few of the everyday illnesses that threatened the men in the South Pacific. Jungle rot was a fungus that was very common and difficult to cure. Al Exner got a case of it on one of his legs and spent weeks treating it with sulfa powder and sunshine, the only remedies available to him.

Of all the tropical diseases, malaria threatened our forces the most. This mosquito-borne disease crippled Americans in Bataan, leading to the Army's surrender to the Japanese there. The trend continued during battles in Papua, New Guinea and Guadalcanal, where a division commander needing every available man ordered every Marine to continue fighting unless his temperature was over 103 degrees.

Since Japan cut off the supply of quinine (the cure for malaria), the next best thing was Atabrine, a drug that Dad distributed to his men. Atabrine had the unusual side effect of turning the men's skin a bright shade of yellow. Ed Knight recalls the guys in his company lining up to receive their dose, then being ordered to open their mouths to make sure they had swallowed it.

After the war, when Ed succumbed to the disease himself, he suffered 106-degree fevers and chills. Huge doses of Atabrine tablets, thirty-two per day, finally calmed his illness. His entire body must have been bright yellow. He suffered from recurrences of the disease for over a year after his return home to the States.

But while many men took care of themselves, the huge network formed to treat the wounded rolled out across the theaters of war. In the field or on the high seas, medical battalions assigned to infantry or fleet divisions treated and evacuated casualties from within a specific zone of action.

As an Army medic, Ed and others like him followed the soldiers into every battle to provide first aid, taking their orders from the unit's commander. When the troops weren't engaged in battle, Ed acted as the family doctor, giving aspirin for headaches, treating jungle rot, and watching for signs of illness. When in battle, he was on the front line, answering the frantic cries of "medic, medic!" by applying tourniquets, administering morphine, and applying sulfa powder and bandages.

Each medic carried a heavy tool kit; Ed recalled that his

usually contained dozens of sealed cans of plasma, bottles of distilled water to use with dried plasma, rolls of gauze, adhesive tape, ointment, syringes, and anything else that was available and could be useful.

It is unclear if Ed had much access to penicillin, which was not in widespread use when the war began. After Japan attacked Pearl Harbor, it became imperative to find a way to mass-produce the drug in order to save the lives of wounded combat soldiers. The Pfizer company invested millions of dollars to convert a plant and soon produced over five times as much penicillin as originally projected. After successful military tests in spring 1943, this new "wonder drug" began saving countless lives from infections on battlefields and in hospitals around the globe.

No matter what was in (or missing) from their tool kits, Ed and his peers in the mobile medical units were the first to rush in to help wounded soldiers and Marines wherever they fell. An injured man in any theater of war was treated and evacuated in similar fashion—a practical protocol that took him from the point of the original trauma to successive points closer and closer to home.

Ed regularly carried little syrettes or packets of morphine that he pressed and injected right through the clothes of the seriously injured men. It should be noted that medics and doctors used morphine with caution on the battlefield, because once administered, the patient could no longer walk on his own, rendering him unable to assist in his own evacuation.

In addition to the professionals such as doctors, nurses, and dentists, many regular GIs served as medics, stretcher bearers, and ambulance drivers. A lot of people volunteered for these positions because of pacifist or religious beliefs.

Teams of stretcher bearers hand-carried patients out of the action and to the first available transportation—a job made treacherous by the rugged battlefield terrain. Sometimes the litter bearers needed to rest every three to five hundred yards as they picked their way along, raising the odds that the patient might die before reaching further assistance.

Ed described how difficult removing the injured or dead was in remote areas where vehicles couldn't enter. Despite the challenges of the heat and terrain, of heavy packs and loaded rifles, Ed and the others considered it a show of honor to transport the dead back to a jeep.

He told me the story of one liaison officer who was killed by friendly fire on a remote mountain in rugged terrain, several miles from the waiting jeep. Evacuating his body in a steady pouring rain took five hours. Ed recalled, "Dead weight is much more difficult to carry than a live, wounded soldier. It took eight of us to carry this body on a litter over the slippery inclines. You were always aware that the enemy might intercept along the way, and it was a real relief to finally reach the waiting jeep."

Jeeps became a familiar sight in every theater of war because their low center of gravity made traveling easier over almost any surface. A jeep could carry three or four stretchers along with an ambulatory patient. The Ford Motor and Willys-Overland companies produced nearly 700,000 such vehicles during the war. Famous correspondent Ernie Pyle said the jeep was "as faithful as a dog, strong as a mule, and agile as a goat."

*Photo courtesy: National Archives CPU 2 #85*

Air evacuation of casualties took on greater importance as the war progressed. Both the Navy and the Army ramped up facilities and personnel to fly patients with critical needs to hospitals. Those needing neurosurgery, ophthalmology care, and plastic surgery became prime candidates for air evacuation. Those with chest or abdominal wounds could not be flown due to the negative effect of high altitude on those patients.

When flying wasn't an option for the most critical cases requiring major surgery, portable surgical hospitals were set up very close to the front, regularly under enemy fire themselves. The staff in these units had to be ready to move in an instant's notice, and in fact, the whole setup of tents, equipment, and personnel could usually be packed up in two hours' time. The 1970s television show *M*A*S*H* depicted the work of this type of unit during the Korean War.

After surgery, patients would then be moved to an aid

station or mobile hospital (these could also be aboard small landing craft), where they could be treated more fully and stabilized. The Naval mobile hospitals were a vital medical innovation, completely equipped and transportable. This type of facility had room for up to 500 beds and was fully self-contained, set up with water purification, power, laundry, and x-ray and dental labs.

From there, the wounded soldier or sailor was yet again transported farther away from the front lines, either to a clearing station that was more sanitary and better equipped to take on major surgery, or to an evacuation hospital or hospital ship.

At the onset of the war, the Navy had just one hospital ship, the USS *Relief,* held over from WWI. There was an immediate need to care for and evacuate the injured, but disputes between the Army and the Navy over who should build and control them delayed their production and delivery until late in 1943. The hospital ships were Army-controlled but Navy-built, commanded and operated.

The ships' exteriors were painted completely white with a

*Wounded from Guadalcanal strapped into stretchers on a landing boat to be taken to a hospital ship. Photo courtesy: National Archives CPU-2 #62*

huge red cross insignia in the center of the hull. Hospital ships sailed under the rules of the Geneva Convention that stated that soldiers no longer participating in the fight (the wounded) should be protected. Under this blanket of security, thousands of seriously injured soldiers and sailors made their safe return to the United States to convalesce.

Hospital ships were invaluable—they not only took on the injured in the fleet, but they filled the role of floating warehouses carrying vital supplies such as plasma, medicine, bandages, and whole blood. They also stood in as doctors' offices for the everyday medical and dental needs of the Navy personnel serving nearby. The Navy drafted many doctors to serve on board ships and many had officer status—sometimes all the way up to captain. Their experience and age factored into their rank.

While Al Exner was busy saving lives on the USS *Lubbock* during the invasion of Iwo Jima in February 1945, his high school friend Art Johnson served on the USS *Bountiful*, one of two hospital ships assigned to the area. After the battle, Johnson told him that the Japanese disregarded the Geneva Convention and fired a torpedo toward the ship. The crewmembers saw the wake of the rapidly approaching torpedo and in alarm sped up, turning just in time to avoid being struck. The USS *Bountiful* wasn't stopped that day and earned four battle stars during the war.

From Australia to Japan, the Philippines to Burma, from New Guinea to Hawaii and all across the Asia/Pacific theater, the complex system of field, mobile, Naval base, and general hospitals, along with naval transport and hospital ships, got our wounded men out of the jungles and on their way home.

USS Bountiful *in 1944 or 1945.*
*Photo courtesy: Naval History and Heritage Command #103572*

It wasn't always just our troops either. The United States' medical personnel provided the same care to prisoners of war (POWs) as to the Americans. Al Exner and the other personnel at Netley Hospital in England gave no preference to wounded Americans to be cared for over the German POWs being treated there.

Dad described his own run-in with a German POW in his journal: *When we arrived at Long Beach, California, I developed a terrible toothache and was able—with difficulty—to get an appointment for a probable tooth extraction. Young Navy dentists weren't in the business of preserving one's teeth—too much work. While I was laid out in the chair, I heard a lot of strongly accented German-English. It was one of our POW's literally demanding treatment. He got it—Americans are really suckers. The Germans*

*and Japanese treated their prisoners of war worse than animals—*
*we treated ours like human beings. In fact, a lot of them migrated*
*here after the war—former POWs that is.*

Back in America, Naval convalescent hospitals popped
up to take care of sailors and Marines who no longer needed
hospital care, but simply needed more time to rest, good
food, and physical therapy before returning home. Many were
located in former luxury resorts and hotels. In Atlantic City,
Chalfonte-Haddon Hall Hotel became the Thomas England
General Hospital. Wounded servicemembers returned home for
treatment there, eventually making it the largest soldier hospital
in the United States.

Out in California, the Navy sought a place for wounded
sailors to heal and soon leased the Santa Cruz resort hotel Casa
Del Rey. By spring of 1943, the hotel started to receive the
injured men and by the time it closed in 1946, 18,000 men
convalesced there, riding horses, playing golf, and using the
indoor plunge pool for therapy.

In Yosemite National Park, the Navy leased the spectacular
and tranquil Ahwahnee Hotel for use as a healing place for men
to rehabilitate before reentering civilian life. However, it soon
became clear that the crushing isolation and boredom had an
adverse effect on those trying to recover from shellshock and
trauma. Because of this, morale among the staff and patients
grew so low that a new commander was brought in to make
drastic changes. Captain Reynolds Hayden, formally head of
the Navy hospital at Pearl Harbor, spearheaded a program that
added a library, bowling alley, pool hall, basketball and tennis

courts, a store with a soda fountain, and craft and woodworking shops. Yosemite Special Hospital, as it was called, became the only Naval hospital that the Secretary of the Navy granted permission to sell beer!

While the medical department put together a practical plan to take care of the sick and wounded, chaos and unpredictability in the system often still reigned. For example, the lack of hospitals or inadequate medical facilities close to the battlefields sometimes prevented soldiers from getting the care they needed. Inventories of medical supplies were often limited, and sometimes in the confusion of moving to a combat area, essential items were left behind. Unmarked containers forced medical personnel to claw through them looking for what they needed, leaving behind a trail of hopelessly mingled supplies.

On the water, limited or inaccurate communication between the ships caused mayhem in the system of evacuating the injured. What should have been a coordinated effort to divide casualties among waiting vessels became an imbalanced flow of patients, overcrowding some ships while others were left partially unused. Sometimes the landing craft simply delivered the wounded automatically to the nearest ship, regardless of whether it was flying the flag indicating it could take on patients at that moment.

Even with all these difficulties, scores of doctors and nurses selflessly offered their expertise and dedication to the war effort, often forgoing lucrative salaries and the safety of back home. Young medics fearlessly followed the troops into battle, determined to help their fallen brothers. Folks like Dad did their best to keep those under their supervision as healthy as possible. In the end, the Medical Department of the Army and Navy achieved remarkable success making sure as many soldiers and sailors as possible made it back home.

*Photo courtesy: National Archives 80-G-181842*

# AFRICAN AMERICANS FIGHT TWO WARS

One of the greatest ironies of World War II was that the Americans joined in a fight to stop Hitler, the most racist man in the world, using a completely segregated military force. In the 1930s and into the 1940s, black and white citizens were used to living in a separated America fully supported by the government across all aspects of society. The divide between black and white Americans became crystal clear during the war, and it forced our government and its people to consider that African Americans deserved equal treatment, both at home and while serving.

Growing up in Madison, Wisconsin, and Freeport, Illinois, my dad did not likely encounter many African Americans during his youth. It's also likely that he didn't understand much about segregation or racism. His journal is speckled with thoughts about coming face-to-face with the reality of how black Americans were treated during the war.

It's important to go back to fully understand the critical role African Americans played in winning the war, both on the home front and around the globe.

In December 1941, just before the U.S. entered WWII, America's defense industry companies were already fielding lucrative contracts to build equipment and arms for sale to

England, as well as for beefing up security at home. The expected growth in these businesses demanded tens of thousands of new employees to produce the goods, yet companies routinely denied black Americans these jobs.

In 1941, civil rights trailblazer A. Philip Randolph joined with other prominent African American leaders in planning a march on Washington to insist on desegregation of the defense industry. As the July march approached, close to 100,000 African Americans stood ready to participate. Sensing the public relations nightmare of a huge black American protest, First Lady Eleanor Roosevelt, and later the President himself, pleaded with Randolph to call off the march, to no avail.

Just one week before the march was to take place, Roosevelt signed Executive Order 8802, banning employment discrimination in both defense industries and government, and set up a temporary committee to ensure that manufacturers hired without prejudice. Many believe that with this one victory, African Americans sowed the seeds of the civil rights protests of the 1950s and '60s.

After Japan attacked Pearl Harbor and the U.S. entered the war, over 2.5 million African American men registered for the draft. The draft boards consisted mostly of all white members, and they often passed over African Americans, choosing the white draftees instead. The National Association for the Advancement of Colored People (NAACP) finally pressured FDR to require that African American enlistments should equal the percentage of black Americans in the population, at the time over ten percent. While this goal was never fully realized, the number of black Americans in the armed forces did begin to grow significantly during the war years.

Most African Americans who served early in the war years worked behind the scenes in support roles, segregated from the fighting forces. The bulk of them ended up in the Army, where they worked in non-combat units fulfilling needs for maintenance, supply, and grave digging.

Dad weighed in from his viewpoint: *Black men in the Navy could only act as stewards—serving food to the officers, cleaning, making up bunks etc. Generally, the only black men we encountered were assigned to unloading cargo onto our ship.*

The Navy was particularly slow to follow FDR's order, until forced to start recruiting African Americans in April 1942. That June, the first black American recruits arrived at Great Lakes Naval Training Center in Illinois, the site the Navy selected to train African American sailors. For a time, the facility remained segregated so thoroughly that it even had its own African American blood supply. While thousands of recruits went

through boot camp at Great Lakes, separating the races created African American classes that were well under-strength, some with only four or five students. By 1944, classes slowly were integrated and by mid-1945, all classes were successfully mixed.

*Photo courtesy: National Archives 80-G-469560*

Even though the Navy tried to comply with FDR's order to enlist ten percent African Americans, black American sailors never made up more than five percent of the entire naval force during the war.

The trickle of African American men entering the Navy eventually grew strong enough to worry commanders about the lack of black American officers to lead these new sailors. In early 1944, the first group of sixteen officer candidates, culled from the Navy ranks, went through the same intensive training as Dad had to become ensigns. Every single man passed the course, but only thirteen received commissions. Those rejected were never told why. Some believe that the Navy, accustomed to a normal rate of failure for officer candidates, didn't want it to appear as if the African American men had performed better than the white men.

The Golden Thirteen, as the thirteen new officers became known, worked on ships crewed by mostly African American sailors or trained other black American recruits in keeping with the Navy's segregated system of the time.

*There was one rare time when a young black arms lieutenant was in charge of an unloading party of white men. We actually thought there was going to be a mutiny. The air was blue with epithets hurled at the black lieutenant. That was pretty much how Tom Brokaw's "greatest generation" treated the black man. Years later, while working as a CPA [I had] a client Pierce Bitker [who] pointed out that life as a young Jewish lieutenant wasn't that comfortable either—Pierce was Army, I believe.*

*The Golden Thirteen (one officer is missing from the photo)*
*Photo courtesy: National Archives 80-G-300215*

As the war raged on and the number of troop deaths mounted, the Army was forced to put more African Americans into fighting positions. It's a little-known fact that almost 2,000 black soldiers hit the beach at Normandy with the 320th Barrage Balloon Battalion, whose job was to set up explosive-rigged balloons to deter German planes and protect the troops from aerial attack. Waverly Woodson Jr. was a corporal and medic with the battalion and years later told the Associated Press about his landing craft that hit a land mine on the way into Omaha Beach. He said, "The tide brought us in, and that's when the 88s [German 88mm guns] hit us. They were murder. Of our twenty-six Navy personnel there was only one left. They raked the whole top of the ship and killed all the crew. Then they started with the mortar shells." Woodson, though wounded himself, spent the next thirty hours on the beach tending to other fallen soldiers.

African Americans also fought valiantly in the Battle of the Bulge after General Eisenhower, desperately needing troop replacements, allowed them to take up arms and fight in combat. African American drivers steered most of the thousands of trucks in the "Red Ball Express" company that supplied Patton's army with much-needed gasoline and supplies. The road to the front stretched up to 400 miles from Normandy at times, and brave soldiers like Howard Gray made hundreds of runs back and forth.

In 1998, students at Washington High School in Washington Court House, Ohio, interviewed Gray and other African American WWII veterans and later shared their interviews with History.com. They found out that Gray, a sergeant in the company, was ordered to Bastogne to get the remaining troops out. Leading a convoy of twelve trucks, he stood as they were loaded one at a time. He later recalled, "I had to stick to [the watch] or I would be killed. Honest to truth. I had to stay there, and I did by the grace of God. I stayed there until my last truck came out, and I boarded that truck. That was Bastogne . . . And we brought 'em out of there. What . . . what was left."

The Army Air Force all-black 99th Fighter Squadron, known as the heroic Tuskegee Airmen, flew over 15,000 missions in Italy, receiving many citations and awards. But when member Lowell

Steward, a hero who had earned the Distinguished Flying Cross, returned to Los Angeles after the war, he was repeatedly denied bank loans to purchase a house simply because he was black.

Even well-known African Americans were treated unfairly. Jackie Robinson, who became the first African American to play in Major League Baseball, served in the Army during the war. College-educated and an excellent marksman, he was denied entry into officer training until Heavyweight Champion Joe Louis complained to the Department of War. Robinson finished the training and became a second lieutenant in the cavalry. Later transferred to a heavily racist Army post in Texas, his frustration built until he refused to sit in the back of the post bus, just as Rosa Parks would do eleven years in the future.

Unfortunately, this is the way it was. The African American men and women supporting the war effort lived, trained, and ate separately from their white peers. Many recounted experiences of being mistreated or jeered at by their fellow Americans. Many leaders in the armed forces thought that white soldiers, particularly those from Southern states, would resist any form of racial integration.

My father lived a somewhat sheltered life in the cities where he grew up, so he had little experience with overt racism. The war opened him up to some realities he had never before considered. *I spent some of the Mardi Gras holiday in 1946 in New Orleans and even in its diminished form—due to wartime shortages—it was quite a spectacle. I encountered firsthand real racism in New Orleans. I always walk to the back when I board a bus—which I did. There was an uncomfortable pause and then the bus driver announced to me, "I will not move the bus until you step to the front of the bus." Like a sheep, I did.*

*Later, during the drunken orgy at the Mardi Gras parade, I was surprised to see black folks served liquor but only out the alley doors of the bars. I never knew any black people in Freeport or Madison. I didn't know that only blacks sat in the back of the bus. The drinking fountains labeled 'white only' and then 'colored only' were another revelation.*

The National WWII Museum posted online an interview with former Mississippi Governor and Army veteran William Winter, whose experiences with segregation while serving in the Army changed his whole perspective on race. This excerpt sheds some important light on the norms of the time:

> The army was as segregated as Mississippi was. I was assigned as a white officer. All white . . . all black enlisted men, all white officers. And so I found myself at Fort McClellan in October of 1944 training black troops for infantry service. The white officers, however, were soon integrated in an experiment by the army . . . with the addition of a great many black officers. And so I found, for the first time, myself living, working in close, in very close relationships with black people. I had grown up with black youngsters, but I had never worked, uh . . . in an integrated, socially equal situation. And, so, that was an educational experience for me, a very productive one. One that . . . caused me again to reassess the system of segregation that I had grown up in and

to realize the unfairness of it, and to realize that we were, we were limiting ourselves as a people when we did not embrace fully the concept of equal rights and equal opportunities for people, regardless of race.

So I developed some very warm relationships there with these newfound friends who were black. On the post, things were integrated. One thing, however, that caught my eye early on, and that was on weekends, when we would get a pass to go into Anniston, Alabama. We would get on a bus, a civilian bus, and the black officers, my black officer friends, would have to go to the back of the bus. And then, of course, when we got into Anniston, we couldn't have a hamburger together, we couldn't go to a movie together, couldn't even go to church together, and it was hammered into my head at that time how grossly unfair our system of segregation was. And I became convinced at that point, that as soon as the war was over we were going to see some changes in the way we lived in the South.

Mr. Winter's experience seems much like my father's in that if not for WWII and leaving home, the two of them might not have witnessed firsthand the inequalities between black and white Americans. Like Mr. Winter, Dad saw the unfairness of it, and for the remainder of his life, impressed upon all his children that all people should be treated the same, with respect and dignity.

Perhaps this reality in the 1940s would have to change as one white person at a time became more enlightened. Maybe the powers that be in the military were reluctant to take on this second "battle" in the midst of trying to win the war. But it didn't stop African Americans from beginning to stand up for themselves back home.

It all started with a letter to the most popular African American newspaper in the states, the *Pittsburgh Courier*. In January 1942, James G. Thompson wrote, "Should I sacrifice my life to live half American? Is the kind of America I know worth defending?" In his letter, Thompson proposed that black Americans should fight for a double V victory—to beat oppressors both here and abroad. The editors of the *Courier* got behind Thompson's idea and encouraged African Americans to get behind the war effort while also urging them to stand up for equal rights and treatment—liberties granted to every other American.

The paper quickly released an official Double V insignia and passionately declared, "In our fight for freedom we wage a two-pronged attack against our enslavers at home and those abroad who would enslave us. WE HAVE A STAKE IN THIS FIGHT . . . WE ARE AMERICANS TOO!"

Pittsburgh Courier
*archives*

The paper ran the Double V Campaign weekly, gave American flags to new subscribers, and encouraged people to buy war bonds. The campaign soon wove its way into popular culture, as photos of "Double V girls" and actresses (Lana Turner was one) cropped up in magazines and postcards. There were even Double V hats, dresses, and pins. More importantly, the *Courier* published numerous photos of whites standing with blacks as they flashed the Double V sign, driving home the notion that to win the war, Americans must unite. Although the campaign was wildly popular, the federal government still monitored the African American press to make sure no efforts for civil rights superseded the main goal of winning the war.

With one "V" taken care of after the Allies won the war, a Single V took over—there was still work to be done for African Americans to gain equality. They had done their part serving in the military and working in defense industries back home. The campaign had given voice to people who desired the end of discrimination in this country. Now their efforts could be geared toward making a case to end segregation in this country.

Almost a million African Americans served here and abroad in uniform, and thousands of women served in the women's auxiliaries. In the States, the wave of the Great Migration of African Americans leaving the South crested during the war as folks relocated to pursue the burgeoning job opportunities in the defense industry. Almost half a million people relocated to the West where shipbuilding and aircraft manufacturing facilities dotted the coastline from Washington to California.

For many African American men and women, holding a skilled job changed their lives forever after.

It wasn't all smooth sailing, however. Even though African Americans worked in the factories side by side with whites, it was still impossible to avoid anti-black slurs and segregated housing. Word trickled (inaccurately) to my father about one major event that took place back home.

*There was a mutiny in 1944 in [Port] Chicago when a group of black cargo unloaders refused to unload cargo. There had been a major explosion a few days earlier in which some of the crew were killed. The mutineers were tried and given dishonorable discharges. We discussed this mutiny vigorously on our ship. We finally agreed that although the* [black] *men were ill prepared for their assignment, they should have followed orders. We being me, Jim Harnack, and the entire crew. The enlisted men on our ship were very emphatic. They stated in their letters "they should hang the yellow bellied 'cocksuckers.'" I'm sorry about the language but that's what they wrote.*

*Almost all of us did the best we could. We would never have demanded that the Army stop unloading shells, bombs, bullets, etc. even though their constant thumping on our steel deck was most annoying. The great majority of the cargo unloaders we encountered were white men, not black—*[the white men were] *not the best-trained men we dealt with. In fact, it was obvious that this was just plain grunt work. I believe they endured it because it was a lot better than the other option—getting killed in regular action and because they chose to follow orders.*

*As far as I can see free choice is not one of the options you have in a war unless, of course, you are a member of the very powerful elite group that runs things. That's just the way it was.*

The reality was that the explosion at Port Chicago, California, was the largest home front disaster of the war, resulting in fifteen percent of all African American deaths attributed to WWII. The base had been built quickly at Port Chicago to meet the tremendous demand for munitions, the location chosen due to its proximity to San Francisco where many ships embarked for the South Pacific. On the night of July 1, 1944, two ships were at Port Chicago, ready to be loaded with high explosives, depth charges, and ammunition. Several thousand tons of ammunition were to fill their holds, with another 429 tons held on nearby railcars on the pier.

The base officers, all white, and the enlisted men, all black, received minimum training in cargo handling—though certainly not enough to safely manage dangerous materials. Adding to the lack of experience was the pressure to stow as much cargo onto the ships as possible in every eight-hour shift. According to Evan Andrew's article "Port Chicago Disaster Stuns the Nation, 70 Years Ago," sailor Joseph Small recalled, "The officers used to pit one division against the other. I often heard them argue over what division was beating the others."

Safety standards grew lax and morale declined as officers encouraged competition between the cargo gangs to load more than the previous shift.

Civilian longshoremen officials weighed in after witnessing the careless handling of explosives by Navy Pier workers. They saw that the men who operated the winches that lifted the cargo had little or no training. The longshoremen union offered to send in experienced handlers to provide training to the young sailors, but the Navy declined.

This powder keg of munitions and low morale erupted in disaster at 10:18 p.m., as a series of explosions sent a tremendous pillar of fire and smoke into the air above the base. All 320 men on the ships and working on the dock that night were killed instantly, and both ships and every structure around the pier completely disintegrated. African American workers accounted for nearly two-thirds of the dead.

The blast was felt as far away as Boulder City, Nevada— hundreds of miles away. Falling debris injured nearly 400 more, including those living in the enlisted men's barracks a mile away from the blast site.

Naval leadership set about on a course to get the base, critical for supplying forces in the South Pacific, up and running again as quickly as possible. Some of the Port Chicago survivors who weren't working that evening were assigned the traumatic and grisly task of cleaning up the disaster site. Cleaning up was one thing, but going back to loading munitions without any changes to safety protocols was another. The survivors and other replacements refused to load munitions, saying they would follow any order but that one.

The Navy court-martialed several hundred men, holding them in a nearby barge. Admiral Carleton H. Wright warned them that refusing to work was mutiny, a crime punishable by death. Of these men, all but fifty decided that returning to the dock was preferable to facing a firing squad. Those holdouts, the Port Chicago 50 as they became known, were charged with mutiny.

The NAACP and others took note of the trial that seemed plagued with racial overtones. Future Supreme Court Justice Thurgood Marshall sat in on the last few days of the six-week hearings, and according to Evan Andrew's article, said, "This is not 50 men on trial for mutiny. This is the Navy on trial for its whole vicious policy toward negroes."

Despite the protests of Marshall and others, most of the Chicago 50 received sentences between eight and fifteen years of hard labor. After the war, following a flood of letters from concerned citizens, including Eleanor Roosevelt, the Navy gave the fifty mutineers clemency, but the entire episode showed the profound cost of racial discrimination.

Would the result for the men have been different if the crews had been white? The trial brought the plight of black members of the military to the public's notice—the Navy finally recognized that mostly African American sailors performed the dangerous work of loading munitions. The NAACP investigators found that these sailors saw themselves as "little more than expendable laborers working under egregious conditions."

Following the disaster at Port Chicago, the Navy slowly began making changes to procedures and training that resulted in safer handling of dangerous materials. They also reexamined segregation in their ranks and began integrating units by 1945, three years before Truman would demand desegregation in the military.

Half a world away, Dad and his shipmates clearly heard a

skewed version of the truth that *"several* of the crew were killed," when the tragic event at Port Chicago actually caused the single largest loss of African American lives during the war. Was the unvarnished truth kept from *LCT-977* and others in the Navy on purpose? It seems that even after he returned to the mainland, Dad never heard all the true details of this tragedy.

Dad's comments show he believed the loss of free choice during wartime was more to blame for the results of the Chicago Mutiny than race —that it had nothing to do with the color of the men's skin. Having been indoctrinated with Navy protocols and rules, I believe Dad viewed following orders during wartime to be more important than anything else.

While Dad might not have seen much racism while the war raged on, after it was over he saw firsthand proof that it was still prevalent in the South. After the war ended, Dad was reassigned to a larger ship that brought troops home from the South Pacific. At the end of the last trip, a problem arose. *We sailed to Lake Charles, Louisiana, for the final decommissioning of the ship. By this time, I was in command and two months into my tenure as commander, our young black steward was charged with stealing a white woman's purse. In Lake Charles that made him guilty (just the accusation of it, that is). Fortunately for the young man he was remanded to our ship for trial. A guilty verdict would have meant a dishonorable discharge, but one of the three officers I selected as jury refused to agree that he was guilty. At least our steward got a decent discharge. The young lad served his time in the Navy to help "save the world" but the southern whites didn't need him—nor the Northerners for that matter.*

What Dad is trying to say here is that even though this young man served, it still wasn't enough to stop the racists back home in the States from treating him as a second-class citizen, or to change the reality of a still-segregated America.

Before the Japanese attacked Pearl Harbor, there were fewer than 4,000 African Americans in our military. Afterward, over two million vowed to participate by registering for the draft. By the end of the war, over 900,000 black Americans proudly served in the military, becoming part of the great "Arsenal of Democracy" that won the war.

Many returned stateside to find continued segregation and discrimination and discovered that the single V victory for equal treatment remained an elusive thing.

# SECTION FOUR: WAR'S END

As the war in Europe drew to a close, the Allies began to set their sights in earnest on ending the war with Japan. Trying to stave off a full invasion of Japan, the Allies spent the spring and summer of 1945 hammering Japanese cities with bombs from the air and from ships. An estimated 100,000 tons of explosives were used on this ultimately unsuccessful goal.

"Operation Downfall," planned to commence in November 1945, was the military name for the plan then devised for the potential invasion of Japan. The huge operation was to take place in two phases and would include the entire U.S. Navy in the Pacific, several Air Force divisions, the entire Marine Corps, and millions of combat soldiers.

Fresh in the minds of the American military commanders tasked with planning the operation was the April 1945 Battle of Okinawa. It was there that the Japanese revealed their stubbornness, savagery, and willingness to lose over 100,000 of their own men. The bloodiest battle in the Pacific, the Japanese either injured or killed almost 50,000 Americans, painting a grim portrait of how much worse an invasion of the Japanese mainland might be. Personnel at the Department of the Navy estimated total American losses of anywhere up to 800,000 men—it would be the deadliest battle of the war.

In the first phase, "Operation Olympic," Marines would land (with air and sea support) at Kyushu, the heavily defended southernmost Japanese island. The goal was to secure Kyushu and its airfield to use as the Allies' platform for the second phase, "Operation Coronet." This phase, much larger than the first, would attempt to assault the main Japanese island Honshu in an effort to finally obtain the unconditional surrender of Japan.

War diaries show that roughly 1,000 LCTs were in the Pacific in August 1945, including those in California and Pearl Harbor. The plan was to send most, if not all, of the LCTs already in the Pacific theater (including Dad's *LCT-977*) toward Japan as part of Operation Downfall to attempt to wrest surrender from the last remaining Axis foe.

The LCTs' role in Operation Downfall would be to follow the initial invasion waves to the beach, delivering the tanks, vehicles, and heavy equipment needed to establish the beachhead (like at Normandy). They would supply ammo, fuel, additional supplies, food, and potentially additional personnel. The LCTs' main task would be to resupply the troops heading inland in the days and weeks following the initial invasion. Anchoring at the water's edge, they would have become easy targets on the beaches of Japan just as they had been in New Guinea and the Philippines.

The veterans I interviewed recalled dreading an eventual move toward mainland Japan because they had already witnessed firsthand the ferocity and tenacity of the enemy. They knew the Japanese were willing to do almost anything to avoid defeat, especially after seeing the kamikaze attacks become commonplace in the summer of 1945. Dad knew his LCT would be headed that way soon, but as luck would have it, early that summer he was granted a leave to travel home to marry my mother.

In the midst of the planning for Operation Downfall, on July 26, 1945, the Allied leaders issued the Potsdam Declaration, offering the Japanese the chance to surrender. There were thirteen points in the declaration, eight of which were the conditions required for surrender. The main thrust of the document was that everyone responsible for planning and carrying out Japan's goal of world conquest in WWII would be replaced by a new order stressing peace and justice for all. The hope was that democracy would be revived, with free speech, religion, and respect for life prevailing.

Allied leaders warned the Japanese that if they turned down this offer, their military and homeland would face *"prompt and utter destruction."* Japan refused the offer.

Harry S. Truman, perhaps haunted by Operation Downfall casualty estimates, decided instead to drop the first of two atomic bombs on Japan on August 6, 1945, devastating the population of Hiroshima. Several days later, the second bomb fell on Nagasaki.

The next day, the Japanese government formally accepted the terms of the Potsdam Declaration. In the afternoon of August 15 (August 14 in the United States) the Japanese people heard a recorded radio broadcast from Emperor Hirohito, whose voice many of them had never heard before, urging them to accept the surrender. Hirohito declared, "Should we continue to fight, it would not only result in the ultimate collapse and obliteration of the Japanese nation but would also lead to the total extinction of human civilization."

That same day, President Truman announced Japan's surrender in a press conference from the White House. After years of conflict, Americans excitedly declared August 14 to be VJ-Day or Victory over Japan Day. Operation Downfall was not to be, to the relief of millions of servicemen.

Soon after, the huge task of bringing our men back home began.

## A V-J DAY LIKE NO OTHER
### Chaos in San Francisco

Dad came a long way since that summer day three years before when he headed to the Chicago Naval recruitment center to enlist. From his training at Notre Dame and Columbia universities to his duty serving on his LCT mainly in New Guinea and the Philippines, he was gone from home a long time. But where was he on that August day in 1945 when the Japanese surrendered and the war finally came to an end?

He was in San Francisco, making his way home for the leave he received. A major port for disembarking to the South Pacific, San Francisco funneled about 1.6 million personnel through it during the course of the war. The military population at the area's many Naval, Air Force, and other military bases soared in the months before the war's end once the war in Europe drew to a close and efforts ramped up against Japan. In mid-August, the city was brimming with young men poised to leave for the Pacific theater.

While most American cities erupted in joy at the news that the long and bloody war was finally over, the celebration in San Francisco began peacefully but ended with eleven deaths and over 1,000 people injured. Dad witnessed the chaos for himself and yet made just one brief entry in his journal regarding the spectacle: *I was in San Francisco when peace finally struck (8/15/45 I believe—I had spent 18 months in the South Pacific). We had at last caught the attention of the "Japs" as we still called them.*

In San Francisco, as the official news of Japan's surrender spread, thousands of workers spilled out of office buildings downtown. The sounds of factory whistles, car horns, and church bells filled the air as shredded paper rained down on the revelers below. Throngs of people converged on Market Street with everyone kissing, laughing, and radiating joy and relief that the war was over.

The original V-J celebration lasted until the wee hours of Wednesday, August 15, and resumed later that afternoon. This time around, fueled by alcohol, many of the revelers began to riot—smashing windows, looting businesses, starting fires. Thousands of unsupervised, drunken military personnel and civilians wreaked havoc on the city's downtown. Market Street, lined with bars, was now littered with smashed bottles and trashed war bond machines.

*There were riots in San Francisco and it became very dangerous to be out on the streets especially if you were a military officer. There was a lot of animosity from the enlisted men toward the "brass," so we weren't just "one big happy family."*

The mob disabled thirty of San Francisco's municipal streetcars, and tragically, one of the workers was killed. All automobile and bus traffic in the downtown area came to a halt.

Many of the rioters were young male civilians. Former Deputy Police Chief Kevin J. Mullen said, "If you pull all restraints off and add liquor, that's what happens. These were not veterans; they were young people who hadn't been in the war. They hadn't seen the war, and now they didn't have to. There would be no invasion of Japan, no long casualty lists. These young men would not see combat. So they got drunk."

The majority of these young men were most likely waiting for their draft number to come up. Others might have already enlisted and were awaiting their orders to ship out. What a relief it must have been for them to realize that their futures would not include fighting in the war.

One witness reported a naked redhead dancing at the base of the Native Sons' Monument after servicemen tore off her clothes. Other eyewitnesses reported numerous rapes and even some gang rapes, but none were reported to the authorities. This was human nature at its worst.

Eleven people were killed during the melee. One tragic incident involved Stella and John Morris, a Navy seaman, who had waited for the war's end before marrying. Within hours after their wedding at 4:30 p.m. August 15, a drunk driver struck them as they crossed the street, killing Stella and badly injuring John. The driver was never found.

According to the September 7, 1945, issue of *Yank*, the Army weekly magazine, Marine Private First Class James Prim, thirty-four, who had survived unimaginable campaigns in the South Pacific, fell down a set of stairs in the early hours of August 15 and died of a skull fracture.

The San Francisco police were completely unprepared for the events that unfolded. *The Chronicle* reported that the Army military police, the Navy shore patrol, and the San Francisco police had initially received official orders to "let the people do anything within reason, and keep property damage down."

But the situation quickly spiraled out of control. Finally, late in the evening on August 15, thousands of police officers, both civilian and military, began to bring order to the chaos. The San Francisco Police Department called in all local and military police reserves to assist, and the armed services ordered all military personnel back to their ships or bases. *After several nights of drunken celebrations and brawling, the Army and the Navy grounded all enlisted men to their bases or ships and life went on.* If Dad was out on the street, I'm sure he was relieved to hear these orders, although I will never know.

Criticism rained down on the San Francisco Police Department for being unprepared to control the events as they escalated. District Attorney Edmund Brown announced a grand jury inquiry to determine who was responsible for the debacle, but nothing ever came of it. No one filed charges for any of the murders, rapes, or riotous acts of property destruction.

In fact, everyone seemed to move on and forgot the riot. Within a month, General Jonathan Wainwright (a war hero and POW who had been held by the Japanese) led a huge parade on Market Street. Estimates are that about half a million people attended the parade, without incident.

By the time of the parade, Dad was back home and a newlywed, ready to shake off the experiences of the previous years, including the events of his unfortunate stopover in San Francisco.

# THE GI BILL – Our Men Come Home

At the close of WWI, servicemen received sixty bucks and a train ticket home—barely a pat on the back for their bravery and sacrifice. Now it was time for the United States government to determine what would become of the millions of soldiers and sailors returning home from this second world war.

Following the first Great War (now known as WWI), grateful Congress members believed that those who helped win the war deserved some compensation to make up for their lost income. In 1924, over Coolidge's veto, Congress approved a bonus for WWI veterans that was set up like a bond—veterans could use it as collateral for loans, but they couldn't cash it until it matured in 1945.

But before long, scores of veterans were out of work, broke, and hungry because of the Great Depression. The men needed the money now, not in 1945. Tens of thousands, many joined by their families, headed to Washington, D.C. to demand their bonuses. They settled into makeshift shantytowns for months before the Army violently chased them out and burned their ramshackle houses and tents to the ground

In 1944, with this disastrous episode barely in the rearview mirror, congressmen eyed their options for taking care of the coming crop of returning soldiers. They had a chance to both redeem themselves and stave off the potential economic crisis caused by millions of men returning without jobs waiting for them. Dad had an opinion about the congressional idea that came to fruition: *I always looked at the G.I. Bill as a masterful stroke—not only to prevent a massive employment glut but to reward those who chose to finish their schooling. There were also benefits available other than college training in the trades and other technical fields.*

President Roosevelt signed the Servicemen's Readjustment Act of 1944—commonly called the GI Bill of Rights—into law on June 22, 1944. It was broken down into four main components:

- Allowance while unemployed, also known as the 52-20 club
- Tuition & living expenses to pursue college or to complete high school
- Vocational/on-the-job training
- Loans to buy a home, business, or farm (commonly called VA Loans)

The GI Bill almost never made it to the President's desk, mostly because of the first provision for unemployment pay. The proposed bill provided twenty dollars per week for up to fifty-two weeks while the veteran looked for work—a "readjustment allowance." Some called it a form of welfare or saw it as a disincentive to working. House members and senators disagreed over the provision and were deadlocked as the committee prepared to vote on June 10.

A congressional committee, led by known racist Representative John Rankin of Mississippi, took on the task of hammering out the differences. Rankin opposed the unemployment insurance because African American veterans would receive the same compensation as whites. He believed that the majority of the 50,000 black American veterans from his state would remain unemployed for the entire year.

As chair of the congressional committee, Rankin refused to cast the absentee vote he held for one of the other members— Rep. John Gibson of Douglas, Georgia. Gibson had returned home several weeks before the official vote to recuperate from an illness and was unaware that Rankin intended to withhold his vote. Attempts to reach him by telephone failed, so members of Georgia's American Legion led a statewide effort to locate him and get him to Washington in time for the vote. A police motorcycle escort rushed him through a downpour on a harrowing 90 mph ride to the Jacksonville, Florida, airport where an Eastern Air Lines plane was waiting. Off he went to Washington just in time for the vote. During the plane ride, his anger grew, and he strode into the committee chamber at 10 a.m. to cast the tying vote, saying, "Americans are dying today in Normandy in the greatest invasion in all history [D-Day being just four days earlier]. I'm going to hold a press conference after this meeting and castigate anyone who dares to vote against this bill!"

During WWII, millions of men spent their formative adult years under the constant fear of the unknown or in brutal combat, yet if they appeared able-bodied upon their return, they were expected to easily resume their old lives. Post-traumatic stress disorder would not be recognized until many years later, yet it was under this undefined cloud that WWII veterans came home to experience the stress and difficulty of reacclimating to civilian life. Even though the 52-20 could be construed as a form of welfare, it offered a "leg up" and some empathy to veterans returning home and transitioning back into civilian life.

Dad finally made it home at the start of summer of 1946, with plans to complete his last two years of college beginning that fall. *Needless to say, I came home very quietly in June of 1946 and spent a nice summer on the dole. Mom worked while I was a member of the 52-20 club which gave each veteran $20 tax free a week for 52 weeks as long as they were unemployed or not under the G.I. Bill in college. As a returning veteran, I was entitled to my summer job at Burgess Battery Company. They had been paying me $18 a week, which less Social Security netted me $17.82 for 40 hours of work. I had three months to kill before going back to college in September, Mom worked and our little furnished apartment was less than $75 a month. I received terminal leave pay of $900 and an Illinois veteran's bonus of $800. Other than a halfwit, who would have gone back to work for $17.82 a week? My only regret— too late now—was that Mom continued to work. She was always so loyal and honest that she felt she owed the Company for having hired her in late 1945.* In the 1940s, twenty dollars per week was a lot of money. Minimum wage at the time was thirty cents an hour. For context, people could buy both a loaf of bread and a gallon of gasoline for twenty-five cents.

Between 1944 and 1949, just over half of the sixteen million eligible veterans took advantage of the twenty dollars, and like

Dad, most of them did so for just three or four months. In the end, the government distributed less than twenty percent of the funds originally estimated for the program.

*The* [GI] *bill enabled hundreds of thousands of young veterans to get a full college education (or training with trades) on the government and, of course, paid for by the taxpayers. I'd say this was a small price to pay for the folks, who to quote Tom Brokaw, "saved the world." I kind of considered it back pay for them* [the veterans] *having worked their butts off for 3-5 years, at slave labor pay, eating food that, to put it bluntly, was crap, and with generally speaking, terrible medical care. I always felt that most of the enlisted men deserved a lot more credit than they got for their forced labor.*

*Officers, in general, were treated fairly. By the time I mustered out as a Lieutenant Jr grade, I was earning about $275 a month plus food, clothing, and quarters. That was not a bad salary in 1945 for a young man. In 1943, for example, a bright young college graduate with a degree in accounting could expect an annual starting salary of $980 - $1140. There was no overtime pay for these salaried folks. They were, after all, "white collar" workers.*

Dad was an accountant for his entire career and included a passage from his journal under the title *"How I made the Big Bucks in the Navy."* It's important to have some context in order to understand what the GI Bill offered. In this section of his journal, Dad divided his salary for 1945 by the number of hours he worked to discover he made just $1 per hour while he served—or even less. *Actually the $1 per hour figure . . . is wrong. Essentially, we were on duty 24 hours a day come rain or shine—no time and a half for overtime or double time for Saturday* *and Sunday. On 5/11/07 I'm still beefing about the $6.60 for life insurance. By the way, I was supposed to file an income tax return for 1945—I never did get around to that.*

Scores of veterans took advantage of the GI Bill to get an education. Eventually, over two million went to college, many the first in their families to do so. Prior to the war, colleges and universities were almost exclusively private institutions, attended by only the wealthiest Americans. In the 1940s, graduating from high school was uncommon, and most citizens certainly never dreamed of furthering their educations beyond that.

The GI Bill benefits were generous—any veteran who served a minimum of ninety days could receive up to four years of full-time tuition up to $500. The Veterans Administration paid for tuition, fees, and books. Students also received a monthly stipend for their living expenses, with married veterans receiving a greater amount.

Even so, initial interest in the program fell flat—when veterans didn't rush back to school, politicians grew alarmed that their idea would fail. Part of the problem was that many veterans didn't know about the benefits entitled to them, or if they knew, they didn't know how to go about receiving them.

But before long, the program caught on, and the veteran enrollment in the country's universities swelled with the new students flooding these institutions and changing the campus landscapes. People from different backgrounds, races, and religions began blending together. For the first time, married students could attend—even those with children—something unthinkable prior to the war.

There were detractors of the educational component of the GI Bill. Some college leaders, most notably the presidents of both Harvard and the University of Chicago, thought their schools would be overrun with unqualified people and that some colleges might want to let veterans in just for the income. These fears proved unfounded. The vets, grateful to be home, became mature and studious students. Many veterans, who would not have been considered good candidates for college prior to the war, took to school with relish and thrived in the academic environment. According to Milton Greenberg in his book *The GI Bill: The Law That Changed America*, wounded Senator Bob Dole of Kansas said, "We knew it was for real. If we were going to do anything in life, we had to settle down, get to work, and study."

Of course, not every veteran took easily to going back to school. Al Exner returned from his years in the Navy and with the GI Bill enrolled at UW–Parkside in Racine, Wisconsin. He was in classrooms with professors who couldn't relate to his experiences in the war and with students who hadn't really lived much yet and didn't take life seriously. He had just spent years trying to save the lives of men this same age, so he became disillusioned with school and decided to go to work instead.

It took Dad two additional years to complete his accounting degree, and just months prior to earning it, he astonished my mother by enrolling in law school. It seems he ran into a friend near the old law building on Bascom Hill at the University of Wisconsin–Madison who had just enrolled and encouraged Dad to do the same. This friend dropped out within the first month, but Dad made it all the way through, becoming a lawyer who never ended up practicing law a single day in his life.

*I was not a bad law student but clearly no Clarence Darrow nor future Supreme Court judge. We roomed and boarded with my aunt Nelly. This was a tough time for Mom since Nelly was not an easy person to please. I used to tell Mom that fifty years from now you'll look back and laugh. Mom has looked back—but never laughed up until 1997, that is; 1999 now, 2000 now, 2001 now, 2002, 2006. It was great being a student under the GI Bill, having a beautiful wife and not a care in the world.*

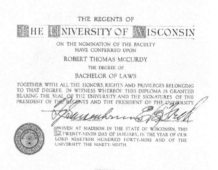

THE REGENTS OF

THE UNIVERSITY OF WISCONSIN

ON THE NOMINATION OF THE FACULTY
HAVE CONFERRED UPON

ROBERT THOMAS MCCURDY

THE DEGREE OF

BACHELOR OF LAWS

TOGETHER WITH ALL THE HONORS, RIGHTS AND PRIVILEGES BELONGING TO THAT DEGREE. IN WITNESS WHEREOF THIS DIPLOMA IS GRANTED BEARING THE SEAL OF THE UNIVERSITY AND THE SIGNATURES OF THE PRESIDENT OF THE REGENTS AND THE PRESIDENT OF THE UNIVERSITY

GIVEN AT MADISON IN THE STATE OF WISCONSIN, THIS TWENTY-NINTH DAY OF JANUARY, IN THE YEAR OF OUR LORD NINETEEN HUNDRED FORTY-NINE AND OF THE UNIVERSITY THE NINETY-NINTH.

*Law school graduation photo*

Ed Knight told me he thought the GI Bill was one of the best things that ever happened to him. As I wrote earlier, he spent several harrowing years as an Army medic under the grimmest conditions in the South Pacific, contracting malaria while serving there. Once home in Arkansas, he received disability for two full years until the disease stopped recurring, so he never needed to join the 52-20 club. Upon his return from the war, he spent a quiet summer living with his brother while he recovered before enrolling in college that fall. The GI Bill opened up the door to the University of Arkansas to him where he earned a degree in 1948 as well as a master's in 1954.

John Eskau took advantage of his benefits at the Milwaukee School of Engineering where he gained the skills needed to pursue a successful career in Construction, Real Estate, and Development.

Universities throughout the United States churned out waves of doctors, lawyers, scientists, and other professionals in this period after the war. In later years, at least ten Nobel Prize winners would be traced back to men who used their veteran educational benefits. Neil Armstrong might never have stepped onto the surface of the moon if it weren't for the engineers working on NASA space flight—almost half of them attended college on the GI Bill.

A far smaller percentage of GI Bill students than civilian students dropped out—only about twenty-five percent—and even then, most left due to financial reasons. This may have been the root of the now commonly held American belief that attending post-high school education is the best way to secure a brighter future.

If a veteran chose not to go to college, they could attend trade, business, and even art schools. Before their stints in the military, loads of men were unskilled laborers. Sometimes wartime assignments exposed them to specialized areas such as communication or medicine. If their experiences sparked an interest in that field, they now had the chance to pursue it and build on their skills. Al Exner enjoyed a long career with pharmaceutical giant Wyeth Laboratories. His medical knowledge came in handy as he built rapport with the doctors he met on the job.

Some veterans used the opportunity the GI Bill presented to finally get their high school diplomas. Any extra education might now help them compete for jobs.

All of these newly school-wizened adults were ready to resume their lives, to find jobs, marry, start families, and buy places of their own. The baby boom of the late 1940s attests to how quickly our veterans married and had children, but buying a home became a more difficult goal to attain.

After the war, veterans commonly returned home and stayed with relatives, like my dad and mom did, as they sought to establish themselves. There was a critical housing shortage at the time. Because of the rationing of building materials during the war, many existing homes had fallen into disrepair or were abandoned. In cities that hosted wartime ship and manufacturing efforts, housing units already burst at the seams from workers who had relocated there for jobs.

To help returning soldiers transfer from renting to owning, the GI Bill included a Home Loan Guarantee program. It helped them build up a credit rating on the same level as men who hadn't gone into the service during the war. The Veterans Administration loans guaranteed fifty percent of the loan amount at only four percent interest. By backing the veteran loans, the government reassured bankers and developers to proceed with lending money and building houses.

On a smaller, though still important scale, the VA also offered business and farm loans. This part of the benefits package allowed people to invest in machinery and livestock for their farms or to start up their own businesses.

Between the introduction of the GI Bill and 1960, almost seven million home loans were arranged through the VA, and a major shift to the suburbs began. Huge neighborhoods consisting of small plots of land and tiny, partially pre-fabricated houses sprung up nationwide. The most famous was in Levittown, New York, where folks snapped up a $7,500 slice of heaven in the seven-square mile tract of farmland that was previously full of onions and potatoes. By the end of the 1950s, over 65,000 people lived there.

Many new homes in America were taken care of by the hundreds of thousands of women who had also served during the war, themselves entitled to all the benefits of the GI Bill. However, most of these ladies expected to come home from the war and become wives and mothers instead of pursuing further education or careers. It is unknown how many women took advantage of the bill. The Veterans Administration didn't keep records, and frankly, many women didn't even know they were eligible for the benefits.

The GI Bill was intended to be race neutral, but African American veterans soon discovered structural discrimination in the program. Though the government funded the GI Bill, the states implemented it, so veterans came up against segregationist Jim Crow laws when they applied for benefits. VA staff, mostly white, routinely brushed off African American requests, denying them tuition benefits and instead steering them toward vocational training. In an article in *The Journal of Blacks in Higher Education*, author Edward Humes said, "The counselors didn't merely discourage black veterans. They just said no. No to home loans. No to job placement, except for the most menial positions. And no to college, except for historically black colleges, maintaining the sham of 'separate but equal.'" Prior to the war, very few African American people went to college, and if they did, they usually attended the historically black colleges and universities (HBCUs) in the South. Outside of the South, colleges either applied quotas for African Americans or simply did not accept them at all. Because there were so few HBCUs, they strained under the sudden influx of students. Even though the government provided financial aid to them to expand their footprints or update their facilities, many were still forced to turn away prospective students because their resources were spread to the breaking point.

While college was not the path most African American veterans chose, many did eagerly seek out vocational training and GED benefits. The number of vocational schools teaching trades such as construction, plumbing, and electrical grew rapidly, but some refused to admit African Americans or claimed that they lacked the sufficient equipment to train both black and white people together.

The VA home loans also weren't powerful enough to

overcome the discrimination still rampant in American cities. For example, neighborhoods such as Levittown prohibited African Americans from moving in. In their standard lease that included an option to buy, it stated that the home could not "be used or occupied by any person other than members of the Caucasian race." While this clause was later dropped, the neighborhood, and many others like it throughout the United States, continued to adhere to this racist standard. This left black Americans with few options to move out of less desirable neighborhoods they found themselves in or to simply buy a house there. Even with the federal guarantee, banks still refused to loan money to African American applicants.

While black Americans experienced difficulty claiming their benefits, almost three million other veterans decided not to take advantage of the GI Bill benefits at all. Some had already completed their schooling before the war or had good jobs to return to. Others didn't want to take what they saw as a "handout" from the government. Some who didn't participate still received indirect benefits through medical treatment at VA hospitals, a network of which had been set up before the bill.

Still, the transition to life back home was difficult in many ways. Veterans spoke of how their lives were disrupted and put on hold because of their service. Some called the war years "the lost years." In many communities, returning soldiers and sailors faced businesses that complained bitterly about the perceived "handouts" of the GI Bill. Many vets resented those who had not served and had trouble reconciling the lives that had been forced upon them during their service with the lives of those who were allowed to stay home. Dad wrote about his perception of the outspoken anti-GI sentiments of his hometown's chamber of commerce, as well as those of his first employer in 1949.

*To this day I have never quite reconciled myself to the terrible inequities between those who served and those who stayed home. I never spoke out on this or complained—just quietly thought about it. I believe over 450,000 servicemen were killed or wounded in action or during training. Lots of my peers never got a chance to be married, to reproduce or do anything else really. Many of the recruits were under 21 and therefore not entitled to vote, nor could they even buy themselves a glass of beer. I think, I could be wrong, in some parts of the country they couldn't even get married—without parental consent.*

*Meanwhile back on the home front those with physical defects, over age* [too old to enlist or be drafted] *or with a wife and kids got a free ride. My brother Keyes, for example, got a better paying job and his main problems were the shortage of cigarettes, certain kinds of liquor, shoes, gas for cars and other trivial matters (meat and butter were rationed but beating the system was no real challenge). My brother Phil . . . had a wife, two kids, a nice home, a good income—he was 36 and, of course, safe from the draft. He could easily have been forced to serve in some capacity. It was, after all, our nation's war and it shouldn't have been left to a bunch of kids doing all the hard stuff against the "Krauts" and "Nips."*

*I mentioned my brothers Phil and Keyes because they were people I knew. There were millions of chaps scattered around the country who were in the same category—got a three to four-year jump start on people who could have been competitive in the field of* *commerce (and life in general). I left the service with <u>absolutely no</u> <u>bitterness</u> and was thrilled to get back to a normal life. (I'm entitled to bitch now—just a little.) I suspect that most of the other 16.5 million veterans felt the same way. It's only been in the last few years that I've started beefing about some of the inequities—to myself.*

I'm glad that Dad took full advantage of the benefits he had earned while putting his life on hold overseas for three whole years. For the servicemen who were able to use the bill, life-changing outcomes became possible. Some men took the time they needed to recover from the trauma they had faced overseas and gradually eased back into life stateside. Many received the education they had always dreamed of and furthered their future success in business or the trades. Many achieved their piece of

the American Dream by owning their own homes in which to raise their families.

Dad, of course, did all of the above.

*Dad wrote under the photo of my mother: "Obviously, the young bride. 8/23/45. She made possible all the good things that ever happened to me. The bad things were my fault."*

*Dad putting in the lawn at their first house*

# I LEAVE YOU WITH THIS

It was one thing to discover that I had a book inside me but quite another to get it out onto paper. At the beginning, my ultimate goal was to write something that provided readers with information about both the interesting and mundane aspects of military life during WWII, focusing on the human side of the story. I wanted Dad (and the other veterans) to tell their stories in their own voices while I stayed mostly on the sidelines providing further background and details.

While I was taking aim at those original goals, I discovered that though I could mostly keep myself off the page, I could not keep the experience itself from having a profound and personal effect on me. To begin with, I discovered that I had the determination and discipline to finish what I started—I felt I owed it to Dad to see it through. I couldn't deny the affection and gratitude I felt toward the surviving veterans whom I was lucky to forge relationships with. My respect for and awe of the WWII generation grew with each new story I researched. But most importantly, throughout it all I could not avoid the emotions that washed over me as I interacted with and interpreted Dad's words.

From the very beginning, it was important to me that the book do justice to the veterans whose steady and brave efforts won the war, particularly the 407,316 men and women who never made it home. At times, this felt like too huge and weighty a responsibility. I was determined to make sure I told every veteran's story as accurately as possible. When those who experienced WWII firsthand are gone, it will be up to oral and written historical records like this one to guide people, answer their questions, and correct misperceptions.

My father's generation is a dying breed. The National WWII Museum's most recent statistics for the year 2017 indicate that of the over sixteen million Americans who served in the war, just over half a million remain to tell their stories—likely many fewer by the time I write this as 2019 begins. The museum is in a race against time to try to record as many first-person accounts as possible. As Dave Phillips of *The New York Times* wrote, "The past can be as acrid and hard to grasp as battlefield smoke." I couldn't agree more.

Every single day, hundreds of sons and daughters of WWII veterans share the experience I had as they stand at the bedsides of their fathers to witness their final moments. I thought of these peers of mine often while I wrote, wondering what, if anything, their fathers passed along to them about their experiences fighting America's most devastating war. I wanted to provide these "kids" with even a small glimpse of what those men went through if their fathers, like mine, never uttered a word about their experiences while they were alive.

With each passing year as the war recedes even further into history, the task of impressing upon America's youth the bravery, perseverance, and commitment of the WWII generation gets more difficult and abstract, and therefore more critical. I found this to be true with my own children, and I know that many readers would agree. I was compelled to do my part to keep the story alive and to encourage others to make sure that the sacrifices made by the millions who served in WWII (and the wars thereafter) are not forgotten.

I constantly thought about Dad when I sat down to write, and as his daughter, it was important to me to properly honor him in the book. I often dreamt of him, once most memorably on an October night almost eight years after Dad took his final breath in December 2010.

In the dream, I lifted his seemingly weightless body onto his narrow hospital bed and then clambered up to join him there, settling back to cradle his head in my arms. He'd already pulled the breathing apparatus out of his nose in one last defiant effort to take control of his own destiny.

In the dream, we lay there together, listening to Jim Hall's iconic "Concierto De Aranjuez"—a mellow song with guitar, trumpet, and piano riffs of its tender melody. As Dad closed his eyes and his breathing slowed and finally stopped completely, his body relaxed and sank into the soft sheets and blankets. I should have felt sad, but for some reason I was overcome with a sense that everything would be okay, a feeling that remained when I awoke.

Of course, the reality of his death was much more complicated and painful. Dad's deterioration began six months earlier with a fall that fractured bones and also unfortunately brought on sudden onset dementia. From that point on, he was ready for his life to be over, often expressing his feelings to my sister, Liz, and me. We did our best to comfort him, but he made up his own mind about it by refusing to eat.

One morning about a month before he died, I followed beside Dad's wheelchair as the hospice nurse rolled him toward the dining room of the nursing home. Just as she was about to push him across the threshold, his arms shot out from his sides, palms pressing firmly into the doorframe to stop his forward motion. The last thing that he could control was whether or not he would be forced to eat, and although I left in tears that day, I was proud of him for his strength in taking a stand.

Recently, I was struck by a comment Malcolm Gladwell made on an episode of his podcast, *Revisionist History*, when he wonders, "What is a child's obligation to his parent? I took my father's presence for granted for as long as he was alive, and when he died, the first shocking realization was that I had to find a way to keep him alive in my heart, to honor his memory."

Of course, I hoped that I had fulfilled my obligations to my dad and had been a loving daughter to him while he was alive. We were very close, particularly in his final years when I was his principal driver. When I found Dad's journal over four years after he died, his written words brought him back to life for me. He had taken the time to record his thoughts and recollections about WWII, and now I was determined to honor his memory by sharing them with others.

It is my hope that this book that Dad and I wrote "together" will be a source of interest, information, and discussion for history buffs and families of WWII veterans—their kids and grandkids—sitting down to read it, a little Tommy Dorsey or Glenn Miller playing in the background to set the 1940s mood. I hope they find themselves in the shoes of the brave Americans who fought for life, liberty, and the pursuit of happiness and truly understand the inevitable great and tragic loss that occurs when evil rears its head.

I must admit that for some reason I didn't want to complete the last few chapters of this book, finding myself easily distracted and unable to sit down and write. It finally dawned on me that by reaching the very last entry in Dad's journal, the "conversation" between the two of us would officially be over. There would be no new words or paths to follow, and this wonderful, four-year, daily interaction with my late father would at last come to a close.

It's been a great ride. 'Bye Dad.

## ACKNOWLEDGMENTS

I am forever grateful to all of the generous World War II veterans who shared their experiences in person, in archived oral accounts, in books, and in letters. Your generosity of spirit, selfless service, and never-ending desire to live life to the fullest, even under the most challenging conditions, will continue to inspire us all. Having access to these first-person accounts not only helped me to better understand the WWII years but also contributed to bringing this book to life.

I am beyond indebted to the many people who offered me encouragement and direction while working on this project.

Karen Roelke at the Wisconsin branch of the Honor Flight referred me to John Eskau, the first veteran I had the pleasure to meet. John served on the same type of ship as my Dad, so he was instrumental in answering specific questions I had about the mechanics and layout of the LCT.

Arriving at his well-tended home in Waukesha, a tin of cookies in hand, I spent the next several hours hearing John's story and looking through his scrapbooks and photo albums. In John's bright smile and twinkling eyes, I saw a hint of his mischievous 17-year-old self. In those eyes I saw the kid who thought that going off to war was a great adventure.

The second veteran I spoke with many times was Al Exner. Both Howie Magner of Milwaukee Magazine and Meg Jones at the Milwaukee Journal had previously written articles featuring Al and kindly arranged an introduction. Al has spent his retirement years sharing his war story with interested students throughout the Milwaukee area.

Al really took me under his wing—meeting with me for coffee, sending me things in the mail, and inviting me to a VFW luncheon. I am also so grateful for his willingness to read through the first draft of this book to check for accuracy. Al has supported me one hundred percent of the way, and I think of him as a surrogate father who was there to answer all my questions when my own father could not.

My dear friend, Kristine Masta, introduced me to the third veteran I interviewed, Ed Knight. She made his acquaintance on a long flight and went on to exchange holiday cards with him for years. She asked if he would be interested in sharing his story with me.

A few weeks later, I answered the phone to hear a lovely southern voice on the other end of the line. Ed and I talked for almost two hours—me frantically scribbling notes as he spoke, him pausing over the most difficult memories. We connected several times after that first night, and he happily answered every question I posed. It was with great sadness that I learned of his passing on March 22, 2018.

The wonderful Mary Lou Roberts, professor at the University of Wisconsin-Madison, invited me to sit in on her History of WWII lecture and encouraged me to tell Dad's story, and by extension, the story of millions just like him. Her students are lucky to have her.

Kim Suhr and the round-table participants at Red Oak Writing have their fingerprints all over this book. Sharing the chapters in progress and receiving honest feedback improved my manuscript in so many ways. I would particularly like to thank Myles, Susie, Jennifer, Nancy, Deborah, and Joel for not holding back with their suggestions, critiques, and encouragement. Kim is an inspiring leader, and her help with putting together my book proposal was just one of the many ways she supported me during this process.

Jean Stein and Ron Curtis read early versions of the manuscript, and I am grateful for their diplomatic corrections and excellent suggestions for improving the book. I'd also like to give a shout out to all the folks working at Colectivo Coffee shops in the Milwaukee area. It was you who kept me fueled when I showed up needing a change of pace from writing at home.

All the folks at Orange Hat Publishing deserve a round of applause. I am forever thankful that owner Shannon Ishizaki saw something in my pitch. Her enthusiasm for books flows through everyone on her staff, and the whole team is devoted to making an author's dream come true. Denise Guibord, my editor, made what could have been a painful process, one that felt like a collaboration. The beautiful book you are holding is proof of Lauren Blue's top-notch proofreading and layout abilities as well as Kaeley Dunteman's obvious design skill. Veronica Davis-Quiroz helped me navigate the waters of marketing and getting the book into the public eye.

No writer can become a true author without the support of her family. If my daughter, Lena, had not had that History class assignment, none of the events of the past several years would have taken place. She and my son, Elijah, are the ultimate two-person fan section. They've kept me motivated to finish this project and always encourage me to view myself as a real writer.

Finally, all the thanks and love in the world go to my husband, Josh, who has supported every crazy idea I've had for the past 30 years. He's always believed that I can accomplish anything I put my mind to, and in this case he was right. Love you, babe.

# ABOUT THE AUTHORS

### Robert Thomas McCurdy

Robert Thomas McCurdy was born on May 7, 1921 and spent his youth in Madison, Wisconsin and Freeport, Illinois. After serving three years in the Navy, he returned home to earn his Accounting and Law degrees from the University of Wisconsin-Madison. He married Muriel in August 1945, and they soon settled in Milwaukee where they raised five children.

While his career as a CPA kept him behind a desk, he had many favorite pastimes such as gardening, crossword puzzles, bonfires, and baseball—he had an almost photographic mind for Major League statistics. He loved to travel, too—family road trips and annual vacations to Hawaii, with Muriel later on, were two of his greatest joys. Miles Davis and other jazz greats were the soundtrack of his life.

He spent numerous hours hand-writing the family history as well as his WWII memoirs. While he claims his two boys had no curiosity about his exploits during the war, they remember "playing war" constantly as children. Like many veterans, he simply chose not to glorify his time in the service.

He passed away peacefully in 2010.

### *Julia Gimbel*

Julia Gimbel lives in Milwaukee, Wisconsin with her husband, Josh, and their two pugs who snore peacefully at her feet as she writes. She is proud of her two adult children, Elijah and Lena, who are establishing themselves respectively at work and school. She has been published in "Family Stories from the Attic" (2017), "Creative Wisconsin" (2017 & 2019), and "Wisconsin People and Ideas" (2019).

Julia shares little-known WWII stories with thousands of followers on her facebook page, @JuliaWritesWWII. She is currently pursuing her Masters degree in World War II Studies.

# REFERENCES

## SO IT BEGINS:

Schneider, James G. *The Navy V-12 Program: Leadership for a Lifetime.* Boston: Houghton Mifflin Company, 1987.

Somogyi, Lou. "The Ties that Bind: Navy truly kept Notre Dame afloat during World War II." *Blue & Gold Illustrated.* October 27, 2011. http://www.und.com/sports/m-footbl/spec-rel/102711aah.html.

First Down Moses, "Notre Dame and Navy: Why We Play, Part 1." One Foot Down. October 31, 2013. http://www.onefootdown.com/2013/10/31/5047760/notre-dame-navy-football-why-we-still-play-series-history-part-1.

Alison, Carolyn. "V-12: The Navy College Training Program." V-12 Program. Accessed March 4, 2015. http://homepages.rootsweb.ancestry.com/~uscnrotc/V-12/v12-his.htm.

*The Notre Dame Scholastic Football Number.* December 10, 1943. 80(4). http://www.archives.nd.edu/Football/Football-1943s.pdf.

## MIDSHIPMEN'S SCHOOL:

"World War II Midshipmen's School: A Piece of Northwestern History." *Northwestern University News.* February 3, 2009.

http://www.northwestern.edu/newscenter/stories/2009/02/midshipmen.html.

"World War II." Columbia University Roll of Honor. Accessed February 26, 2015. http://www.warmemorial.columbia.edu/wars/world-war-ii.

Kwon, Beth. "Six Who Served: Sixty years after the end of World War II, Columbia Veterans Remember." *Columbia Magazine.* Accessed March 12, 2015. www.columbia.edu/cu/alumni/Magazine/Fall2005/ww2.pdf.

Foss, Michael. "Home on the Heights: 100 Years of Housing at Columbia." *Columbia College Today.* September 2005. https://www.college.columbia.edu/cct_archive/sep05/cover.html.

"Naval Terms and Phraseologies." De La Salle University. Accessed March 31, 2015. http://www.dlsu.edu.ph/offices/osa/rotc/pdf/ms2/naval-terms.pdf.

"The Magnetic Compass." Royal Museums Greenwich. Accessed March 31, 2015. http://www.rmg.co.uk/explore/sea-and-ships/facts/ships-and-seafarers/the-magnetic-compass.

Cutler, Lieutenant Commander Thomas J. US Navy (Retired). 1994. "Those Other Grads." *Naval History Magazine* 8(2). https://www.usni.org/magazines/navalhistory/1994-04/those-other-grads.

## A LOT OF GOODBYES:

Gailey, Harry A. *The War in the Pacific: From Pearl Harbor to Tokyo Bay.* Novato, CA: Presidio Press, 1995.

Steinberg, Rafael. *Return to the Philippines.* Alexandria, VA: Time-Life Books, 1979.

Giangreco, D.M. and John T. Kuehn. *Eyewitness Pacific Theater: Firsthand Accounts of the War in the Pacific from Pearl Harbor to the Atomic Bombs.* New York: Sterling Publishing Company, 2008.

Lennon82. "The Battle Off Samar." World of Warships forum. August 16, 1014. http://forum.worldofwarships.com/index.php?/topic/10256-the-battle-off-samar/.

"Henry Kaiser's Escort Carriers and the Battle of Leyte Gulf." Kaiser Permanente. April 2, 2015. https://about.kaiserpermanente.org/our-story/our-history/henry-kaisers-escort-carriers-and-the-battle-of-leyte-gulf.

Overy, Richard. *War in the Pacific.* London: SevenOaks, 2010.

Gregory, Ted. "Ship's Survivors Fading Away." *Chicago Tribune.* October 5, 2003. https://www.chicagotribune.com/news/ct-xpm-2003-10-05-0310050303-story.html.

"USS Ommaney Bay (CVE-79)." Hullnumber.com. Accessed April 14, 2015. http://www.hullnumber.com/CVE-79.

"Navy Seabags." Naval History and Heritage Command. Accessed March 15, 2016. http://www.history.navy.mil/browse-by-topic/heritage/uniforms-and-personal-equipment/navy-seabags.html.

Tessmer, Staff Sergeant Robert. "Life Aboard a Troop Transport." The 100th Infantry Division. Accessed March 15, 2016. http://www.100thww2.org/anecd/TRANSPORT.html.

Ruch, John. "Gedunk." Stupid Question (TM) Archives (blog). March 29, 2008. http://stupidquestionarchives.blogspot.com/2008/03/gedunk.html.

## LCT-977:

Baker, William D. *The LCT Story: Victory in Europe Plus the Letters of a Young Ensign.* United States: Xlibris Corporation, 2001.

Swanson, Ron. 2013. "Mare Island Naval Shipyard: First Navy Base on the West Coast." *Flotilla: Newsletter of the LCT Flotillas of World War II* 14(1).

"LCT Mk5 History." Accessed April 30, 2015. http://lct376.org/history.htm.

"Landing Craft, Tank (LCT)." GlobalSecurity.org. Accessed April 21, 2015. http://www.globalsecurity.org/military/systems/ship/lct.htm.

"Landing Craft Tank." Revolvy. Accessed April 3, 2018. https://www.revolvy.com/main/index.php?s=Landing%20craft%20tank.

Wolfert, Ira. "LCT I Love You." *The Saturday Evening Post.* January 8, 1944.

Hickman, Kennedy. "World War II: The Liberty Ship Program." About.com. Accessed April 21, 2015. http://militaryhistory.about.com/od/industrialmobilization/p/libertyships.htm.

"Liberty Ships and Victory Ships." National Park Service. Accessed February 11, 2015. http://www.nps.gov/nr/twhp/wwwlps/lessons/116liberty_victory_ships/116facts1.htm.

"United States Navy Losses World War II." NavSource Naval History. Accessed June 4, 2015. http://www.navsource.org/Naval/losses.htm#lst.

Swanson, Ron. 2008. "Ensign Mel Eiben – O-in-C LCT-804." *Forks in the Road* 9(3).

## CAST OF CHARACTERS ON LCT-977:

Prepared by the Bureau of Naval Personnel. "Specifications for LCT Officer and Enlisted Billets." August 1944. http://ww2lct.org/history/documents/billets.htm.

Prepared by the Training and Operations Staff, Landing Craft School, Amphibious Training base, Coronado, California, in cooperation with the Bureau of Naval Personnel, Instructor Training Program. *Skill in the Surf: A Landing Boat Manual.* February 1945. https://www.history.navy.mil/research/library/online-reading-room/title-list-alphabetically/s/skill-in-the-surf-a-landing-boat-manual.html.

Baker, William D. *The LCT Story: Victory in Europe Plus the Letters of a Young Ensign.* United States: Xlibris Corporation, 2001.

## THE NAVY WAY:

Baker, William D. *The LCT Story: Victory in Europe Plus the Letters of a Young Ensign.* United States: Xlibris Corporation, 2001.

Prepared by the Training and Operations Staff, Landing Craft School, Amphibious Training base, Coronado, California, in cooperation with the Bureau of Naval Personnel, Instructor Training Program. *Skill in the Surf: A Landing Boat Manual.* February 1945. https://www.history.navy.mil/research/library/online-reading-room/title-list-alphabetically/s/skill-in-the-surf-a-landing-boat-manual.html.

Connell, Cdr. Royal W. and Vice Adm. William Mack. *Naval Ceremonies, Customs, and Traditions.* Annapolis, MD: Naval Institute Press, 2004.

Chen, C. Peter. "Line Crossing Ceremony." World War II Database. Accessed January 15, 2018. https://ww2db.com/image.php?image_id=6203.

Wildewberg, Thomas. 2014. "Neptune's Band of Brothers." *Naval History*, 28(6). https://www.usni.org/magazines/navalhistory/2014-12/neptunes-band-brothers.

Sullivan, Denise. "What is a US Army ASR Score." Chron.com. Accessed January 17, 2018. http://work.chron.com/army-asr-score-22134.html.

"The Points System or Advanced Service Rating Score." Custerman.com. Accessed January 17, 2018. http://www.custermen.com/AtTheFront/Points.htm.

"History of Other Than Honorable Discharges." U.S. Veterans Lighthouse. November 19, 2015. https://otherthanhonorabledischarge.wordpress.com.

"The Service Flag of the United States." The Flag of the United States of America. Accessed January 30, 2018. http://www.usflag.org/history/serviceflag.html.

"Blue Star Banners." The American Legion. Accessed January 30, 2018. https://www.legion.org/troops/bluestar.

McMachen, Chris. "Burying the Dead in WWII: The Quartermaster Graves Registration Service." Warfare History Network. March 27, 2017. http://warfarehistorynetwork.com.

"US Navy Personnel in World War II: Service and Casualty Statistics." Naval History and Heritage Command. Accessed January 15, 2018. https://www.history.navy.mil/content/history/nhhc/research/library/online-reading-room/title-list-alphabetically/u/us-navy-personnel-in-world-war-ii-service-and-casualty-statistics.html.

"US Military Personnel." National WWII Museum. Accessed January 15, 2018. https://www.nationalww2museum.org.

## FORCES COMBINED YET ALSO CONFLICTED:

Giangreco, D.M. and John T. Kuehn. *Eyewitness Pacific Theater: Firsthand Accounts of the War in the Pacific from Pearl Harbor to the Atomic Bombs.* New York: Sterling Publishing Company, 2008.

"Seabee History." Seabee Museum and Memorial Park. Accessed January 17, 2018. https://www.seabeesmuseum.com/seabee-history.

Geroux, William. "The Merchant Marine Were the Unsung Heroes of World War II." Smithsonian.com. May 27, 2016. https://www.smithsonianmag.com/history/merchant-marine-were-unsung-heroes-world-war-ii-180959253/.

"The U.S. Merchant Marine." Armed-guard.com. Accessed January 17, 2018. www.armed-guard.com/about-mm.html.

Cutler, Lieutenant Commander Thomas J. "Those Other Grads." *Naval History Magazine.* April 1994. www.usni.org/magazines/navalhistory/1994-04/those-other-grads.

## FEEDING THE FORCE:

Baker, William D. *The LCT Story: Victory in Europe Plus the Letters of a Young Ensign.* United States: Xlibris Corporation, 2001.

Mitchel, Patricia B. "WWII Navy Food Remembered." foodhistory.com. Accessed January 18, 2016. www.foodhistory.com/foodnotes/leftovers/ww2/usn/pla/.

Green, Hardy. "How K-Rations Fed Soldiers and Saved American Businesses." *Bloomberg*. February 20, 2013. www.bloomberg.com/view/articles/2013-02-20/how-k-rations-fed-soldiers-and-saved-american-businesses.

Koehler, Franz A. *Special Rations for the Armed Forces 1946-53 [QMC Historical Studies Series 11, No. 6]*. Washington, D.C.: Historical Branch, Office of the Quartermaster General, 1958.

"Ration D Bars." Hershey Community Archives. Accessed November 23, 2015. www.hersheyarchives.org/essay/details.aspx?EssayId=26.

"The History of Rations." US Army Quartermaster Foundation. Conference notes prepared by the Quartermaster School for the Quartermaster General. January 1949. Accessed November 23, 2015. www.qmfound.com/history_of_rations.htm

"The K Ration." U.S. Army Field Rations. Accessed November 5, 2014. www.armymodels.com?ARTICLES/Rations/krations.html.

Butler, Stephanie. "D-Day Rations: How Chocolate Helped Win the War." History.com. Accessed June 20, 2016. www.history.com/news/hungry-history/d-day-rations-how-chocolate-helped-win-the-war.

Food For Fighters. "US Office of War Information Video 1943." Accessed January 10, 2017. https://www.youtube.com/watch?v=c34s1ntOmZE.

"Our Pacific Tour: Darold Beckman Skipper LCT-1150." 2007. *Flotilla: Newsletter of the LCT Flotillas of World War II* 8(2).

## SMOKE 'EM IF YOU GOT 'EM:

"WW2 American Prisoner of War Relief Packages." WW2 US Medical Research Centre. Accessed April 4, 2016. https://www.med-dept.com/articles/ww2-american-prisoner-of-war-relief-packages/.

Zebrowski, Carl. "Smoke 'Em if You Got 'Em." America in WWII. Accessed April 4, 2016. http://www.americainwwii.com/articles/smoke-em-if-you-got-em/.

"Tobacco Industry and The Connection to the Military." Florida Tobacco Prevention Training for Educators. November 11, 2011. https://tobaccopreventionk12.wordpress.com.

"Making Decisions Regarding Tobacco Use." R.J. Reynolds Tobacco. Accessed June 10, 2016. http://www.rjrt.com/tobacco-use-health/public-health-information.

Taylor, Ben. "The Cost of Cigarettes the Year You Were Born." Mooseroots. Accessed June 13, 2016. http://cpi.mooseroots.com/stories/13907/cost-cigarettes-history#Intro.

Brown Hamilton, Tracy. "The Nazis' Forgotten Anti-Smoking Campaign." *The Atlantic.* July 9, 2014. https://www.theatlantic.com/health/archive/2014/07/the-nazis-forgotten-anti-smoking-campaign/373766/.

## BOYS AND THE BOOZE:

Brown Jr., C.K. "Charles K. Brown – Seaman LCT-783." 2016. *Flotilla: Newsletter of the LCT Flotillas of World War II* 17(1).

"Ralph P. Avery." 2015. *Flotilla: Newsletter of the LCT Flotillas of World War II* 16(3).

"Our Pacific Tour: Darold Beckman Skipper LCT-1150." 2007. *Flotilla: Newsletter of the LCT Flotillas of World War II* 8(2).

"Bill Miller – Ships Cook LCT-804." 2008. *Flotilla: Newsletter of the LCT Flotillas of World War II* 9(3).

"Recollections of Edward Jensen MotorMac on LCT-730." 2014. *Flotilla: Newsletter of the LCT Flotillas of World War II* 15(3).

Baker, William D. *The LCT Story: Victory in Europe Plus the Letters of a Young Ensign.* United States: Xlibris Corporation, 2001.

US Naval Institute Staff. "A Hundred Years Dry: The U.S. Navy's End of Alcohol at Sea." *USNI News.* July 1, 2014. https://news.usni.org/2014/07/01/hundred-years-dry-u-s-navys-end-alcohol-sea.

Hall, Jake. "A Farewell to Sobriety, Part Two: Drinking During World War II." *Molotov Cocktail.* June 5, 2015. http://warontherocks.com/2015/06/a-farewell-to-sobriety-part-two-drinking-during-world-war-ii/.

Moen, Alan. 2002. "Beer Goes To War." *All About Beer Magazine* 23 (4). http://allaboutbeer.com/article/beer-goes-to-war/.

Mattise, Nathan. "How Nazis and WWII Changed Cocktails Forever." *Paste Magazine.* July 20, 2015. https://www.pastemagazine.com/articles/2015/07/how-nazis-and-wwii-changed-cocktails-forever.html.

"Torpedo Juice: "The Madness & the Myth." *World War Two Flashbacks* (blog). February 28, 2009. http://worldwartaoflashbacks.blogspot.com/2009/02/torpedo-juice-madness-myth.html.

Ostlund, Mike. *Find 'Em, Chase 'Em, Sink 'Em: The Mysterious Loss of the WWII Submarine USS Gudgeon.* Guilford, CT: Lyons Press, 2006.

Holl, Richard E. *Committed to Victory: The Kentucky Homefront During World War II.* Lexington, KY: University Press of Kentucky, 2015.

Budge, Kent G. "Alcohol." *The Pacific War Online Encyclopedia.* Accessed August 10, 2016. http://pwencycl.kgbudge.com/A/l/Alcohol.htm.

Madigan, Tim. "Their War Ended 70 Years ago. Their Trauma Didn't." *The Washington Post.* September 11, 2015. https://www.washingtonpost.com/opinions/the-greatest-generations-forgotten-trauma/2015/09/11/8978d3b0-46b0-11e5-8ab4-c73967a143d3_story.html.

Druley, Keith A. and Steven Pashko. "Posttraumatic Stress Disorder in WWII and Korean Combat Veterans with Alcohol Dependency." *Recent Dev Alcohol.* 1988, 6:89-101.

## THE TIES THAT BIND:

Baker, William D. *The LCT Story: Victory in Europe Plus the Letters of a Young Ensign.* United States: Xlibris Corporation, 2001.

Carroll, Andrew. *War Letters: Extraordinary Correspondence from American Wars.* New York: Scribner, 2001.

"V-Mail is Speed Mail." Smithsonian National Postal Museum. Accessed September 10, 2015. http://postalmuseum.si.edu/VictoryMail/index.html.

"Dear John letter." World Wide Words. Accessed October 13, 2015. http://www.worldwidewords.org/qa/qa-dea5/htm.

"Irene Rich's 'Dear John' Old Time Radio Program." Golden Age of Radio. Accessed October 13, 2015. http://www.goldenageradio.com/2014/02/irene-richs-dear-john-old-time-radio.html.

"Censorship!" American Experience, PBS. Accessed May 17, 2016. http://www.pbs.org/wgbh/americanexperience/features/general-article/warletters-censorship.

Schultz, Colin. "You Actually Can Die of a Broken Heart." Smithsonian.com. May 20, 2013. http://www.smithsonianmag.com/smart-news/you-actually-can-die-of-a-broken-heart-66606700.

## BOREDOM + INGENUITY = FUN:

Baker, William D. *The LCT Story: Victory in Europe Plus the Letters of a Young Ensign.* United States: Xlibris Corporation, 2001.

"Our Pacific Tour: Darold Beckman Skipper LCT-1150." 2007. *Flotilla: Newsletter of the LCT Flotillas of World War II* 8(2).

"Ed Jensen." 2014. *Flotilla: Newsletter of the LCT Flotillas of World War II* 15(3).

Brown Jr., C.K. "Charles K. Brown – Seaman LCT-783." 2016. *Flotilla: Newsletter of the LCT Flotillas of World War II* 17(1).

"Contemporary Libraries: 1940's." Eduscapes. Accessed October 20, 2016. www.eduscapes.com/history/contemporary/1940.htm.

Meyer, David. "What is the Dead Man's Hand?" July 12, 2012. http://www.davidmeyercreations.com.

"A Map Inside the Cards." Bicycle Cards. Accessed October 31, 2016. www.bicyclecards.com/article/a-map-inside-the-cards/.

Brandner, Eric. "USO Shows in Prose: Entertainment During World War II." United Service Organizations. October 15, 2015. www.uso.org/stories/61-uso-shows-in-prose-entertainment-during-world-war-ii.

"History." WWII USO Preservation Association. Accessed April 20, 2016. http://www.ww2uso.org/history.html.

Winchell, Meghan K. "Good Girls, Good Food, Good Fun: The Story of USO Hostesses during World War II." University of North Carolina Press. Accessed April 20, 2016. www.uncpress.unc.edu/browse/page/567.

Scherrer, Lessa. "There's No Place Like Home: An Overview of the USO in World War II." ww2homefront. Accessed June 30, 2016. www.ww2homefront.com/junkie6.html.

"Entertaining the Troops." Bob and Dolores Hope Foundation. Accessed June 30, 2016. http://bobhope.org/bob-dolores-hope/bob/.

"Glenn Miller: 'Sustain the Wings.'" Wartime Entertainment in WWII. Mt. Holyoke College website. Accessed October 30, 2016. https://www.mtholyoke.edu/~knigh20c/classweb/miller.html.

"Bob Hope First in the Hearts of Servicemen." Wartime Entertainment in WWII. Mt. Holyoke College website. Accessed October 30, 2016. https://www.mtholyoke.edu/~knigh20c/classweb/hope.html.

## WASH.DRY.FOLD.REPEAT:

Baker, William D. *The LCT Story: Victory in Europe Plus the Letters of a Young Ensign.* United States: Xlibris Corporation, 2001.

"Our Pacific Tour: Darold Beckman Skipper LCT-1150." 2007. *Flotilla: Newsletter of the LCT Flotillas of World War II* 8(2).

Brown Jr., C.K. "Charles K. Brown – Seaman LCT-783." 2016. *Flotilla: Newsletter of the LCT Flotillas of World War II* 17(1).

## DANGER LIES IN WAIT:

Baker, William D. *The LCT Story: Victory in Europe Plus the Letters of a Young Ensign.* United States: Xlibris Corporation, 2001.

Rickard, J. "Battle of Buna, 19 November 1942-2 January 1943." November 20, 2008. http://www.historyofwar.org/articles/battles_buna.html.

"Return to the Philippines – LCT Flotilla 22 at Leyte and Luzon." 2014. *Flotilla: Newsletter of the LCT Flotillas of World War II* 15(4).

## "MEDIC, MEDIC!":

"Brief Overview of the Medical Department." WW2 US Medical Research Centre. Accessed October 3, 2018. https://www.med-dept.com/articles/brief-overview-of-the-medical-department/.

U.S. Marine Corps. "The History of the Medical Department of the United States Navy in World War II." Accessed October 8, 2018. http://www.theblackvault.com/documents/wwii/marine1/1212i.pdf.

"USS Bountiful Hospital Ship." World War II Troop Ships. Accessed October 8, 2018. http://ww2troopships.com/ships/b/bountiful/default.htm.

"WW2 Hospital Ships." WW2 US Medical Research Centre. Accessed February 11, 2018. https://www.med-dept.com/articles/ww2-hospital-ships/.

"Convalescent Hospitals of WWII." Navy Medicine. Accessed January 8, 2019. https://www.med.navy.mil/bumed/

nmhistory/Pages/showcase/WWII_Convalescent_
Hospitals/main.aspx.

"WW2 Military Hospitals: Pacific Theater of Operations and Minor Theaters." WW2 US Medical Research Centre. Accessed February 11, 2018. https://www.med-dept.com/ articles/ww2-military-hospitals-pacific-theater-of-operations/.

"Return to the Philippines – LCT Flotilla 22 at Leyte and Luzon." 2014. *Flotilla: Newsletter of the LCT Flotillas of World War II* 15(4).

## AFRICAN AMERICANS FIGHT TWO WARS:

Sheinkin, Steve. *The Port Chicago 50: Disaster, Mutiny, and the Fight for Civil Rights.* New York: Roaring Book Press, 2014.

Allen, Robert L. *The Port Chicago Mutiny: The Story of the Largest Mass Mutiny Trial in U.S. Naval History.* Berkeley, CA: Heydey Books, 1993.

Andrews, Evan. "Port Chicago Disaster Stuns the Nation, 70 Years Ago." July 17, 2014, updated August 30, 2018. https://www.history.com/news/port-chicago-disaster-stuns-the-nation-70-years-ago.

Schneider, James G. *The Navy V-12 Program: Leadership for a Lifetime.* Boston: Houghton Mifflin Company, 1987.

Rampersad, Arnold. *Jackie Robinson: A Biography.* New York: Ballantine Books, 1998.

"African Americans in WWII." National Museum of the Pacific War. Accessed March 12, 2017. www.pacificwarmuseum.org.

"African Americans in World War II: Fighting for a Double Victory." The National WWII Museum. Accessed March 2, 2017. www.nationalww2museum.org.

Taylor, Clarence. "Patriotism Crosses the Color Line: African Americans in World War II." The Gilder Lehrman Institute of American History. Accessed March 2, 2017. http://new.gilderlehrman.org/history-by-era/world-war-ii/essays/patriotism-crosses-color-line-african-americans-world-war-ii.

The Editors of Encyclopaedia Britannica. "Golden Thirteen: First African-American Naval Officers." Encyclopaedia Britannica. Accessed April 18, 2017. www.britannica.com/topic/Golden-Thirteen.

Santana, Rebecca. "Fighting Germans and Jim Crow: Marylander Waverly Woodson Jr was among black troops in combat on D-Day." *The Baltimore Sun.* June 6, 2019. https://www.baltimoresun.com/maryland/bs-md-d-day-black-troops-waverly-woodson-0605-story.html.

"General Patton's Forgotten Troops: African-American Soldiers in WWII in their own words." History.com. Accessed July 12, 2019. https://images.history.com/images/media/pdf/AfricanAmericanWWII_Study_Guide.pdf.

OHair, Jennifer. "African Americans in World War II, the Asiatic-Pacific Theater." Texas Historical Commission. February 5, 2014. http://www.thc.texas.gov/blog/african-americans-world-war-ii-asiatic-pacific-theater.

Gates, Henry Louis Jr. "What Was Black America's Double War?" PBS. Accessed April 18, 2017. https://www.pbs.org/wnet/african-americans-many-rivers-to-cross/history/what-was-black-americas-double-war/.

Harper, Dale P. September 2001. "A Massive Explosion and a 'Mutiny' at Port Chicago Brought Race Relations to the Forefront." *World War II* 16 (3).

"Port Chicago Mutiny (1944)." Black Past. Accessed April 18, 2017. https://www.blackpast.org/african-american-history/port-chicago-mutiny-0/.

"World War II and After in the Black West." The Schomburg Center for Research in Black Culture. Accessed May 9, 2017.http://www.inmotionaame.org/migrations/topic.cfm;jsessionid=f8304669915313370815968?migration=6&topic=9&bhcp=1.

Chief of Naval Personnel Public Affairs. "Navy Celebrates 2017 African American/Black History Month." January 31,2017. https://www.navy.mil/submit/display.asp?story_id=98648.

Vanden Brook, Tom. "Pentagon's Elite Forces Lack Diversity." *USA Today.* August 6, 2016. https://www.usatoday.com/story/news/nation/2015/08/05/diversity-seals-green-berets/31122851/.

## A V-J DAY LIKE NO OTHER:

Fracchia, Charles A. *City by the Bay: A History of Modern San Francisco.* Encinitas, CA: Heritage Media Corp, 1997.

Mullen, Kevin J. *The Toughest Gang in Town: Police Stories from Old San Francisco.* Novato, CA: Noir Publications, 2005.

Nolte, Carl. "The Dark Side of V-J Day: The story of the city's deadliest Riot has been largely forgotten." SFGate. August 15, 2005. http://www.sfgate.com/bayarea/article/SAN-FRANCISCO-The-dark-side-of-V-J-Day-The-2647870.php.

History.com Editors. "V-J Day." History.com. October 14, 2009, updated March 14, 2019. http://www.history.com/topics/world-war-ii/v-j-day.

Article from *Yank, The Army Weekly*. September 7, 1945. http://oldmagazinearticles.com/article-summary/vj-day_in_san_francisco_1945.

"Japan Surrenders, bringing an end to WWII." History.com. February 9, 2010, updated August 29, 2019. https://www.history.com/this-day-in-history/japan-surrenders.

Smith, Charles R. "Securing the Surrender: Marines in the Occupation of Japan." Marines in WWII Commemorative Series produced by The Marine Corps History and Museums Division. Accessed February 25, 2019. https://www.nps.gov/parkhistory/online_books/wapa/extcontent/usmc/pcn-190-003143-00/sec1.htm.

**THE GI BILL:**

All Things Considered. "The Bonus Army: How A Protest Led to the GI Bill." National Public Radio. November 11, 2011. https://www.npr.org/2011/11/11/142224795/the-bonus-army-how-a-protest-led-to-the-gi-bill.

Greenberg, Milton. *The GI Bill: The Law that Changed America*. New York: Lickle Publishing Inc, 1997.

"How John Gibson Helped Save the G.I. Bill." *Statesboro Herald*. November 20, 2006. https://www.statesboroherald.com/life/how-john-gibson-helped-save-the-gi-bill/.

"Education and Training." US Department of Veteran Affairs. Accessed September 19, 2017. https://www.benefits.va.gov/gibill/history.asp.

Altschuler, Glenn C. and Stuart M. Blumin. *The G.I. Bill: A New Deal for Veterans*. New York: Oxford University Press, 2009.

"The Bonus Army." Eyewitness to History. Accessed September 19, 2017. http://www.eyewitnesstohistory.com/snprelief4.htm.

Blakemore, Erin. "How the GI Bill's Promise Was Denied to a Million Black WWII Veterans." History.com. June 21, 2019, updated September 30, 2019. www.history.com/news/gi-bill-black-wwii-veterans-benefits.

Lambert, Bruce. "At 50, Levittown Contends with its Legacy of Bias." *The New York Times*. December 28, 1997. https://www.nytimes.com/1997/12/28/nyregion/at-50-levittown-contends-with-its-legacy-of-bias.html.

Luders-Manuel, Shannon. "The Inequality Hidden in the Race-Neutral G.I. Bill." JSTOR Daily. September 18, 2017. https://daily.jstor.org/the-inequality-hidden-within-the-race-neutral-g-i-bill/.